SEARCHING FOR SGT. BAILEY

Saluting an Ordinary Soldier of World War II

By James Breig

PARK CHASE PRESS

Dedicated to
Mary and Kate,
whose belief and support
sustained and encouraged me

✷ ✷ ✷

'I don't say he's a great man. [He] never made a lot of money. His name was never in the paper. He's not the finest character that ever lived. But he's a human being, and a terrible thing is happening to him. So attention must be paid. He's not to be allowed to fall in his grave like an old dog. Attention, attention must finally be paid to such a person.'

FROM 'DEATH OF A SALESMAN' BY ARTHUR MILLER

Printed and bound in the United States of America

2 3 4 5   First Edition

Library of Congress Control Number 2011940153

ISBN 978-1-885938-43-5

Published in 2011 by

 Park Chase Press
P.O. Box 777
Baltimore, Maryland 21203

PUBLISHER: Christopher Gunty
COVER AND BOOK DESIGN: April Marie Hornbeck
PRINTED BY: Catholic Print Solutions

SEARCHING FOR SGT. BAILEY

Saluting an Ordinary Soldier of World War II

By James Breig

CONTENTS

FOREWORD

This book was born of a whim.

In December 2008, my wife, Mary, and I were driving from our home in upstate New York to Colonial Williamsburg in Virginia, where we had honeymooned many years before. The trip, which we take at least once a year, involves an elaborate ritual that includes leaving I-95 South, a maneuver never made with regret, and concluding the final leg of our journey on a quiet country road. As part of our secular liturgy, we pause shy of our destination to stretch our legs by strolling around Market Place Antiques, located at the end of an outdoor mall in Gloucester County.

Wandering through the aisles this time, I spotted a stack of small pages that were resting in a china bowl. They were half the size of a normal sheet and slick to the touch. Realizing what they were, I cradled them in my palm, brought them to the cash register, counted them out and asked their cost. On a whim, thinking they might provide the makings of a magazine article, I handed over my credit card.

Somehow, Sergeant James Boisseau Bailey's World War II V-mails—letters home from overseas that had been reduced on microfilm to save shipping weight and then enlarged when delivered in the U.S.—had ended up among thousands of old and discarded items scattered in the various booths in the shop. As I read the letters when we got home, my interest was piqued. Who was Bailey? Why was he called Boisseau and not Jim? Who was his mother with the unusual name of Rella? What was his hometown, Prince George Courthouse, Virginia, like? As I learned the answers, my interest evolved into a fascination and then into an obsession to reclaim the story of a man who had been in the war.

Within weeks, I would be standing in front of the house he grew up in.

Millions of men like Boisseau marched away from home in the 1940s. Most returned to little acclaim. They hugged their wives, ignited the Baby Boom, resumed their jobs and trudged through the decades. If asked what had happened to them and how it affected them, they seldom answered in depth. In those days, people generally didn't disclose their private lives for public consideration, and men were even more laconic. Lately, they have been dubbed the Greatest Generation, but the sobriquet is often applied only to heroes: the boys of Pointe du Hoc, the Marines of Iwo Jima, the sailors of Midway, the airmen of fiery raids over Germany and Japan.

But there are other kinds of heroes, including those who do their duty, regardless of what it is, well and faithfully. Behind each traditional WWII hero filed a long line of heroic support troops, such as quartermasters who supplied and fed them, medics who tended to their wounds, mechanics who repaired bombers. Their stories need to be told. If the stories are allowed to fade, so, too, will the men who lived them. So, too, will the history they made.

Too many veterans have kept silent about their service, some of them believing they did nothing special or worth remembering. They didn't parachute into enemy territory in a dank Pacific jungle, jump into frozen foxholes during the Battle of the Bulge or fire at diving kamikazes from the sea-washed decks of flaming ships. One supply sergeant, who served in Guam, told me that, because he was not shot at, "I never thought I was in the service."

But he most definitely was. Like so many others, he diligently did was he was asked to do. Many men are trained to remain strong and silent, and many veterans of WWII dare not speak about what happened to them because they might break down. So they kept—and keep—their secrets. After telling me his story for this book, the first time he had shared details of his service to his country, one veteran vowed, "I will never speak of this again."

On October 4, 1943, Gerald Fox, a Massachusetts quartermaster serving in Italy, wrote his parents in a V-mail:

> *Have met a bunch of fellows here in the hospital and have heard many a story. They say they will not talk about it when they get home. I don't want to hear or say a darn thing about it when I get out either, and I haven't seen very much action in comparison to some of the boys.*

As the remnants of that generation hurry toward sundown, their stories—of all sorts—must be preserved because they are personal, familial and national histories. Their letters home are one resource, as are their own in-person testimonies, perhaps recorded by descendants, students and historians—or writers who happen on their letters in a consignment shop.

By reclaiming the story of Sergeant Bailey, supplemented by letters from dozens of other servicemen as well as personal interviews with veterans, I hope to salute the millions who went to war and were never properly memorialized. In 1943, novelist John Steinbeck wrote:

> *The battalion of men who are moving half-tracks from one place to another, doing a job that gets no headlines, no public notice, and yet which must be done if there is to be a victory, are forgotten, and they feel forgotten.*

They were forgotten, in part, because they kept their silence, but also because writers of magazine articles, newspaper stories, books, TV shows and films detected little that was significant in their actions, less that merited reporting and nothing worth preserving.

On May 21, 1945, only two weeks after Germany surrendered, Sergeant Ben Courtright, a Kansan who learned to recognize planes by the sound of their engines as he repaired bombers in France, reflected on his time overseas. To his wife, Liz, and their toddler, Jimmie, he wrote some poignant lines with faint echoes of "The Star-Spangled Banner":

> *Oh say darling I have seven battle stars, besides my Bronze Star. So you can see we have done a lot to help win the war. However I never went on a mission. I dont have much glory myself. But I have worked pretty hard to keep my ship in the air.*

And then, like most of his generation, he added, "I dont suppose you are interested much in that sort of thing."

But I believe that we are. And that's why this book, sparked by a whim, exists....

CHAPTER ONE

THE BOISSEAUS OF PRINCE GEORGE

On September 21, 1914, the first full day of autumn in the northern hemisphere, a teenage girl stepped off a celebrated train that had arrived from Richmond, Virginia, at Union Station, the recently completed Beaux-Arts terminal in Washington, D.C. One of her first acts in the nation's capital was to lie to The Washington Post.

Her name was Irella Olivia Boisseau.

Thirty years later, her son, an Army sergeant, wrote letters to her. Called V-mails, they were dispatched from New Guinea in the southern hemisphere, bearing complaints of temperatures "hotter than the hinges of hell" and reports of recurring bouts with ringworm. He always signed his letters with "Love," followed by "Boisseau." Like so many first-born southern males, he had been given his mother's maiden name as a middle name.

He was James Boisseau Bailey.

This is the story of that mother and a son....of a war and a distant island....of an ordinary man from a small town who found himself in the middle of one of the most cataclysmic events of the 20th century and wanted only one thing: to go home to the place of his birth, a place that formed him and contributed so much to who he was.

Rella, as she was called, and Boisseau were both tightly rooted in Prince George Courthouse, Virginia, a place so small that it wasn't so much a town as a neighborhood. She lived there all of her too-short life, and it's where he would return after being shipped thousands of miles away during World War II. He came back, if his letters are any indication, in search of the normal life he constantly dreamed of while stuck on a god-forsaken island planted thick with disease and danger. But normal life seemed to escape him. As did Jane, who slipped from the collective memory of Prince George to become an apparition of love.

The reasons home and love eluded him might have been beyond his control; place, time and events can snatch away what people most desire. Or perhaps the causes lurked inside him, hidden away for a lifetime until

1

teased out by an analysis of who he was, an assessment based on the clues he himself unconsciously concealed in his letters.

Those letters were all addressed to Prince George Courthouse, the seat of Prince George County, Virginia. Located about 25 miles south of Richmond, its tight cluster of public buildings, small businesses and old houses rest on mostly flat farmland. When folks say that someone lives "up on the hill," they point to a small swell in the earth that seems to rise little higher than a pitcher's mound.

As with many counties in Virginia, the courthouse building itself was the hub of action for more than 250 years. Through the decades, it was where accused criminals and runaway slaves were jailed, the site of trials and hangings, the scene of events that were noisily gabbed about in taverns and printed in newspapers, topics like tobacco and slave auctions, sales of cattle, corn, linen and land, and horse thefts and cock fights.

The authors of a recent application to designate the structure as an historic site delved into the importance of courthouse towns:

> *The county courthouse of Virginia not only served as the center of the local government, but played important roles in the political, social and economical aspects of a community as well. Monthly meetings of court, primarily for the administrative business of a county, also provided regular opportunities for the gathering of local residents. Court days in a rural community drew those with official business, but also voters, buyers, sellers, or traders of crops, horses, dry goods as well as those who wished to be entertained by speeches.*

In the 18th and first half of the 19th centuries, scratch farmers in the county subsisted in hovels and huts, while black slaves made do in small, crowded, hot cabins. Merchants and their families—with surnames like Ramsay, Russell, Hood and Duncan—lived behind or above their small stores. The upper classes built manor houses that were palatial by comparison. In 1752, one man described the many buildings on his plantation:

> *One Dwelling-house 38 by 25, containing 4 Rooms and 4 Closets, with 2 Brick Chimneys plaister'd and white-wash'd, also*

*another Dwelling house 38 by 18, with a Stack of Chimneys in
the Middle, 2 Rooms on a Floor, and a large Closet, plaister'd and
white-wash'd, a good Dairy, Meat-house, Smoak-house, Kitchen,
Quarter, Spinning-house with a Brick Chimney, one 40 and one
32 Feet Tobacco Houses, a large well-fixed Store, with several
other convenient Houses and Orchards; and on each of the other
Plantations are two 32 Feet Tobacco Houses, an Overseer's House,
and Negroe Quarters.*

In the 1860s, the Civil War spilled into the county as northern soldiers invaded Virginia, lifted balloons into the sky to spy on Confederate movements, culled information from fleeing slaves about the whereabouts of enemy troops and, at nearby Petersburg, settled into one of the longest sieges of the century. When they departed, the Yankees would leave behind scorched courthouses, happily freed slaves and lingering hard feelings.

In the early decades of the 1900s, the town, small, neat and tight, was the sort of place where everybody appeared not only to know everybody else but also to be related to them—if not by blood, then by marriage. Surnames reappeared as middle names, and middle names were repurposed as married names. Epps was one of those names. Sometimes rendered as Eppes or Epes, the variations suggest common heritage from a time when spelling was not a precise art. But a long-time resident, when asked if a man whose first name was Fenner was related to a family whose last name was the same, said dismissively, "That's another pack of dogs." Strangers had to be careful not to make assumptions about relationships.

For a century or more, names like Epps, Munt, Burrow and Temple were common in positions of power and influence in Prince George. One official document, dated September 30, 1905, lists W.D. Temple as the court clerk, F.A. Epps as the superintendent of the poor and R.C. Burrow as the commissioner of revenue in Prince George Courthouse. Eleven years later, the report would catalogue Temple, Epps and Burrow in the exact same roles.

Such political inbreeding was, in part, due to the nature of Virginia county government. In 1915, LeRoy Hodges, a statistician who studied the state government, observed that "the county of Prince George,…which in 1910 had a population of only 27 to the square mile—the total being less than 8,000, of which 58 per cent were negroes—has over 60 officials holding positions of public trust. Thirty-five of these officials are elected by the people, while the appointment of 23 is either directly or indirectly controlled by the Circuit Court. This condition is typical of every county in Virginia."

With the local judges appointing more than one-third of the county officials, cronyism and the inheritance of offices within families are invited. In keeping with the times, all of them were white males. Some historians have referred to cliques of this type as a "courthouse ring" (historian Gordon Wood has used the phrase "county court oligarchies"), and they dominated local politics in the South for generations.

For generations, no one had to check who the sheriff was in Prince George. William Epes Boisseau held that title for more than 40 years. (His middle name is spelled "Epes" on his gravestone, but "Eppes" in a newspaper article about him.) A former teacher, he was the sort of big-hearted man who could take in a stray white pointer with black ears, place an ad in the newspaper to find its owner and return it, asking only that the ad be paid for. But he was also the sort of cold-hearted man who could ceremoniously hand his loaded service pistol to a friend in order to invite an unarmed man to meet him nearby to settle a dispute with fists.

A happy occasion was celebrated at his home on September 14, 1931, when he and his wife, Mary (nicknamed Mollie), marked their golden wedding anniversary. The couple sent out a fancy invitation, informing friends they would be "at home" that evening "from eight to ten o'clock" to receive guests. Members of the Bailey family, including Rella and 16-year-old Boisseau, were likely present, for their home lay across the street. More to the point, the sheriff was Mrs. Bailey's uncle and appears to have often been her savior, most recently when the Baileys had suffered a tragic loss seven months earlier.

Boisseau—pronounced "BOY-saw" in the region—means "bushel" in French. The Boisseaus, many of them descended from Rev. James Boisseau, a French Huguenot clergyman who came to Virginia in the late 17th century, could be found scattered like wind-blown seeds throughout

Virginia and North Carolina. In 1857, the Virginia House of Delegates included a James Boisseau (as well as a James M. Bailey, a hint of a name combination that lay ahead). Since many slaves took on their masters' names, black Boisseaus could be discovered as easily as white ones.

From that stock came Sheriff Boisseau, a third great-grandson of the minister. The sheriff also sat on the county's draft board during World War I and presided over a clan that wielded a great deal of authority in the county, which in the early 1900s contained 8,000 people spread over 280 square miles. His deputy—following the keep-it-in-the-family tradition of the area—was his younger brother, George Johnson Boisseau. George, who also farmed and was a future voter registrar, was Rella's father and Boisseau's grandfather.

On November 6, 1907, the sheriff's daughter, Marywood, wed Sidney Floyd Brown in a ceremony The Washington Post and The Richmond Times-Dispatch took note of. The Richmond newspaper dubbed the bride a "Young Prince George Lady." The church, the article said, was gaily but tastefully decorated with "palms, chrysanthemums and autumn leaves beneath the soft glow of many candles arranged with exquisite taste." They "formed a bower of beauty within the church." Marywood was "attired in an elegant gown of white embroidered chiffon over taffeta, tulle veil caught with orange blossoms." She "wore a necklace of diamonds and pearls, and carried Bride roses and violets." The bridesmaids were "beautifully gowned in white French batiste, with empire girdles."

Leading Marywood—sometimes rendered Mary Wood—to the altar was the maid of honor, Annie Johnson Boisseau, eight-year-old Rella's big sister. It was the sort of grand wedding that Rella would not experience when her own marriage occurred seven years later.

Two of the four ushers at Marywood's wedding were also Boisseaus: the bride's brother, Richard, and Rella's brother, George, who was named for their father. In 1918, tragedy would strike the Boisseau family when Richard's speeding car collided with a work car of the Washington-Virginia Railway in Alexandria County. He was 31 at the time of his death.

It sometimes seemed as though strange deaths stalked the Boisseaus. As boys, W.E. and George had been devastated by their mother's violent death when she was struck by lightning. As an adult, George barely survived after being kicked by a mule. Striding down the street, he lost his hat to a gust of wind, which tumbled it under a wagon. When he tried to retrieve it, the crotchety animal objected. The deputy came away "badly injured," according to the Richmond Times-Dispatch, and sported "an ugly scalp wound" that arced above a fractured skull. While his condition was given as "critical," the newspaper assured readers that "there is, however, no internal bleeding, and he is thoroughly conscious."

Recovery from the kick allotted George five more years of life. In June 1916, according to his obit, he "dropped dead" at 62 "while seated on his porch." When he passed away, The News-Leader in Richmond recorded that he left behind his widow, Lena, a son who was his namesake and two daughters—Mrs. Thomas A. Munt and Rella. He was also survived by his grandson, Boisseau, who was not yet one and would never know his maternal granddad. But he would come to know the harsh blows that death could deliver.

From those roots, planted deep in Virginia soil and so often stained with sorrow, Sergeant Bailey sprang.

CHAPTER TWO

ALL ABOARD CUPID'S SPECIAL

In the 1840s, the city of Richmond, Virginia, population 20,000, bustled with open-air shops where noisy vendors hawked live animals, with disreputable theaters that crowded out more genteel establishments, with boisterous banter among men over horse races and politics, with whispered gossip among women about upcoming balls, with subscriptions belatedly being taken to erect a statue to native Virginian George Washington, with slaves scurrying along to complete assignments on the orders of their masters or being led in chains to be auctioned at the slave market, and with charitable and literary societies that assembled with the aim of improving the community.

Known for their air of superiority, Virginians were already proud of breeding U.S. presidents, a pride that came doubly when, on March 4, 1841, two Virginians—William Henry Harrison and John Tyler—were sworn in as president and vice president. A month later, the latter would succeed the former, who had died suddenly. The next year, English novelist Charles Dickens visited the city to much acclaim. At a dinner in his honor, he lifted a toast to the men who had feted him:

I say the best flag of truce between two nations having the same common origin and speaking the same language is a fair sheet of white paper inscribed with the literature of each. Throughout all my travels in these parts I shall think of the pleasure which I have enjoyed in the bosom of your society.

Speaking 30 years after the War of 1812, Dickens might have expected that his audience included veterans of the last Anglo-American conflict.

Recalling the capital's earlier days, one of the city's residents told of the Amicable Society of Richmond, which had been formed in 1788 "with the benevolent object of relieving strangers and wayfarers, in distress, for whom the law makes no provision.... On the formation of the Male Orphan Asylum, the Amicable Society made a donation to it of $1000."

The institution opened in a small house in 1844. Two years later, the Virginia law that formally incorporated the Richmond Male Orphan Asylum allowed "the father of any white male infant child" and the capital's "overseers of the poor" to place the minor in the asylum, where the boys, 6-12, would be "instructed in literature, science and morals"—as well as such marketable skills as cigar-making—before being bound out as apprentices.

Around the same time that the private asylum was created, a baby girl was born to the Cunningham family. She would one day become its superintendent as well as the originator of an ingenious way of raising money to support the under-funded institution. That infant grew up to be Mrs. James R. Gill, who had the notion of expanding the budget with income from train excursions. She first ran vacationers to the seashore at Norfolk and persuaded Governor Fitzhugh Lee to go along to help promote the trips. Her next brainstorm was to load trains that chugged from Richmond to Washington, D.C., and back again, connecting the capitals of the War Between the States, the term preferred by Southerners for what the North called the Civil War. With the money she made from the trips, Mrs. Gill planted trees, installed gardens and erected buildings that enhanced and enlarged the orphanage.

Some of her passengers, who had more personal purposes in mind, transformed the outings into inexpensive honeymoons. The Washington Post, in 1909, described how couples would hop off the train and meander "hand in hand through the Capitol, the Congressional Library, and the White House, with their hearts attuned to the music of the spheres or something like that." As a result, the excursions, which began in 1895 and occurred two to four times annually, were soon nicknamed Cupid's Special. They attracted hundreds of riders who filled several special cars appended to the train. Jammed with young ladies in a romantic mood, the trips could also lure sporty young men eager to advertise their fevered availability. On one occasion, Mrs. Gill, accustomed to dealing daily with unruly orphan boys, ejected two swains from the cars after they had hopped aboard wearing home-made labels in their buttonholes that cheekily declared, "Come on in, girls, the water's fine. We make $25 a week and have no bad habits."

After she showed them the door, Mrs. Gill, a proper Victorian lady who dressed like a widow and scolded like a schoolmarm, sniffed, "Such impudence. These are ladies and gentlemen on this trip. I always cater to the best, but sometimes those without manners slip in unawares."

On a late-September excursion to Washington in 1914, just weeks after Europe had exploded into a hellish conflict that would eventually become known as World War I, a young man and his much younger girlfriend seem to have heeded Ms. Gill's advice to "make up their minds quickly to marry." He was James Benjamin Bailey, and she was Irella Olivia Boisseau, the deputy sheriff's daughter who had been named after her maternal grandmother. The couple arrived in Washington with a smaller trainload than usual because election day in Richmond had trimmed the numbers willing to leave town. Mrs. Gill, who hadn't taken that fact into consideration when she scheduled the tour, voiced her ready excuse on arrival in D.C., "I am not a suffragette, and do not think about politics."

Among those disembarking from Cupid's Special on that September 21 were several couples intent on returning to Richmond as husbands and wives. Two pairs of them hastened to catch a train to Baltimore, where they had relatives waiting to attend their nuptials there. The other men and women, eager to get to the D.C. City Hall in Judiciary Square to obtain their licenses, had to shoulder their way past one final obstacle in the form of a reporter from The Washington Post.

Two of the lovebirds were 50-year-olds from Blackstone and Petersburg, Virginia. Another pair, in their 20s, lived in Richmond. Due to their geographical proximity, the remaining four might have known each other. Alan L. White, a 34-year-old carpenter, and Ophelia O. Kelsey, 28, hailed from tiny Disputanta in Prince George County. From the same county came James B. Bailey, who would turn 30 in two weeks, and his companion, Irella. The son of a farmer from tiny Newville, he was called Ben by those who knew him well. She was Rella to all.

Was the journalist hard of hearing? Was the train bellowing and belching too loudly? Or were the couple nervous and speaking in low tones? James' middle name was Benjamin, but the newsman (or woman) recorded it as "James E. Bailey." As for his soon-to-be wife, the writer mistook her name as Isabella. Had she blushed and answered his request for her unusual name by stammering softly in her high-pitched voice, "I-I- Irella," so that he jotted down in his notebook, "Isabella," a name he was more familiar with? Or had James spoken for her, fooling the journalist to his beloved's secret delight?

What is certain is that someone lied about her age. Rella—or Ben, speaking for her—told the scribe that she was 20. She was, in fact, only 16. The lie would soon be repeated with Heaven as a witness.

On a surprisingly hot day for Washington in late September (the temperature would peak at 92), the mid-teenager and her nearly 30-year-old boyfriend made their way from the station to City Hall, one of the oldest buildings in D.C., where the groom-to-be "solemnly" swore an oath, "so help me God," that his wife-to-be was 20. The couple had a reason for their charade. While the Commonwealth of Virginia permitted girls to marry when they were as young as 12, they needed parental permission to do so. A woman had to be 21 to marry without their elders' consent. In their hometown, where everybody knew everybody else, the couple never would have gotten away with faking Irella's age. In D.C., on the other hand, 18-year-olds could wed without needing an okay from mom and dad. Thus, with her fib, Rella gained four years and a ring. James and his bride were eloping. Entraining for Washington in order to take advantage of its more lenient regulations was common among young lovers in Virginia.

With License No. 66943 in hand, the two hastened to Wesley Chapel, a Methodist-Episcopal church at the corner of Fifth and F Street, just a brief walk from City Hall. There, the minister, Rev. Howard F. Downs, pronounced them man and wife, and signed their dubious document. For Irella, there would be no grand chiffon-and-tulle wedding like her cousin Marywood's or even her sister Annie's. Still, it was official, and when the "I do's" were spoken, the elopement instantly joined the Eppses, Baileys, Boisseaus and who knows how many other Prince George families through the confused cousinry of the region. The tangle could be found in Rella's own ancestry. Her father and uncle, who were brothers, had married sisters, Lena and Mollie Birchett.

In a time before TV, radio and even recorded music, Virginians, like others around the world, made their own entertainment. An example occurred that fall:

An occasion of wide interest in social circles is the "the dansant" to be given by the U. D. C. [United Daughters of the Confederacy] at Prince George Courthouse Friday night, Nov. 6th. A fine band of music will be in attendance for the benefit of those who wish to dance and other amusements will be provided for those who prefer more sedate enjoyment. Oysters, sandwiches, ice cream, cake and coffee will be served, and a good time is assured all who attend. Everybody is invited, and a number from Petersburg are expected to be present.

When Germany invaded Belgium in August 1914, some Prince George County citizens formed a Belgian Relief Fund to succor the refugees who were fleeing from the brutal battles and attendant atrocities. Clothing was collected, with people credited for being "very liberal" in their generosity.

Some creative souls then combined the notion of an evening of entertainment with their desire to aid the oppressed. Thus, on November 3, 1914, a "Musical Tea" fundraiser was held in a home in Petersburg, located just up the road from Prince George Courthouse. The result "was very successful from every standpoint," said that city's newspaper. It was also described as "a real pleasure to all who availed themselves of the invitation to be present."

Next, an amateur vaudeville show was slated in order to bring in additional money for the Belgians. Among those taking part was a new bride, as reported in the Petersburg Daily Progress on November 21, 1914, two days before her 17th birthday and precisely two months after her D.C. wedding:

A lecture recital was given at the Prince George High school last night for the Belgians. It was well attended and greatly enjoyed by every person present. Judge J. F. West, of Waverly, and Mr. Paul Pettit of Petersburg, gave some delightfully humorous sketches.... Mrs. Ben Bailey, who as Miss Rella Boisseau, won

*such fame by her recitations, made a wonderful impersonation of
the darkey of ante-bellum days.... Fifteen dollars and a half were
deposited as the proceeds of the concert to the account of the Prince
George Committee Belgian Relief Fund.*

The new Mrs. Bailey led off the night with her skit, titled "Old Time
Religion." As she stepped before the audience, perhaps in the blackface
makeup that was popular then in minstrel shows, she carried a secret: She
was pregnant. Eight months after the show and ten months after their
wedding—were the soon-to-be grandparents nervously calculating on
their fingers?—Rella and Ben brought a new addition into the tribe.

On his birth certificate, dated July 11, 1915, the infant's natal place
was given as the Templeton District of Prince George County, located
south of the courthouse. On the document, his mother gave up her true
age of 17. Daddy was 30. The baby, given both family names, was James
Boisseau Bailey.

The child—who would grow to love baseball, traverse an ocean and
be involved in a second global war—would be known to all as Boisseau, a
name that would be his signature on all of his letters home from Oro Bay,
New Guinea, Army Post Office 503, c/o the postmaster in San Francisco.

When the letters were delivered to Prince George Courthouse, she
eagerly tore them open because, by then, she was the postmistress.

CHAPTER THREE

NUMBER 33119894

Through the opening decades of the 20th century, through seasons that swung from oppressive southern humidity in August that made the air so moist that it seemed to lie on the skin like a damp dishrag to unexpectedly arctic chills in January (one resident remembers the deep and wide James River freezing over and a Model T being driven over it), Boisseau, a hale and hearty soul, grew up and delighted everyone.

He was the jolly Pied Piper who led the guys into the cellar of the courthouse through an unlocked door to shoot craps near the boilers. He danced at the school socials and drove girlfriends to Petersburg to have barbecue and take in a movie. Sometimes, Edwina was beside him in his car, and sometimes, it was Jeannie or Naomi. No one can recall a girl named Jane. In the summer of 1936, when he turned 21, he and his date could have bought tickets to see Gary Cooper in "Mr. Deeds Goes to Town," "Modern Times" with Charlie Chaplin or "Red River Valley," starring Gene Autry. All of the films were preceded by cartoons, coming attractions and a newsreel, maybe showing Jesse Owens winning a gold medal at the Olympics in Berlin, or Franklin Delano Roosevelt—FDR in headlines—being nominated for a second term as president, or the dirigible Hindenburg arriving, safely and uneventfully, in Lindenhurst, New Jersey. A year later, that could not have been said.

"Red," as Boisseau was nicknamed because of the sandy hair above his pale, freckled face, was the daring one who raced through town with a noisy muffler. Who was going to ticket him? He was the grandson and grand-nephew of sheriffs, and best friends with the kid of the new sheriff, Basil Belsches, who had succeeded W.E. Boisseau and even rented the house W.E. had owned, the one across the street from the Bailey place and its adjacent post office.

The sheriff's son, Shelton, was among Boisseau's collection of boyhood pals. He was taken in by the Baileys—an open-door and open-hearted habit that Charlotte, Red's sister, would continue years later when she

13

was married. Shelton remembered a night in 1933 when he and Joe Sebera Jr. joined a bunch of older guys—Boisseau was almost certainly among them—to overnight in a wilderness cabin while unaware of an approaching hurricane. As the waters of the nearby river kept rising, they nailed the door shut to fend off the wind and piled their goods on tables to keep them dry. The blissfully clueless gang passed a .22 around to shoot at floating watermelons. The next afternoon, a rescue crew arrived in a boat, Judge Temple, the sheriff and Joe Sebera Sr. among the occupants. A day later, the cabin was submerged. "We were highly insulted" by the rescuers, Shelton recalled. "We did not want to leave."

Beginning some time after graduating from high school, Boisseau became a driver-salesman for the Petersburg Coca-Cola Bottling Works at 255-57 East Bank Street, just a short distance west of the courthouse and his home. On November 27, 1936, about 15 months after President Roosevelt had signed the ground-breaking Social Security Act, 21-year-old Boisseau filled out a form to apply for his account number: 226-07-4124. He identified his father as "James Ben" and his mother as "Rella." He placed a checkmark next to "male" and a much larger one next to "white." He signed the application "JBBailey," eschewing punctuation and allowing no break between the letters.

As someone he much later told about his job recorded it, probably using many of Boisseau's own words, "[I] traveled a regular route checking on customers to make sure that they always had an adequate supply of Coca-Cola on hand. [I also] solicited new customers whenever possible and answered complaints if necessary."

He also traveled another itinerary, one that was very familiar and often just as rewarding to him: trolling for girls. A man who was in grade school in the mid-1930s recalls Boisseau frequently arriving just as classes ended in order to pick up the teacher for a date. Lennie Barnes, a Surry County woman who double-dated with him in those years, remembers that "young people didn't have to do a lot for entertainment in those days. We'd go to a place near Petersburg that had a jukebox and dance or to the movies. Sometimes, we'd go to a wharf along the James and have fun, just laughing and talking." Her memories of Boisseau are of a young man "a

14

little on the wild side. He drank beer. We were rural people and thought of Prince George as a city. He always had more than we had when we were young, like a new car. He was happy-go-lucky, a jolly good guy—and very sophisticated to us."

A younger man remembers Boisseau's medium build, his ruddy complexion and even the curly reddish hairs on his arm, as well as his penchant "to kind of laugh when he talked. He was seldom real serious about anything." He also remembers Boisseau's distinctive voice, not raspy or "growly," but sort of husky with a gargle in it, and his tendency to "walk kind of fast."

The 1940 U.S. Census recorded that Prince George County was made up of 12,226 people, a jump of about 2,000 over the 1930 count, a remarkable gain that was due, in part at least, to new industries in the region. Fifty-seven percent of the population were males, and 62 percent of the total were whites. Only about 350 people in the region were foreign-born.

Approximately 4,000 people were employed, the plurality on farms. Other men—only one-fifth of the women were in the labor force—worked in construction, manufacturing and retail trade. One man reported that he worked in "automobiles and automobile equipment"—Joe Sebera, the mechanic, perhaps.

The most populous part of the county was the Bland District, where the Baileys lived. It held 5,575 people, four-fifths of whom were whites. Nearly 800 members of that section's population were in Boisseau's age cohort, 25-34, and 551 of those were males.

Many of them were about to have their life-plans interrupted.

On October 8, 1941, two days after his favorite baseball team, the New York Yankees, clinched the World Series, Boisseau climbed out of the Coke uniform he donned for his job and climbed into a brand new outfit. That was the day his life was turned upside down for the next four years, one month and 22 days. He was drafted, caught in the call-up of men that Congress, anticipating America's involvement in a world war that had already begun in Europe, had authorized in September 1940.

The favored only son, the cut-up and pal, the kid with connections was reduced to a number: 33119894. Those eight digits, which appeared at the top of every letter he mailed home from the South Pacific, formed his Army Serial Number, with the "33" denoting that he had been drafted in Virginia. When he reported for induction in Richmond, the Army described him as 70.5 inches tall and 155 pounds heavy with hazel eyes, red hair and a ruddy complexion. He had no other distinguishing marks. Along with other Virginians, he was sent to Camp Lee in Petersburg, only a saunter from his hometown.

Another Virginia recruit, in a postcard home, described what happened next in a few words, "Got here at five o'clock Monday. Got uniforms today. Also shots in the arm."

It is not known how Boisseau parted from his family or what their reaction was. Perhaps the worried minds of his mother and two sisters were calmed a bit by Brigadier General Charles D. Hartman, commandant of Camp Lee, where Boisseau was sent for training. Under the headline, "Dear Mother: Here's What Camp Lee Does for Your Son," he wrote in The Washington Post:

> Your son knows why he is in the Army of this Nation, which believes in "the right" to vote, to choose an occupation, to live decently. He knows we must now show that a democracy can have military as well as commercial and domestic strength.... Some reasonable restrictions will be placed on his movements. Except for emergencies, he will not be granted a furlough during his [13-week] training period.... You can hold up your end by letting him know frequently that his family and friends are thinking of him.

Stationed at Camp Lee, Private Herbert McDavit clipped the article and mailed it to his wife, Mary Ellen, in New Jersey. She wrote back, "Shouldn't it have gone to your mother?" Realizing that he was trying to share what his life was like, she struck out that line and continued, tongue-in-cheek:

> Just started reading on farther—now I get it. I see there's a full athletic program and my boy can compete in any sports which happens to be his favorite.... Let me know your first golf score & how many fish you catch, huh. I also see you will be placed in the

class where your ability and experience will best fit you. You'll get 3
stars then in 6 weeks, huh?

In his autobiography, Pulitzer Prize-winning poet Karl Shapiro described, in third person, what it was like to be drafted in 1941 and sent to Camp Lee:

> *He is practically kidnapped off the streets of freedom and*
> *is removed in one day from home, job, school, friends…to the*
> *desolation of Petersburg, Virginia…. How could he be drafted into*
> *a non-existent army when there was no war?*

Boisseau wasn't the only Prince George County resident putting on khaki. The Rev. Marshall M. Milton, rector of venerable Brandon [Episcopal] Parish, took leave from his church to ferry bombers to Britain. Shelton Belsches, the kid who recalled the hurricane and watermelons, voluntarily joined the Army Air Corps and served in the Panama Canal Zone. Carlton Figg from Burrowsville went to Camp Lee, Fort Knox and then Normandy after D-Day, moving easterly through Europe as the end of the global conflict neared. After becoming a quartermaster at Camp Lee, Virginia, Alexander Johnson wound up in combat in the Pacific, including on Saipan. As a black man serving in a segregated unit and then traveling home after the war, he experienced racism in new ways and exotic places.

Camp Lee, which sprawled just about two miles from his and Boisseau's homes, provided quartermaster basic training. Every three months, 10,400 men, most of them from east of the Mississippi, passed through the camp to be taught one of 117 occupations. Vocational interviews and aptitude testing sorted the thousands into classes in such categories as cooks and clerks, painters and plumbers, truck drivers and motorcyclists, warehousemen and carpenters.

As the recruits entered Camp Lee, they were issued clothing and equipment, and sternly warned that they were financially responsible for any "loss or damage." As they paraded through the Recruit Reception Center, they were handed two dog tags, a raincoat, towels, five cotton drawers, two khaki shirts and two neckties to go with them, a pair of wool gloves, a toothbrush, and assorted other items.

17

The men were in the Army now.

Founded in 1917 as the possibility of entering World War I heated up for America, Camp Lee—named for Robert E.—boomed into a massive facility that housed 60,000 men. After the Armistice was signed in 1918, the cantonment was demolished, and the site ceded to Virginia, which transformed it into a game preserve. The impending Second World War caused the government to reclaim Camp Lee as a town-sized facility specializing in training quartermasters. At the cost of $8,000 apiece, barracks after barracks appeared, built the help of workers from Prince George Courthouse.

The resurrection was put more colorfully in a brochure handed out to recruits:

When the Axis began butchering Europe and the national
emergency was declared in 1940, Camp Lee sprang to life again.
Almost overnight the sound of marching feet and the crack of rifle
fire replaced the song of the birds.

Rebuilding on the massive grounds created more than barracks, exercise fields and a hospital. There were also three service clubs (one set aside for "colored soldiers") where dances and other live entertainment were offered, three libraries, a post office, a bank, firehouses, five movie theaters, a dozen PXs, seven chapels, and organized leagues for everything from baseball to ping-pong. The recruits' brochure took pride in announcing that "one of the newest additions to the camp's sport buildings is the Second Brigade Field House, used by colored troops."

For $1.50 a month, trainees could have their laundry done. Through two telephone centers that were staffed with operators, soldiers could place long-distance calls to their families. Off base in Petersburg, three miles away, there were four more USO centers, again with one set aside for blacks.

An issue of the Quartermaster Professional Bulletin marking the 50th anniversary of World War II described the camp as

U-shaped. A Avenue formed a big "U" that ran nearly five
miles from tip to tip.... If you had been among the thousands

*of raw recruits arriving on post 50 years ago, you would likely
have come through the main gate past the MP (military police)
checkpoint, and seen immediately before you a bewildering
patchwork of signs pointing in all different directions, where
various activities were located.*

*Turning left on A Avenue, past the big water tower, would
bring you into the Quartermaster Replacement Training Center,
the heart and soul of Camp Lee.... Laid out in grid fashion,
one street after another was lined with company barracks, PT
(physical training) areas, supply rooms, motor pools, small PXs
(post exchanges), and administrative buildings. [Beyond those lay]
warehouses, classrooms, equipment stands and empty railroad cars.*

On and on, the camp stretched. It would even become home to 1,000
German POWs who had been taken in various European battles. In a
January 4, 1945, letter to an Army buddy, a corporal stationed at Camp
Lee revealed, "I have been bumming around here in Lee since last August
and I am still unassigned. I am chasing garrison prisoners every other day."
On May 5, 1944, one of the POWs, named Wilhelm Roder, wrote to Ilse
(probably his wife), in Fahrnau, Germany. Two of his lines were blacked
out by a censor, but the remainder shows how lonely soldiers could be:

*I still did not get any mail from you. My comrades already
received some. I am counting on tomorrow or the day after that a
little letter from you will be there.... Waiting for it is not very easy
for me but I cannot change this, just wait and wait again. Daily I
am thinking how you are doing.... I am well here. Do not worry
about me.*

The absence of mail and the expectant waiting for letters would be a
repetitive theme in Boisseau's own messages from New Guinea.

The naming of the camp for Lee, a Virginian who had fought against
the federal government less than a century earlier, was a controversial honor
but allowed. Naming the camp newspaper The Traveller after Lee's horse

19

was also tolerated. A step too far happened in 1941 when the Quartermaster Corps submitted a proposed insignia to the War Department that contained the Stars and Bars, the design of the Confederacy's battle flag. The insignia was rejected. (After the war, the massive center became permanent and was renamed Fort Lee, which still includes a Quartermaster School as well as a Quartermaster Museum.)

In his address to the mothers of recruits, General Hartman encapsulated the life of each trainee:

He will be here 13 weeks. He will spend half of his eight-hour working day in basic military training, so he can protect himself and our country, if necessary, against forces which are opposed to everything we stand for. As for the other half of his basic training—well, what did he do in civilian life? Was he a mechanic, professional man, clerk, baker, or salesman? Camp Lee's quartermaster replacement center has close to 100 subjects in which men are trained for the streamlined quartermaster corps. Your son will be placed in the class where his ability and experience will make him feel best fitted to serve in our modern Army. After specializing in one field of technical knowledge, he will be better equipped for his future in civilian life.

The wartime training incorporated standard drilling, parading, map reading and preparation for battle. The mock battles could be terrifyingly authentic, as reported by Time magazine in 1942:

Outside historic Petersburg some 800 hog-dirty, dog-tired soldiers of the.... Quartermaster Training Regiment were sleeping soundly. A soft north-northeast breeze fanned the damp air; the lonely flashlight of a patrolling officer threaded the dark Virginia night; somewhere a mongrel pup howled plaintively. Suddenly came the long, heart-chilling shriek of dive-bombers, the rattle of machine guns, the dull, stomach-curdling thud of high explosives. Over the camp rolled clouds of black, evil-smelling smoke. Up went a cry: "Gas! Gas! Gaaaasss!" Out of their tiny olive-green tents tumbled soldiers, stuffing heads into gas masks, grabbing at pants.

In a few minutes it was over. In this spectacular way the
Quartermaster Corps tested rookie reaction to unexpected night
attacks. The gas was simulated by smudge-pot smoke. The horrific
noises were recordings taken during the bombing of London,
amplified to life size. All this was explained to the somewhat
shaken rookies, who were then given a round of back-pats for good
work. The camp went back to bed. Half an hour later hell broke
loose again. This time the gas was real tear gas. Again the boys
behaved well, though some ended up with smarting eyes, patches of
irritated skin, and rumpled tempers.

This is not the kind of treatment the men of the Quartermaster
Corps are traditionally accustomed to. Throughout their 167-
year history,… QMCers have not been expected to fight. But
no more. In this war QMCers will be trained as fighting men.
Although quartermaster positions are five to 250 miles behind the
battlefronts, the fluidity of modern battle tactics may expose them
at any time to aircraft, paratroops, fast motorized units.

Popular Science magazine ran an article that demonstrated through
words and illustrations just how realistic and graphic obstacle courses
could become, specifically the one at Camp Lee. Dubbing it "brand-new"
and perhaps erected after Boisseau left for New Guinea, the magazine
described it "a 275-foot, shallow trench of horrors through which trainees
and officers must crawl at night. This twisting, slimy passage…accustoms
men to unexpected happenings and prepares them for situations faced in
actual battle." The course, which the article nicknamed the "jitter-killer,"
included an assault on the senses, such as

sticky, ill-smelling mud,…the rattle of machine guns, the scream
of dive bombers, and one deafening explosion after another.… You
slide head first into a pool of muck at the bottom of a shell crater.…
Sand blows in your face.… Without warning, you are struck by
a stench, and…what appears to be a body in an advanced stage of
putrefaction.… The last lap of the course is a gas-filled chamber."

The magazine said that the purpose of the obstacle course was to prepare men for the worst they would encounter during a real battle. The list began with mud, smells and explosions, and ended with the mingled—and mangled—corpses of friends and enemies.

In the post's own newspaper, a 1943 article about the obstacle course (definitely the one that Boisseau experienced) labeled it as packed with "devices of the devil," including a rope swing, monkey bars, pipes to crawl through, staggered tires to high-step through and net wall to climb. "Upon the completion of the course, the soldier may have an all-over feeling similar to the throb in his head on the day after payday," the paper said drolly.

Private Arthur Hurwit of Connecticut told his wife, Barbara, about the Camp Lee obstacle course in a November 5, 1943, letter:

This afternoon we went through the battle conditioning course or infiltration as some call it.... They had 6 machine guns firing at us and that crap blowing up around us as we crawled over the course and under bobbed wire. It wasn't bad except that it was raining and we crawled, slid and almost swam through mud. You should have seen us when we got through.

There was a purpose to the training, voiced by Colonel George A. Horkan, superintendent of Camp Lee, to National Geographic magazine:

QM troops must be armed to fight, because so often they find themselves right in the thick of battle.... That's why...cadets go in for chemical warfare, work on pistol and rifle ranges, learn use of tommy guns, map reading, jungle and desert warfare, infantry maneuvers, as well as strictly QM problems. We make 'em soldiers first, then quartermasters.

Another aspect of training revolved around keeping recruits busy and habituated to following orders blindly. Ben F. Courtright, a Kansan who trained at the U.S. Army Air Corps Basic Training Center in Fresno, California, told his wife about his daily routine:

We always get up at 5 a.m., make up the beds, sweep the floor and then mop the joint. Then we go to breakfast. Next we go out and take exercises—and boy I about died doing them this

*morning. Next thing we do is march and drill till about ½ hour
before dinner. After dinner, we go back and march untill 5 p.m.
Then we are off to clean up for retreat at 5:30—after retreat we
eat supper. Then if we don't have to go to a lecture or if we don't
have an air raid alarm we are free to go to our barracks to either
write letters or go to bed. The lights are always turned out at 9
p.m. Then bed check at 10 p.m. ... We just march & drill all of the
time. I do mean all the time...being in camp is just like being [in]
jail. It really is Hell.*

Other peeks into what everyday life was like at Camp Lee come from
the testimony of a man who was there and from V-mails written home by
draftees, such as Howard Thomas, a Clevelander, who was sent to Camp
Lee just six months before Boisseau arrived. Thomas was given the rank of
corporal because he had attended a civilian basic training course when he
was a teenager, but that did not exempt him from grunt work.

"It was the same thing every day," he recalled in an interview for this
book, "Reveille, inspection, the mess hall, inspection of rooms and beds.
You could eat off the wooden floors we polished. We had to get used to
using the latrines that handled 10 or 15 guys at a time, with no partitions
between the toilets. One job I had was to separate garbage for the trucks
that came for it."

Private Fox of Massachusetts was at Camp Lee a year behind
Boisseau but when he was still stationed there. Fox, 29, would end up in a
Quartermaster laundry company, serving in Africa, Corsica and Italy, where
he repaired the equipment. For leisure, he took a visitor on a bus ride around
the enormous encampment and went to next-door Petersburg to have his
picture snapped. One soldier described the city in a 1941 letter home:

*Reminds me of Dubuque. Long main street with a little ups
and downs on each side but nothing near so steep. You can see the
whole thing in a couple of hours.*

Arthur Hurwit told his wife in a 1942 letter:

That town [Petersburg] was a sight. That was my first

23

*experience in a city near the camp on soldiers pay day. Wow!! I
waited a half hour in Peoples drug store for a lime-ade. Eating
at any of the restaurants was just out. I went down to the Lewis'
(army store) and sat around a while[;] the whole family and help
waited on soldiers.*

Howard Thomas recalled visiting Hopewell, Petersburg, sites along the
Appomattox, a cemetery with the graves of Civil War soldiers and the
replica of a pirate ship that was tied up to a dock. "Families would invite
you to their homes for dinner and show you around," he said.

Back at the camp, there were laughs to be had. "I heard a good one
the other day," Fox said in a letter home. "A fellow dropped an orange peel
on the floor, and another fellow saw him and yelled, 'Hey pick up that
orange peel, someone will slip and break their leg.' The other fellow said,
'Jesus Christ, wouldn't he be a lucky guy.'" Something unfunny happened
to Fox when "the Colonel walked in yesterday and caught some of the
fellows upstairs playing poker, so the whole barracks are confined to the
Company area for one week.... It don't seem right to confine the whole
bunch of us just on account of a few fellows. We can't go to the show, the
Post Exchange or any place."

Shapiro, with his poet's eye for detail, limned basic training at Lee in
a few lines:

*Except for the endless marching drills, the men sat in class
after class of first-aid lectures and basic information about poison
gas and puncture wounds, bandaging and splinting, shock and
gonorrhea. They practiced safety from strafing and were made to
leap on a signal into roadside ditches, which in Virginia are full of
poison ivy and were sent to the barracks hospital and swathed in
wet bandages.*

Invited by a magazine to write a poem about draftees, he pondered
whether he should write

*about the greasy cutlery, never wiped off,...fried eggs that
had petrified for six hours, bread that was gray...and inedible,*

24

coffee that was not coffee? The drilling? The poison ivy? The endless scrubbing of crude floors, the open toilets, the homosexuals?

That was hardly the image the commandant tried to impart to concerned parents.

On October 28, 1941, Bertram C. Behrmann of Indianapolis was inducted into the Army. By the beginning of November, he was stationed at Camp Lee with Boisseau, who was only a month ahead of him in training. In a November 13 letter to his girlfriend, Behrmann described one of the duties rookies like him and the Virginian pulled:

*We were told first thing Wed morning that the "A" and "B"
[barracks] would draw guard duty for this week-end. It's a hard
job, but I'm glad I will get it so early...because then I won't have
to do it again for a while. This guard duty is actually carrying a
rifle and doing sentinel duty. There are about 6 or seven "posts"
and we will find out in the morning which post we will have. This
weekend trick is the toughest because it is from 12 noon Saturday
until 5 oclock Sunday evening—about 29 hours. We will be "on
duty" all that time—Walking our post 2 hours and resting 4. The
bad part if that we have to stick around the guardhouse during
each of those 4-hour periods because we always have to be available
in case of emergency. I'm not so crazy about it, but every one has
to do it once in a while.... Some of those posts will require loaded
rifles. We will be expected to shoot to kill if the occasion arises....
With the size of this company (225) it is unlikely that I will draw
guard duty again while at Camp Lee.*

Private Behrmann listed easier duties, including policing the barracks area, scrubbing pots and pans in the kitchen, polishing his shoes, and watching "for fires in the wee hours of the morning." As with all recruits, Behrmann—and Boisseau—also had to drill:

*All yesterday we did "Manual of Arms" which means drilling
at place with the rifle—you know "Order Arms—Present Arms.
Right Shoulder Arms, etc."—all the positions it is possible and*

25

permissable to hold a rifle (never call it a gun, he says).... It is a
queer feeling to see all the rifles pointing over the shoulders of the
fellows in front of me. The weight of the rifle is only 81/2 lbs but it
sure hurt my arms and hands and shoulders, too.

When he added it all up, including not having a furlough to make it back to Indiana for Thanksgiving or Christmas, Private Behrmann told his girl, "It's as bad as being in jail or something—always having to be responsible to someone for every thing. I'm not used to that and it's going to take a long time to get used to it if I ever do. I wanta come home."

As December 7, 1941, approached, the leaves had been trimmed to 24 hours, he said, for the reason his lieutenant explained succinctly: "Probably because we are now closer to war than any time since 1918," when America had entered World War I. Behrmann added, "All we can do now is pray for peace and restoration of world order so that the present emergency will be dissolved."

If Boisseau was being trained for his eventual role as a warehouseman in a base depot, The New York Times described how he was being taught:

Khaki-clad men are learning to master the problems of Army
supply in the Warehouse School. Under operation by the soldier-
students, tiny trucks ply between pillars the size of a pencil, dumping
and picking up minute blocks representing crates and packing
cases. It sounds like play but proper management of the model is as
intricate as solving a complicated mathematical problem.

A far more elaborate model was constructed at Camp Lee in mid-1943. The miniature Theatre of Operations collapsed a 2,000-mile front into a space that was 250 feet by 40 feet. The Washington Post described it as "emphasizing with life-like realism all the elements of modern quartermaster supply warfare...from the point of troop debarkation right up to the....fighter crouched in a fox hole at the front."

Built outdoors, the model had risers so lecturers and learners could view the scene in detail. The display also made clear, reported The Post, that "the new fighting quartermaster soldier today is a combat fighter and not just a service soldier and purveyor of goods."

Part of the model contained a waterfront, shipping and warehouses, a scene Boisseau was to become very familiar with.

At the end of their training, the graduates would be shuffled like cards and dealt out to their new units, which were scattered throughout the U.S. in order to be shipped overseas. Private Fox noted that "most of the fellows that were here when I came are gone now; only about 10 fellows [are] left." He obsessed over where he would end up. "I wish the hell I knew what was going to happen, dam it," he told his parents. "If they would only tell me one way or the other I would stop worrying." Meanwhile, he was perfecting tricks to survive in the service:

> *I found out one thing; in the Army the more you do, the more you have to do. Every time I have work to do, I hurry and try to get it over with, and then they will make me help someone that is slow and lazy. After this, I am going to take my time. The other day when we were getting ready for inspection, I helped scrub the floor, and then I washed my window, had my locker clean, cleaned my rifle, in fact everything was spic & span. The Sargeant came along just as I sat down to smoke and said, "Come on Fox, get off your ass, and do a little work."*

As they trained and learned to adjust to life in the service, hundreds of thousands of recruits like Fox and Boisseau fretted over their futures, which they could not control. It was a constant source of anxiety, and no wonder. Hints and warnings of war were in the wind. If Boisseau had paid attention, prior to his being drafted, to the front page of the January 4, 1941, issue of The Bee, a newspaper in Danville, Virginia, he would have read:

> *"There is serious danger of Japanese-German collaboration on espionage that deserves prompt attention.... It could be especially serious when we remember that Pearl Harbor, Hawaii, is the base for our Pacific fleet."*

That warning was issued by Guy Gillette, a Democratic senator from Iowa. On October 13, when Boisseau was in training. the same paper alerted readers that

*If they ever start shooting in the Pacific Ocean, those little
dots on the map called the Hawaiian Islands will be just about the
most important mountain tops in the world to the United States
because out there lies Pearl Harbor, our potent naval base.*

In its December 6, 1941, issue, The Bee headlined a brief article, "Close
Camp Lee to Casual Visitors," and reported that "an order was issued
yesterday closing this army post to all casual visitors. Provision also was
made for placing of additional guards throughout the camp. Civilian traffic
through the camp…has been prohibited. Civilians entering the camp must
have passes from the Military Police Information Station."

The next day, December 7, 1941, just as Boisseau was ending his basic
training and 60 days after he had entered the service, the Japanese attacked
Pearl Harbor from the sky and beneath the waves. It being a Sunday, he
might have heard the news while on leave (if leaves had not been cancelled)
and relaxing in his mother's home. That was Shapiro's experience as he
twirled the dial on a radio in Maryland, desperate to learn the details. As
he did, "it dawned on him that he was in uniform and that the uniform
meant war."

The day after the attack, Major General James E. Edmonds, commandant
of Camp Lee, posted guards to protect against sabotage. Less than two
weeks later, he announced that a public address system had been installed
throughout the facility and assured trainees that "American soldiers such as
you should be told all and you should be told it promptly." News from the
battlefronts would be broadcast thrice daily over the system, he promised.

In the Lee Traveller, Technical Sergeant Jack Tierney expressed the
feelings of the men in a commentary:

> *Well, we're in. … After more than two years of wondering and
> waiting the United States is at war. … America is going to shove
> some American steel into the Japanese at the point where it will
> do the most good. … Of course, there is sorrow, indignant sorrow,
> for the American lives lost in the surprise attack on our Pacific
> outposts. … Those men and women have not died in vain. … The
> surprise raid on Hawaii will be avenged.*

Boisseau and his classmates would be among the avengers.

When he completed his basic training, Camp Lee issued what amounted to a yearbook of the "graduates." The publication, paid for by the members of the various units, contained photos of the new soldiers. His company—all of whose members were Caucasians—was dominated by Pennsylvanians, who made up half of the almost 200-man roster, and Virginians, who accounted for nearly 60 of them. After bunches of soldiers from Maryland (12) and the District of Columbia (19) were figured in, only a few other states were represented—from the Midwest, Deep South and Far West (South Dakota).

Among Boisseau's bunkmates were an electrician and a shoemaker from Pennsylvania, a married man who hailed from the nation's capital, a railroad clerk and a movie projectionist, both from Maryland, a baker born in Tennessee, a primary school teacher out of Wisconsin, and an actor from Richmond.

On page 73 of the yearbook printed for the 10th Training Regiment, Headquarters Company, First Battalion, Company F, between pictures of Private Clarence E. Bailey of Saxton, Pennsylvania, and Thomas B. Baldridge Jr. of Wynnewood in the same state, appears a photo of Private James B. Bailey of Prince George, Virginia. He wears a stern expression of stolid determination, studied seriousness and the toned strength that was evidence of his 13 weeks of tough physical exercise. He looked like a man with a mission.

Outlining that mission, Major General Edmund B. Gregory, Quartermaster General, vowed: "Let me make this promise to the American people. The Quartermaster Corps will never fail your boys! We will deliver the goods. Wherever they go—to whatever point American fighting men penetrate—quartermasters will be by their side."

A mammoth effort would be required to fulfill that promise. Between 1941 and 1945, the corps would produce 28.7 million pairs of boots, nearly 70 million shirts and just as many trousers, 28 million raincoats, 30 million tents, half a billion socks, and 17 billion pounds of canned vegetables. Writing in The National Geographic Magazine's November 1942 issue, assistant editor Frederick Simpich noted, "In all the long, exciting annals

29

of our Army, from Valley Forge to Bataan, no force has played a more important role than the Quartermaster Corps.... However, its great and gallant deeds are often unsung.... The grim, significant thought is, we would lose this war, instantly, but for the QM." Simpich encapsulated the efforts of a quartermaster by writing that "he feeds, clothes, hauls, and comforts the whole Army, shooting with one hand and working with the other."

Colonel Horkan told National Geographic, "Each battle in this global war proves that the speed of moving troops is geared to the speed and efficiency of supply trains. The quartermaster, then, becomes the key man in the solution of today's strategic problems."

But Boisseau's chance to be a "key man" was on hold. For all of 1942 and part of 1943, he remained at Camp Lee as a dining room orderly. If so, a modern-day quartermaster labeled it "a cushy job." Certainly preferable to combat, it had its downside. One soldier at Camp Lee described an orderly as "the unglorified, the unmentionable, the most yelled-at guy in the mess hall."

Still, serving food had its advantages, especially when celebrities appeared for meals. Luscious actress Ann Rutherford dropped by. Next, a trio of blond glamour girls—Madeline Carroll, Anita Louise and Carole Landis—showed up. So did sports stars, including "Rapid Robert" Feller, the major league pitcher from the Cleveland Indians, and boxer Joe Louis, the Brown Bomber. The entire Brooklyn (football) Dodgers team huddled up. In between such visits, there were USO shows, movies and plays to amuse the men.

Life in camp was cushy in many ways for the Prince George soldier. The Lee men drilled with rifles, but no one shot at them. They carried on routine tasks without worrying about malaria or trench foot. When a recruit did die, it was due to an accidental drowning, not to an enemy tank attack.

So, for Boisseau, time ticked away with few cares. The 10th Regiment, his graduating class, took part in tournaments in everything from basketball to horseshoes. They put on shows, opened "Tavern in the 10th," an outdoor beer garden that the post newspaper said "was fast becoming a favorite meeting spot for Lee soldiers," and won first prize in the camp's Christmas decoration contest. The war, however, was never far from the soldiers' minds.

The Camp Lee Traveller, the training facility's weekly newspaper, described the regiment's holiday decoration as "a dramatic presentation of a Bataan battlefield, bearing the legend, 'There Were No Atheists on Bataan.'"

Weekly front-page articles, under the title "Over There," updated battles in Europe and the Pacific, and editorials about the war kept combat in the forefront of everyone's thoughts. Said one in July 29, 1942:

> Let us remember that in far distant lands our comrades
> died yesterday, are dying today, and will die tomorrow. They
> are fighting fiercely to keep from being destroyed themselves....
> To those of us behind the line must come a realization of what is
> taking place over there.

While working as an orderly, Boisseau was accumulating a major debt that would be repaid in the future. He was being held in place until the Army was ready to send him to the Pacific to become part of the military machinery that would invade the Philippines and then Japan. Hints of that could be found in The Lee Traveller (the name was shortened in 1943). In its January 20, 1943, issue, Boisseau would have read:

> Allied air might continued its relentless battering of Jap bases
> in the New Guinea battle zone.... An Allied ground force smashed
> hard at Japs in the Sananada sector of the north New Guinea coast.

In April, he would have seen the name of the exact place—Oro Bay—where he would soon begin spending two years. He would be writing that name at the top of his letters, although he didn't know it yet:

> Last week Japan showed the first signs of major air activity
> since winter. In four days it launched three large scale raids on
> New Guinea bases—Oro Bay, Port Moresby, Milne Bay.

While part of his sojourn at Camp Lee was occupied with the duties of being an orderly, he also was in extended training for the role he would eventually fill in New Guinea. The Army field manual covering a Depot Company, Supply, in which he would serve, outlines the "phases of instruction" for personnel. Beginning with basic training, Boisseau would have passed through "technical and military training" with

> *emphasis on the technical functions of the depot company,*
> *supply.... Each man is taught the essential features of the*
> *operations of the depot company, supply, and is training in his*
> *own assignment. In addition, it is important that each man*
> *should become familiar with at least one job other than his own*
> *in order that the company may later function smoothly in spite of*
> *temporary or permanent changes in personnel.*

Next, the preparation went on to unit training that encompassed technical and military instruction, and field operation, which included experiences "as far as possible under actual field conditions."

As he marked time before going overseas, by meeting stars and going to movies, Boisseau may have attended a performance of "Ten Nights in a Barroom," a war-horse of a play that proved to be a winner in Army camps, including Camp Lee. "Hissing, booing, wisecracking, the boys in the audience get plenty of noise out of their systems," said Time magazine.

He also might have witnessed a quite different play at the base. It was an all-male performance of "The Women," a play (and, later, movie) by Clare Boothe (Luce). The Camp Lee version—with men named Harold, Edward and George playing women named Jane, Sylvia and Nancy—drew national attention from Life magazine as well as a visit to the camp by the playwright herself, who took the stage to declare that the male-cast version demonstrated the similarities of the sexes.

Life noted, "Despite their hairy chests, size-16 shoes and bulging biceps these 'actresses' did a good job with the play.... After the first hour, the audience forgot that 'the women' were men." So successful were the performances at Camp Lee, Life reported, that "as part of a war bond drive the soldiers, in fatigue clothes, lugged the props and scenery 25 miles to Richmond, changed into their girdles and gave two more performances" at the Lyric Theatre.

Boisseau enjoyed an enormous advantage over his fellow recruits. He could easily stay in touch with his mother whenever he was allowed off the base. One person estimates that it was a quarter-mile from the post's back gate to Rella's front door, an easy hike for a soldier familiar with drilling and in the best shape of his life.

She might have been present on the post for a special occasion. When Boisseau's 10th Regiment marked its first birthday with reviews and parties at Camp Lee on October 1, 1942, the newspaper noted that the review parade "will be led by the 'Honor Company,' composed of 150 cadremen who have been in the regiment since its formation. When [it] reaches the reviewing stand it will join a reviewing party, while the remainder of the regiment passes by."

Boisseau would have been part of that Honor Company, and his proud mother would have witnessed her son's achievement. However great their joy, they would have remembered other quartermasters who were overseas and in the thick of fighting. Nearly 5,000 QMs would die in World War II, and two of them received Medals of Honor, including one in what would become Boisseau's region of the Pacific. As that soldier's citation put it:

> Private [George] Watson, a member of the 29th
> Quartermaster Regiment, was on board a ship hit by Japanese
> bombers off the coast of New Guinea on 8 March 1943. When
> the ship had to be abandoned, instead of seeking to save himself,
> he stayed in the water for a prolonged time courageously helping
> others. Weakened by his exertions, he was eventually dragged down
> by the sinking ship and was drowned.

Private Bailey did not bunk with Private Watson, nor did he train with him. That's because Watson was a black man from Alabama. He performed his heroism about 20 miles off Oro Bay, where Boisseau would be stationed about nine months later. The recognition Watson received for his contribution to the war was not typical of the U.S. armed forces. A quarter of a century earlier, during World War I, Negro troops in Army camps were surveyed and their complaints toted up, including

> discrimination as to the issuance of passes to leave the camps—
> that white soldiers were allowed to go at will, while Negroes were
> refused permission to leave; unfair treatment, oftimes brutality, on
> the part of Military Police; inadequate provision for recreation;

33

white non-commissioned officers [being placed] over colored units,
when the colored men were of a higher intellectual plane than the
whites who commanded them; lack of opportunity for educated
Negroes to rise above non-commissioned officers.

In "Scott's Official History of the American Negro in the World War,"
published in 1919, Emmett Jay Scott wrote:

At Camp Lee there was much dissatisfaction among the
colored soldiers. The reports which came to hand embodied the
universal complaint that "the whole atmosphere in regard to the
colored soldier at Camp Lee is one which does not inspire him to
greater patriotism, but rather makes him question the sincerity of
the great war principles of America."…The colored soldiers were
compelled to work at menial tasks, regardless of their educational
equipment or aspirations for higher duties, and discontent
reigned because it was said the white soldiers were given genuine,
intensive military training, while Negroes were not given enough
drilling to give them the simplest rudiments of real soldier life and
were not permitted to fire a gun.

The outraged cries of the black troops echoed in the offices of the
upper levels of the War Department, thanks to "telegrams and protests
[that] were received from representatives of several colored protective
organizations, prominent ministers, leading editors, college heads, and
men of affairs generally," Scott noted. The result was that a retired Army
infantry captain, Louis L. Watson Jr., was hurried to Camp Lee in 1919 on
a fact-finding mission. In his summary report, he confirmed:

There had been relatively few non-commissioned officers,
colored, in the camp and a large percentage of these were corporals
of little ability or promise. It was characteristic of white officers to
ignore men of ability and to make non-commissioned officers of the
illiterate funny fellows who could furnish entertainment for them
in the orderly room with their antics and shameful ignorance.…
Even worse,…in other sections of the camp, where there were not

even non-commissioned officers of this caliber, white officers were
inflicting bodily punishment upon ignorant enlisted men of color.
This of course is contrary to all military law and custom.

What lessened the tension was an infusion of "colored officers." Captain Watson recommended that "a mixed organization of both white and colored officers is a very efficient machine and works out to perfection from a purely military point of view because a man's race pride will not allow him to neglect his duty and thus bring down criticism from officers of the other race."

The post-World War I dismantling of Camp Lee demolished the racial problems as well. But they would rise again when the cantonment was reconstructed. The Quartermaster Corps included a disproportional share of Negro troops during World War II, when the races were segregated into their own units. Erna Risch, in "The Quartermaster Corps: Organization, Supply, and Services," written after WWII, noted that

the War Department—contrary to its declared policy
of equitable distribution—had determined to allot a large
proportion of the Negro inductees to the QMC for the simple
reason that the Corps, presumably because of its service units,
was in a better position to absorb Negro personnel than any other
branch of the Army.

That appears to be a roundabout way of saying that the War Department did not believe blacks were qualified to fly planes, drive tanks or pilot ships, but they were perfect for staffing warehouses and hauling goods. By the time the war ended in 1945, 49 percent of quartermasters were blacks.

During March, April and May of 1945, Risch reports, black recruits at Camp Lee "exceeded quotas by 200 percent." That influx required Camp Lee to adjust to a new world of race relations. As one response, the camp, unlike other Army training centers, placed black and white recruits into integrated classes to learn technical skills. Nonetheless, prejudices continued. For example, Risch notes that "25 percent of all Negroes received at Camp Lee…during the five-year period June 1939 through June 1944, were trained as laborers, in contrast to only 7 percent of whites.... Relatively few were trained as bakers, carpenters, shoe repairmen, machinists, operators of fumigation and bath units, blacksmiths, welders, electricians, draftsmen, and plumbers." The result would be fewer job opportunities for the black soldiers when they re-entered the civilian world.

In "Speak Out, Mr. Roosevelt," an editorial printed on October 6, 1942, The Afro American, a Baltimore newspaper, stated:

> *Two of the choicest morsels of anti-American propaganda*
> *Herr Goebbels could wish for have been issued as orders by the U.S.*
> *Army commanders. The first of these is the infamous memorandum*
> *No. 5 which has been put in the hands of every Camp Lee,*
> *Virginia, soldier. It deals with: 1. Segregation of colored soldiers*
> *on railroads, streetcars, and busses; 2. Racial separation in public*
> *halls, theatres, motion picture shows, and ANY PLACE of public*
> *assembly.... The order...purports to call attention to Virginia's*
> *state and local jim-crow laws and to advise all soldiers that*
> *the "War Department Regulations and Policy" require their*
> *observance.... To the men in United States Army camps you can*
> *say that those camps are on Federal soil, where you shall expect all*
> *soldiers... to be treated as FREE Americans.*

Colonel Horkan, Camp Lee's superintendent, played a small and little noticed role in early efforts to integrate the Army, a process that would not be completed until after World War II. A ticklish problem arose when black soldiers from Camp Lee went into Petersburg for R&R. When it came time for them to return to their barracks, they had the choice of hiking several miles or boarding public buses with segregated seating. Trouble stirred until the white, southern-born colonel devised an ingenious solution. He had the transit company provide buses solely for Army use and ordered that the troops be seated in the order they were picked up, not by color.

While Watson the Quartermaster was giving his life for his country, Boisseau the Quartermaster rested safe in Virginia. But he certainly had the war on his mind along with the ever-present worry about being sent into the fray. He might have felt like Private Joseph Barrington, an 18-year-old combat soldier fresh out of an upstate New York high school and stationed in a Wisconsin training camp. Barrington was on needles and pins. He wrote a letter to his brother, already in the service, and outlined the clues he detected that indicated he was about to be shipped out:

> *I think we are going to move out of his camp. We got all that new equipment that I was telling you about before, and there are no more passes being issued. You know we were out in the field on a month's problem. Well, we were out there 2 weeks when we were rushed in and told that the division was moving sooner than planned. Of course nobody knows where or when, but there is a million rumors floating around here, but none of them worth a thing.*

Barrington would soon be on a ship to England, a stop on his way to France, Luxemburg, Belgium and Germany, countries he tramped through to shove the German army backwards toward the end of the war.

If the experience of Barrington and Sergeant Ben Courtright, the Kansas aircraft mechanic, was typical, Boisseau spent a lot of time speculating on and worrying about his overseas destination. After a ten-day furlough to see his family, Courtright was put on alert. "We were told this outfit was red hot," he wrote his wife. "And we are to be sent out of here in a matter of hours or days. I don't know where we are going yet, but I think it is China. And so does everyone else. We were told we might be gone for three years."

However, scuttlebutt was often wrong. He would not head to the Far East, and he would not be gone for 36 months. Hours and days passed before Courtright, part of a bomber squad, was moved from his camp in Louisiana. Rumors flew as fast as the planes he repaired. First, they were bound for China. Next, they were headed to England. Then they got a lecture on malaria and the atabrine that prevented it, and assumed the South Pacific was their next stop. They were issued knives with eight-inch blades, but their gas masks were collected. What did that bizarre combination signify? Their leather flying gear was confiscated. What could that indicate? The men were not allowed off base. What might that restriction portend?

As the days rolled by, Courtright's letters took on a valedictory tone. "I sure feel blue tonight," he wrote his wife, Liz. "I don't know[;] it is just one of those blue nights I guess. I sure wish I could be home with you tonight." In another letter, he lectured her on how to care for their son, Jimmie, especially how to avoid the colds he was prone to catching. With great specificity, he laid out guidelines on how to handle the household bills without him. "Don't ever buy anything on credit," he warned in one lecture. "Never."

He outlined for Liz the process he would go through before heading out of the country. "Before we go to p.o.e. [Point of Embarkation] we go to what they call a staging area," he explained. "This area is more or less a [physical] training program. And from there we go to P.O.E. The P.O.E. will probably be in New York." Days later, still in Louisiana, Courtright signed off a letter with "Honey, good night & wish me luck—I may need it before this show is over. Good night darling. I'll dream of you tonight. All my love, Ben." He then appended seven X's for the kisses he couldn't deliver in person.

In a week, Sergeant Courtright alerted Liz and Jimmie that "when my letters stop you'll know I am on my way."

Then they ceased.

When his next letter arrived, it contained a new address. He was no longer writing from any of the many bases he had been stationed at in California, Utah, Oklahoma and Louisiana. Now his letters were from the 409th Bomb Gp 640th Sq. APO 9536 c/o Postmaster New York, N.Y. An APO, for Army Post Office, designated where mail was sent to and from. "Due to censorship," he wrote, "I am unable to tell you where I am except that I am in the eastern part of the states. So please don't ask me." He closed this time with "a million kisses sweetheart. Kiss Jimmie for me."

Soon, he was on his way to England, a stopover before going to France.

Like Barrington and Courtright before him, Boisseau's time would come.

CHAPTER FOUR

THE BOY AND THE SHERIFF

As he trained at Camp Lee and waited to be shipped God-knows-where, Boisseau could have lain on his cot, just a whistle away from his mother's home, and thought of how much his life—and hers—had been changed by the war.

At the end of her first 16 years, Irella Olivia Boisseau Bailey—Rella—was married and headed toward motherhood. For the first 26 years of his life, Boisseau was footloose and fancy free. Everyone who encountered him describes him as someone akin to the cowboy comedian and wry commentator of the era, Will Rogers, who said he never met a man he didn't like. "He was a character," said a man who knew Boisseau. "Friendly, outgoing. Nobody was a stranger to him." Added a female contemporary, "He had lots of friends." Said another, "He was a party fella." And another, "He was nice, witty, comical."

Apparently, Boisseau also never met a woman he didn't like. He was a ladies' man even in high school. "He's the only boy I know who took the shorthand course," said a Prince George man, "probably so he could be around the girls." A little wistfully, even 70 years later, a woman who had been interested in him in those long-ago days said, "He went with a lot of girls."

After Boisseau's 1915 birth, two more babies were added to the Bailey family. They were his younger sisters, Charlotte and Virginia, born in 1917 and 1919 respectively. They were not the only major changes to the household. When he and Rella had married, Ben Bailey was a mail carrier. By 1920, he was county commissioner of revenue, succeeding R.C. Burrow. A year earlier, a J.B. Bailey—it might have been Ben—was among the directors of the newly born Prince George County Bank. Other familiar names on the board were Temple, Burrow and Fenner. Thus, the courthouse ring remained sealed to outsiders. With a larger family and more income, Rella and Ben Bailey went looking for a new house. They didn't have to look far.

Sheriff Boisseau's home was located in the central Bland Magisterial District of town, named for Richard Bland, a patriot of the Revolutionary era. The lawman and his wife, Mollie, along with her sister, Lena (who was, thereby, his sister-in law as well as Rella's widowed mother), jointly owned 105 acres on either side of the main road in that courthouse neighborhood. They had bought the land in 1897. On June 10, 1920, the trio sold 38.23 acres that lay across the street from the sheriff's home to Rella Bailey. The agreement held back one acre from the plat because a store owned by R.M. Henry was already situated there. The sale totaled $3,117.25 "cash in hand and secured to be paid." Only Rella's name appeared on the deed, perhaps in an effort to assure that the property stayed in the bloodline and perhaps because her husband had a drinking habit that rendered him untrustworthy.

The house they turned into a home sat atop a knoll, surrounded by often uncut grass that was dotted with wildflowers. A run-off ditch cut along the front of the property and separated it from the tar-and-gravel roadway that led to the courthouse.

After the Baileys moved in opposite the sheriff, one can imagine the little ones, especially the boy, being regaled with violent and lurid tales of sheriffing by their great-uncle, W.E., whom some people called Willie. Since their own law-and-order grandfather, George, had died when Boisseau was only one and since his paternal grandfather lived a distance away, the boy could have easily attached himself to Rella's uncle across the road. Hard evidence that he did lies in his famously undrawn pistol, mentioned in W.E.'s obit. The shooting iron ended up belonging to Boisseau.

Perhaps around a dinner table laden with Rella's fried chicken, a famous plot to slay the sheriff was told and retold. In June 1902, Henry Robinson, serving 90 days for larceny, and Anthony Clayton, awaiting trial for assault on a girl, conspired to murder the peace officer by caving in his skull with an iron bar they had secreted in a stove pipe. They figured their chance would come when he arrived to feed the inmates. With the officer dazed, if not dead, they could break out and flee. The nefarious plan was about to be carried out when a third prisoner called the sheriff aside and ratted out the dangerous duo, who were quickly transferred to a more secure cell.

Maybe the Baileys and Boisseaus spread out along the front porch in the starry summers, sipped icy lemonades and reminisced about the dusty president. On May 19, 1909, President William Howard Taft, journeyed to nearby Petersburg to unveil an obelisk dedicated to Union troops from Pennsylvania who had died there during the Civil War. The rotund chief executive was so large that the ceremonies were delayed at one point to find a chair big enough to accommodate his girth.

No doubt, the sheriff got a laugh from the wide-eyed children when he told how a Virginian rushed forward with a wiggly gift for Taft: a live opossum. The president graciously declined the furry offering. Sheriff Boisseau could also tell how he chose what he called "125 of the handsomest, manliest, and most gentlemanly men in the county" to escort the president from the Prince George County line to Petersburg.

According to The Washington Post, the cohort consisted of "wealthy young men from some of the first families of this section,…mounted on their own blooded horses." In its report of the gala event, The New York Times commented that "the dust along the roads leading through the battlefields was several inches deep, and the President's black cutaway coat and silk hat were of a light brown color when he finally reached the stand" to give his remarks. "The long escort of horsemen and veterans who started ahead of the President finally gave way and allowed the Chief Executive to ride at the head of the column. In this way, he escaped some of the choking clouds of dust." (If it could be found, a newsreel made of the event might contain images of Sheriff Boisseau and possibly Ben Bailey.)

One can only wonder what the southern Boisseaus thought of the dedication honoring northern troops, although the President took pains in his remarks to praise both sides in the months-long stand-off and battle. "We could not," said the magnanimous Taft, "dedicate this beautiful and enduring monument to the volunteer soldiers of Pennsylvania…had they not been confronted by an enemy capable of resisting their assaults with equal vigor and fortitude." What face might have the lawman made and what emphasis might have he placed on the word in noting that the Southerners were termed "an enemy"?

41

As Boisseau grew from toddler to teen, the sheriff could have told stories about what happened before his grand-nephew was born. In 1902, for instance, the sheriff went to Mr. Gosch's farm in the county. The Swede "had failed to respond to a summons" that called on him to pay a fine levied by the court, according to a newspaper account. The fine was imposed after the farmer blocked a public road that ran through his land. Sheriff Boisseau and Deputy Batte arrived to seize Gosch's mules in lieu of payment. When the Swede vowed to kill anyone who touched his animals, the deputy held a gun on him, and the sheriff harnessed the mules. A year later, the lawman arrested Peter Jackson, "a negro boy," for stealing a bag of peanuts from Mr. Temple of the county. Jackson was jailed for 30 days for his theft.

The jail the sheriff oversaw, including, evidently, the locks, had been constructed of wood in 1868. In 1882, every inmate escaped by the simple stratagem of setting fire to the locks. The New York Times revealed that "after the prisoners escaped they extinguished the fire and saved the building from being destroyed." The jail was described seven years later by a reporter who witnessed a hanging there:

It is anything but an imposing or attractive structure. [It] is a two-story frame building with a yard hardly large enough for the execution of a cat much less a human being. Its general ugliness had been enhanced by the addition of a section of fence to the regular barrier, so as to cut off all view from the outside.

That building was replaced by a stouter, one-story brick structure sometime before 1923 (it still stands and is in use for other purposes).

Boisseau was nearly five when his adopted grandpa found himself in the middle of an odd case, one that might have made the rounds of the family at August picnics and Thanksgiving dinners. In 1920, Andrew Bobb, a county resident, was arrested in Petersburg for murdering his wife. The proof was the testimony of his little daughter, who swore that daddy had slain mommy and buried her near their farm. But old, experienced and wily Sheriff Boisseau began sniffing around and discovered Mrs. Bobb alive and well in Dinwiddie, the next county over. On June 6, he left Prince George to retrieve her.

Along the way, Willie might have enjoyed a nip or two. The sheriff was a drinking man, just like Boisseau's father. If alcoholism can be inherited, Boisseau had it flowing his way through family bloodlines. Stories tell of how the sheriff would confiscate liquor during Prohibition, guzzle the contents, toss the empty bottles into the woods behind his house and sleep off his hangover in one of the vacant jail cells. A later owner of the house reported stumbling over the empties, still scattered in the back of the property like headstones in a neglected cemetery.

CHAPTER FIVE

HEADING OVER THERE

Almost all of what is known about Boisseau's time in the Army, between the ages of 26 and 30, comes from his 38 remaining letters home, all but three to his mother. Two went to his sister Charlotte and one to Sis Macy, as his mother's cousin Marywood was known. All but four of the letters cluster in the summer of 1944, providing an in-depth look into his psyche during that crucial period of the war in the Pacific.

The letters are essential skeleton keys to the locked doors of his life because Boisseau's military records were destroyed in a 1973 fire at the Military Personnel Records Center in St. Louis, a conflagration ignited by a discarded cigarette that claimed as many as 18 million documents. Revelatory papers, recently uncovered at the Library of Virginia in Richmond during research for this book, fill in some of the blanks. Those include his Enlisted Record and Report of Separation. Late in the writing of this book, another crucial document surfaced when a relative produced his honorable discharge.

Stationed stateside for two years after he was drafted in 1941, Boisseau—who seems rarely to have left Prince George County before or after the war—eventually set off on the biggest trip of his life, and it wasn't for pleasure. On September 17, 1943, his arm stinging from being freshly inoculated against smallpox, he was marched aboard a ship, perhaps after a brief stay at Camp Stoneman, in Pittsburg, California, north of San Francisco, the main point of embarkation for troops sailing the Pacific.

As Boisseau left, the Lee Traveller back in Virginia printed on its front page the news about "the first step in a new offensive against Rabaul," New Guinea. On the next page, the paper listed the gains being made by Allied troops on that and surrounding islands. On New Guinea, for two years and far away from Prince George, Boisseau would be a supply NCO with the rank of sergeant (TEC 4, Technician Fourth Grade), assigned to the 343rd Quartermaster Depot Company Supply.

Precisely how he travelled from Camp Lee and over the Pacific is unknown, but it was most likely by one of three routes. In his autobiography, Karl Shapiro recounted the one he followed to New Guinea. He began on a train from Camp Lee to Camp Dix in New Jersey, where he switched to a train that chugged to a dock in Boston, where he boarded the Queen Mary, which steamed south in the Atlantic and paused in Rio de Janeiro to refuel and re-provision before cutting east to Cape Town, crossing the Indian Ocean and landing in Australia. The meandering voyage covered more than 18,000 miles over the course of 38 days. Then it was on to New Guinea after stopovers in Perth and Sydney.

Howard Thomas of Cleveland had been sent from Camp Lee to a base in Florida before being brought back up the East Coast and deposited in an embarkation center in New York City, a center that he described as "a city inside a big building. It had everything, including a barber shop. They showed us a room filled with mattresses. They didn't tell us the mattresses were filled with bedbugs."

The troops were then put aboard the U.S. Army transport ship Thomas H. Barry, a converted liner that headed back south and passed close enough to the Bahamas for the passengers to hear band music wafting over the waves. Then they steered into the Panama Canal, steamed to Bora Bora to refuel and finally came to Melbourne, Australia, for a short stay before being sent off to various islands, including New Guinea.

Those were two ways to get to the South Pacific, but Boisseau could not have gone via the Queen Mary because it was soon pressed into service ferrying men only from New York to Scotland. A third and more common method of reaching New Guinea, which is most likely the transit Boisseau made, began with a train ride west across America to Camp Stoneman. One soldier described traveling that way as both "filthy" from coal smoke and long. Another, Corporal Thomas McGee of New Jersey, wrote to a friend about his rail passage to a post in San Francisco:

> I arrived…after nearly 4 days of riding on trains and it sure
> was tough…. To make matters worse the train was 10 hours late in
> getting in…. The reason for it was that the train that was ahead of
> us on the same track we were on was in an accident just outside of

Laramie, Wyoming and several of the cars were derailed and it was
several hours before they were able to get them back on again.

Capturing images of what soldiers like Boisseau spied through the windows during a cross-country ride, Shapiro, the poet, wrote "Troop Train":

It stops the town we come through. Workers raise
Their oily arms in good salute and grin.
Kids scream as at a circus. Business men
Glance hopefully and go their measured way.
And women standing at their dumbstruck door
More slowly wave and seem to warn us back.

The monotony and grimness of life aboard a transport ship, crammed sardine-tight with troops, was described by Private First Class Keith Winston. The Pennsylvania combat medic, whose mail to his wife has been collected in a book titled "Letters from a World War II GI," told her about his trip on the Atlantic:

While we eat only two meals a day, they're pretty
substantial.... In the "holes"—the troops' quarters—it's
disgustingly sickening, since air is lacking, and it's so crowded
you can't move without bumping into some soldier.... The small
percentage of officers on board have as much room as the combined
troops. I have not seen one solitary chair where an enlisted man
can sit down to write a letter.

Many men aboard the transports slept in the open on the decks to escape the stultifying heat below. In his account of sailing the Pacific for 28 days and winding up in Oro Bay, New Guinea, First Lieutenant Miles W. Gale, a paratrooper, wrote:

Below decks it was hot, humid and crowded.... Bunks were
12 tiers high from floor to ceiling and each tier was so tight for
space that the guy in the bunk above was about ten inches over
your nose.... Shipboard food was bad. So nobody asked for seconds.
The two meals a day were just enough to keep one's skin and bones

separated, but barely. . . . Submarine alerts were too frequent to be
true as the [ship] zigzagged and worsened sea sickness cases.

Private Alphonso Amico, who had been drafted before he finished
high school in Connecticut, crossed the Pacific aboard a luxury liner named
America. Refitting and re-christened the U.S.S. West Point, it was capable
of carrying more than 9,000 men at a time, the most of any troop transport.
When he walked up the gangplank, Amico had no idea where he was going.
When he walked down, he was in New Guinea. "It rained every day for six
weeks," he moaned more than 65 years later in an interview for this book.

Thomas, the Ohioan who had trained as a quartermaster at Camp Lee
and was on his way to New Guinea, recalled for this book the horrors of his
six-week Pacific journey:

We ate one meal a day with an orange or apple at night. We
were starving to death. Everyone was sick because the water was
bad. You slept in canvas beds stacked seven high. If the guy above
you was heavy, his butt was in your face. If the guy on top was
sick or drunk, everyone below got the residue of his vomit. One
time, I saw the cook spill a large pot of beef stew on the deck. He
scooped it up and put it back in the pot. I said to myself, "He'll
serve that tomorrow night." He did. I refused to eat it. Everyone
else had dysentery.

Sergeant John Gilday, from upstate New York, recorded his Atlantic
experiences in a self-published memoir:

Many men suffered from seasickness. Thankfully, I was not
one of them. Doubly thankfully, I didn't occupy the lowest bunk
that was subjected to the most vomit from above. This was a very
real problem, especially [during] the time the ship was cutting
through a gale. I vividly recall lying on my cot and feeling the ship
rise and roll to starboard or port until it reached the pinnacle of her
climb and just as the bow starts its plunge into a trough, the ship's
screw (propeller) is churning out of the ocean, causing the ship to
shudder like a dog wagging its tail.

In a letter, written during what he jokingly called his "ferry boat ride" on the Pacific, Private J. Volkman, a member of the Engineers Corps from New York, was careful not to reveal too many details that would violate censorship rules. However, he did provide some more depth about traversing the ocean:

> *We've only had one good storm that made the boat look at times like it was standing on end in the water, but luckily I haven't been the least bit seasick. The best part of the trip so far has been the two stops we made. Each time we were given passes, 3 hours the first time and 5 1/2 the second, so we were able to do a little sightseeing, fill our stomachs with food and ice cream, and best of all, get hot showers. You can never imagine how much you can miss hot showers until you've had to go without them for weeks.*

In a letter to his parents in Washington, D.C., written aboard a ship taking him to Australia before he was assigned to New Guinea, Navy Lieutenant J.L. Avery launched into great detail about boarding and travelling:

> *I had 3 hours notice before reporting for sailing. We reported to one pier and then they loaded us into a bus and took us several miles to another pier. We then went on board.... Anything to confuse the enemy.... We have nothing to do but eat, sleep and put our noses into everything on board.... One of the fellows is making some watercolors of scenes on board.... Another is a magician.... I have gained the nickname of ship's carpenter because of some shelves I built over my bunk and a bench that I made. Anything to pass the time.... It is evening now and most of us are in the wardroom. At one table the inevitable poker game is in progress. A chess game is progressing at snail's pace at another table.*

But not everything went smoothly. The ship's engines turned cranky enough that the vessel turned back toward land for repairs. At another point, danger appeared on the horizon:

> *A ship came astern of us. It was the first one we had seen for several days and because it could not be recognized immediately,*

our ship had a general quarters alarm. All of us passengers went to our lifeboat stations. The gun crews were all ready for action and everybody was tense.... After a few minutes some of us would get up enough nerve to run back for some item we wanted to take in the lifeboat with us. One fellow had some brandy hidden.... Another got a roll of toilet paper, another his pistol, a bottle of mineral oil (for sunburn, I guess), another an Esquire magazine and a Reader's Digest. One of the crew dumped a 100 lb bag of onions in the boat. The cook was more helpful, he brought a sack of potatoes and a case of canned tomatoes.... I got a sack of apples, some unguentine, aspirin, a deck of cards, and my raincoat. By the time we had gotten all this stuff assembled the other ship was close enough that it could be recognized as one of our own.... Some of the actions seemed very funny but at the time all was in seriousness.

Since many soldiers were in the dark about where they were headed, journalist John Lardner decided to make book about their destination. Aboard a troop ship in the mid-Pacific, he posted odds, ranging from Perth, Australia, at 3-1, to Pittsburgh, at 100-1:

I did get one bet on Pittsburgh. From a captain in the Quartermaster Corps. "I've just been shot in the arm for yellow fever and three times for typhus," he said with a scowl, "and I don't think they have 'em in Pittsburgh. But I never passed up a hundred-to-one shot in my life."

Lardner summed up troopship journeys as pretty much all the same:

One floating city is much like another. There are the same bunks in triple tiers, the same long shuffling processions to mess, the same drills, the same blacked-out decks at night, the same ceremonies and services, the same card games and forums, the same alarms and rumors and signs of submarines, the same orders and speeches by commanding officers;...always, I guess, there is the same feeling of adventure and nervous excitement and groping anticipation.

And, to some observers, there were poetic sights to be seen along the way. Gale reported:

> *The breeze was soft and warm. A few dolphins, slick and dark gray, joined us at San Francisco and played around the ship's bow as if doing escort duty. We "Landlubbers" spent hours marveling at the sky colors of sunrise and sunset, after dark the sparkling bioluminescence in the churning water. Its source is the many forms of marine life having luminescent qualities.... In the moonlight the ship's wake would shimmer like a river of liquid silver.*

Boisseau's voyage on the silver river ended somewhere in Australia—there is evidence it was New South Wales—on October 5, 1943, nearly three weeks after leaving America. The next day, on the front page of The Lee Traveller, an article announced that his 10th Regiment, including Company F, had been deactivated because its members were all gone.

The man from Prince George Courthouse, who would soon be leaving Australia for a jungle destination, would not return home for two years.

CHAPTER SIX

THE PLACE HE LEFT BEHIND

As Boisseau steamed toward New Guinea, the Pacific rolling beneath him and the wide skies sun-struck above him, Prince George County could not have been far from his mind. Soldiers, sailors, Marines and airmen all held home close to their hearts as they headed into unknown worlds of unknown dangers. They worried about when they would return—if they would.

His county and small town were all Boisseau knew. He had never lived anywhere else. Prince George was where he grew up and went to school, and it was where he lived and worked. It was even where he trained for two years. The place formed him just as surely as his family, so what it was like discloses something of what he was like.

The county, established in 1702, was "named in honor of Prince George of Denmark, Husband of England's reigning monarch, Queen Anne," according to the county's website (www.princegeorgeva.org). "Formed from Charles City County,…its boundaries stretched from south of the James River down to the North Carolina line."

Two metropolises that loom over the rural county—Richmond and Petersburg—are not formally within it, or any county, due to the habit of the state to establish multiple "independent cities." (There are 42 such cities in the U.S., and all but three of them—St. Louis, Baltimore and Carson City, Nevada—are in Virginia.) Regardless of their formal designation, the two cities' influence inevitably impinges on Prince George. William Byrd of Westover, one of the 18th-century powers-that-be in Virginia, recorded the cities' births in his diary:

> *Sept. 19, 1733.—When we got home we laid the foundation of two large cities, one at Shacco's, to be called Richmond, and the other at the falls of Appomattox river, to be named Petersburg.… The truth of it is, these two places being the uppermost landing of James and Appomattox rivers, are naturally intended for marts where the traffic of the outer inhabitants must centre. Thus we did not build castles only, but also cities in the air.*

53

A sizable slice of what was the preeminent British colony in the New World, Prince George's original area occupied an area that now makes up 17 break-off counties and portions of five more. The county wove in and out of history in the centuries following its creation. Periodically interrupting long years of obscurity, it would suddenly rise into history's notice like an exotic flower that blooms once a century before wilting and returning to the shadows.

In 1752, when George Washington was commissioned an officer by Virginia's royal governor, Robert Dinwiddie, the official papers designated the future president "to be Major and Adjutant of the Militia, Horse and Foot," in a dozen counties, including Prince George. Asked in 1798 if he knew of any accurate histories of the colony and state, Washington, by then an ex-president residing at Mount Vernon, replied:

> I recollect well, to have heard the late Richard Bland of
> Prince George Cty. say, before the Revolution, that he was either
> possessed of, or was collecting materials, and hoped to furnish a
> more correct history of it than any that was then extant. He was
> very competent to the undertaking, being a man of erudition and
> intelligence, long a member of the Councils of this State.

Bland, born in 1710 at Jordan's Point, a James River plantation in Prince George, inherited the property as a child, studied at The College of William and Mary in colonial Virginia's capital of Williamsburg, and graduated with a law degree from the University of Edinburgh in Scotland. In the lead-up to the American Revolution, he inked his quill pen to compose stirring pamphlets against the British and served in the Continental Congress. While he believed, for a time, that the nagging strains and growing antagonisms between the 13 colonies and London could be amicably resolved, he eventually came to advocate the hanging of Lord Dunmore, the royal governor ensconced in Williamsburg. Bland died in the critical year of 1776, after the Declaration of Independence was proclaimed but long before the outcome of the rebellion was known. He is buried on his plantation.

In 1800, writing from Richmond, James Madison, another Virginian, scrawled a hasty note to Thomas Jefferson at Monticello to update him on how the balloting for president was going, an election Jefferson would eventually win. Madison enthused, "The republican ticket has had complete success in this quarter. In Prince George, the vote for it was 197. While it was only 9 for the opposit[e] one." The "opposite one" was the sitting president, John Adams.

In his seminal book, "The Prince George-Hopewell Story," Francis Earle Lutz jotted images of Prince George at the start of the 19th century as

> essentially an agricultural county and not too prosperous a
> one due to the gradual depletion of the soil. The population...
> was 7,429. There were 2,799 white residents and 4,630 Negro
> residents. Of the latter, 250 were free.... The county had no
> incorporated towns.... There were thriving settlements,...but
> these were just straggling accumulations of buildings with no
> governing bodies. Along the Appomattox and James Rivers, stately
> mansions occupied the bluffs and from these were operated the
> larger plantations, for which the county was noted.... One stage
> line passed through the county, but the streams continued to be the
> arteries for commerce and travel.

One of the earliest descriptions of the county was published in 1814 in "The Geographical and Historical Dictionary of America and the West Indies," a translation of a Spanish book by Colonel Don Antonio de Alcedo:

> There are five Episcopal churches in the county, one meeting
> for Friends, and several Methodist meetings. The Baptists have
> occasional meetings, and to this sect the Negroes seem particularly
> attached. It is a fruitful country, and abounds with wheat, corn,
> flax, cotton, and tobacco. Cotton here is an annual plant; and, in
> summer, most of the inhabitants appear in outer garments of their
> own manufacture.

> The timber consists of oaks of various kinds, and of a good
> quality, sufficient to build a formidable navy, and within a
> convenient distance of navigation.... Here is also abundance
> of wild grapes, flowering shrubs, sarsaparilla, snake-root, and

ginseng. Apples are inferior in spirit and taste to those in the
e.states; but peaches have a flavour unknown in those states. The
almond and fig will grow here in the open air, if attended to.
Immense quantities of pork and bacon are cured here, and indeed
form the principal food of the inhabitants. Veal is excellent, mutton
indifferent, poultry of every kind in perfection and in abundance.
The winters are short and generally pleasant.

In 1893, Peter Randolph lifted his pen to record the oppression that he had known decades earlier in "From Slave Cabin to the Pulpit." The account of his life tells of his master, Carter H. Edloe, owner of Mount Pleasant, Brandon and Dandridge's, three plantations in Prince George County. According to Randolph, the slave-owner had signed a secret will in 1838. In it, Edloe set aside all previous wills and declared:

I desire that my estate shall be kept together and cultivated to
the best advantage, until a sufficient sum can be raised to pay my
debts,...and to raise a sufficient sum to pay for the transportation
of my Slaves to any Free State or Colony which they may prefer,
and give to each Slave Fifty Dollars.

Edloe also designated $8,000 for his "female slave, Harriet Barber, and her children." If there wasn't that much money available, he directed his executors to sell land in order to amass the required funds. He also ordered them to give Harriet and her children "their Free Papers." After his death in 1844, Edloe's testament was entangled in courts— and shenanigans—that kept the slaves locked in bondage, according to Randolph's account. After three years, they finally got their manumission papers and $14.96, rather than the promised $50. Randolph grabbed his share and lit out for Boston.

Edloe wasn't the only slave-owner in Prince George to embrace emancipation in a will. As early as 1787, a Prince George resident named Barnaby Nixon worded his will thusly:

Being fully persuaded that freedom is the natural right....
having under my care Negroes of the following names and

ages Jimme aged about 23 yrs, Jacob abt 26 yrs I do therefore
emancipate and set free the said Negroes—and having also under
my care Negroes now in their minority of the following names and
ages vizt Moses (16 yrs), Mille (8 yrs), Polly (3 yrs) whom I also
hereby emancipate and set free, yet I believe it right for me to act
as a guardian over them until the male arrive to the age of twenty
one years and the females to the age of eighteen years.

In 1823, a woman named Jane Barr freed ten black people and bought land for them out of the estate. However, as with Edloe, her living executor failed to carry out her dying wishes.

Freed blacks in the antebellum Prince George County included Easter Gilliam Tinsley, who owned slaves herself. Angelica Chappell, an emancipated slave, remained in the county in the 1830s as a result of support from white citizens, who went against the prevailing practice of forcing ex-slaves to abandon the commonwealth. One historian estimates that "at the beginning of the Civil War there were in Virginia nearly sixty thousand free negroes. That total was far in excess of the number of free colored persons in any other of the great slave States and about doubled the count in North Carolina." But Prince George County was still a place where a northerner who had long lived there was threatened by "a vigilance committee" and advised to leave the state. The cause was the discovery that he was reading The Albany (NY) Evening Journal, an abolitionist newspaper.

During the Civil War in the 1860s, the rural county was repeatedly crisscrossed by troops of both sides. Passing through, a Maine sergeant named Nathan Webb ridiculed the courthouse town as "dreary-looking" and "medieval," adding, "I don't see how people could live here and be contented with such little progress. If any of them ever visited the North they must have been surprised."

In "The Cannoneer," his reminiscence of the war, Augustus Buell described how General George Meade turned the county into a supply resource for his army, work that was the responsibility of quartermasters:

The whole country south of the James, as far as Prince George
Courthouse, was turned into a pasture for vast herds of cattle,

*which were guarded by cavalry and butchered from day to day
to afford fresh meat for the hard-worked troops in the forts and
trenches. Huge piles of baled hay and oats in sacks for the cavalry
and artillery horses lined the railway or were accumulated in the
camps. The camps in the rear of the works became villages. Every
company or battery had log cookhouses. Every regiment had a
bakery, from which the troops got abundance of cooked rations,
including soft bread every day, fresh beef three or four days in the
week, with bean soup or pea soup or dessicated vegetable soup, and
coffee and tea on tap all the time.*

A native son of the county, Edmund Ruffin, a fire-eating slave-holder
who stood four-square for secession, would not have been surprised by the
opinions of ignorant Yankee interlopers, nor interested in the memoirs of
a Union officer. In his late sixties as the war began, he may have personally
ignited it. He claimed in his diary to have fired the first shot in the
direction of Fort Sumter, the April 1861 attack that launched four years of
internecine slaughter.

"I was delighted to perform the service," he wrote. "The shell struck the
fort, at the north-east angle of the parapet. The firing then proceeded...
from 14 different batteries." Inside the besieged redoubt, Captain Abner
Doubleday recorded in his diary that "a ball...lodged in the magazine wall,
and by the sound seemed to bury itself in the masonry about a foot from
my head, in very unpleasant proximity to my right ear. This is the one that
probably came with Mr. Ruffin's compliments."

Ruffin's act was reciprocated later. The August 23, 1862, issue of
Harper's Weekly, a northern paper, printed a Union officer's report that

*a landing was effected [on the James River] by the two
regiments at six o'clock, and in a short time after dense clouds
of smoke were seen issuing from the houses of the secesh [i.e.
secessionists], which were about one mile from the banks of the
river. Ten houses—among others that of the Hon. Edmund
Ruffin—were burned down by our troops.... Cheers rent the air
as the fire was observed breaking.*

City Point, which is today a part of Hopewell, became a focal point of history toward the end of the War Between the States. Located where the James and Appomattox rivers converge, it was chosen by General Ulysses S. Grant as his headquarters during the months-long siege of nearby Petersburg. Between the two lay Prince George Courthouse. City Point soon became one of the busiest ports in the world as tons of materiel passed through. Seven hospitals were erected as well as a sufficient number of bakeries to produce 100,000 rations of bread daily. In his Pulitzer Prize-winning book, "A Stillness at Appomattox," historian Bruce Catton outlines the changes at the site:

> Wharves lined the waterfront for more than a mile, with more docks extending up Appomattox. An average day would see 40 steamboats, 75 sailing vessels and 100 barges tied up or anchored along the waterfront. An Army hospital that covered 200 acres and that could accommodate 10,000 patients crowned a bluff above the river.... The quartermaster general boasted that the facilities here were so extensive that he could easily supply an army of 500,000 men.... To connect this seaport with the army, the government had built a twenty-one mile railroad, complete with freight yards, coal stocks, roundhouse, repair shops, and all the rest.

As one modern author, Scott Reynolds Nelson, summarized the change, "Prince George County, once a sleepy county of woody swamps, ramshackle plantations, and wasted soil [had been transformed] into a bustling transportation hub." (In his book, "Steel Drivin' Man," Nelson argues that the legendary John Henry was based on a real person who spent a great deal of time in Prince George County.)

As the war neared its end in the spring of 1865, President Abraham Lincoln, his wife Mary and their son Tad, just about to turn 12, arrived in City Point by ship. Lincoln, who ignored warnings about the lurking dangers of traveling the disputed waters, conferred with Grant, General William Tecumseh Sherman and Admiral David Porter. After his wife returned to the White House, the president and Tad stayed behind. The Great Emancipator arrived at the site on March 25 and did not leave until

April 8, four days after his son's birthday and less than a week before his own April 14 assassination.

When he learned of General Robert E. Lee's surrender on the day after Lincoln headed back to Washington, the histrionic Ruffin flew into a rage, writing:

> *I here declare my unmitigated hatred to Yankee rule—to all*
> *political, social and business connection with the Yankees and to the*
> *Yankee race. Would that I could impress these sentiments, in their*
> *full force, on every living Southerner and bequeath them to every*
> *one yet to be born! May such sentiments be held universally in the*
> *outraged and down-trodden South, though in silence and stillness,*
> *until the now far-distant day shall arrive for just retribution for*
> *Yankee usurpation, oppression and atrocious outrages, and for*
> *deliverance and vengeance for the now ruined, subjugated and*
> *enslaved Southern States!*

When he finished, he chose suicide over living under Union oppression.

There would be a brief period between the end of the Civil War and the beginning of the 20th century—the Reconstruction era—when white supremacy would weaken and free blacks would rise in Virginia to enjoy what had previously been unimaginable, such as jobs, days off, excursions and even political power. In 1868, as that era entered the state, The Staunton (Virginia) Spectator carried an article about the worries of conservative members of the state constitutional convention. A new constitution was being written for Virginia under federal law and northern pressure.

Southerners who bridled under that domination seized opportunities to throw it off. That group included members of the convention, who listed the overwhelming black majorities in many counties of the commonwealth, such as 5,492 blacks in Prince George County versus 2,918 whites. If suffrage were extended to the negroes, the members noted, votes for county office-holders would go to blacks:

> *Imagine the condition of the whites in a county under such a*
> *system. A negro sheriff, a negro attorney for the commonwealth, a*
> *negro superintendent of the poor, negro supervisors, negro assessors,*

negro collectors, negro school trustees, negro constables, negro
township clerks, negro overseers of the roads, negro magistrates.

The outraged parties complained that "the pivot of the system to
be inaugurated is, of course, negro suffrage. The [proposed constitution]
provides for this on the widest basis. There is universal negro suffrage,
without limitations, except that the party shall be a male, of sound mind,
twenty-one years of age, who has not been convicted of crime, and resided
twelve months in the State and three months in the county where he
proposes to vote."

On top of that outrage, the conservatives added, office-holders had to
take an oath that they "have never voluntarily borne arms against the United
States since [they] have been a citizen thereof; that [they] have voluntarily
given no aid, countenance, counsel, or encouragement to persons engaged
in armed hostility thereto." The result was obvious:

It is well known that there is not one white man in a
thousand in the State that can take this oath. It gives the State
absolutely to the negroes.... The mind is stupefied at the initiation
of negro domination. It is a waking nightmare, whose horrible
shadow cannot be pierced by the struggling faculties—a spell that
neither the senses nor the reason can dissolve.

Reconstruction and black majorities did indeed contribute to a spate
of electoral changes in Prince George County during the final decades of
the 19th century. As early as 1869, a black man was elected to represent the
county in the Virginia General Assembly. A decade later, Richard Bland,
a Negro who bore a celebrated name, was sent to the state's House of
Delegates by the county. In 1880, Virginia Republicans held a convention to
choose representatives to the national presidential convention in Chicago.
Dinwiddie County selected a "colored" man, while Prince George named
another Bland: E.D. Bland, a black state legislator.

In the lead-up to the choice of the Republican candidate for the
1884 congressional election, James P. Evans, a black mailman from
Petersburg, was a heavy favorite, but the party opted for James D. Brady,

61

a white man born in Virginia but raised in New York. He had returned to the state as a Union officer during the Civil War and won the election despite his northern sojourn. Although it meant Evans' loss, Brady was supported by many blacks, including a Prince George teacher named Edward Wellington Browne (sometimes rendered Brown). A minister, businessman, community activist, editor, farmer and physician, Browne was himself elected commissioner of revenue in Prince George, the same post both of Boisseau's parents would eventually hold.

Evans' unsuccessful bid for the Republican nomination presaged a successful run for Congress by a black man. Numbered among Brady's successors in representing the county in Washington, D.C., were two Epeses and John M. Langston, the offspring of a Virginia plantation owner and the slave he emancipated. His father was white, while his mother was black and Native American. During the contentious congressional campaign of 1888, the white Democratic candidate refused to appear alongside his opponent, so Langston toured the towns in the district on his own, speaking, among other places, at Prince George Courthouse.

His adversary seemed to have won the election. However, after a drawn-out dispute over ballot fraud, Langston supplanted him, thus becoming the first black man elected to Congress from the Old Dominion. Because of the length of time required to settle the question of the balloting, he ended up serving only five months in the House of Representatives. Great-uncle of poet Langston Hughes, the congressman was also a lawyer, dean of Howard University Law School, and U.S. minister to Haiti and San Domingo. Nonetheless, when he died in 1897, The New York Times took pains to describe his mother as "a bright mulatto" and him as bearing "the complexion of a creole. His features were good, betraying no African characteristics."

That flowering of political success, fertilized by Republican efforts to lift up former slaves and a warm season when a minority became the majority in areas of Virginia, would fade with the 1800s. White Virginians, as well as other Southerners, reasserted their dominance through such tactics as Jim Crow laws that enforced segregation and poll taxes that squelched black suffrage. Lutz, in his history of the county, said of the rewriting of the Virginia constitution in 1901 and the introduction of a poll tax:

There is no question that it cut Virginia's voting population in half within a brief period. The Negro vote in Prince George was wiped out virtually, or made ineffective for more than a generation.

Jim Crow laws did not die easily. In 1949, Virginia voters defeated a measure to repeal the poll tax by a nearly four-to-one margin. Even the NAACP opposed the repeal because the successor law would have permitted the state legislature to install literacy tests and other regulations in place of the tax. It was not until the mid-1960s that the 24th Amendment to the Constitution and a Supreme Court decision forbade poll taxes. At the time, Virginia was one of only five states that still required payment for the right to vote.

In 1910, Virginia's total population stood at about two million people, one-third of whom were black. In Prince George County, the 1910 U.S. Census found that blacks outnumbered whites, 4,551 to 3,297. Men and women were almost equally divided, while the total population of 7,848 was just about evenly scattered in the county's five districts, named Blackwater, Bland, Brandon, Rives and Templeton.

A 1911 report co-edited by W.E.B. DuBois found disparities in the county's schooling for black and white children:

The colored schools have a term of three months and the whites a term of five months; 1,608 Negro children and 1,700 whites attended school regularly; 25 Negro teachers and 36 white for three Negro schools and five white; seven grades in each. Appropriation for whites annually $20,000, for the colored $10,000. Yet there is a marked improvement over ten years ago. Not much of the $1.00 per capita tax goes to the colored schools. In general Negro public school education here is above the average, and the teachers are well fitted for the work.

Land in Prince George in 1910 was valued at about $7 an acre. "Colored persons," despite being in the majority, owned only 26,000 acres, worth around $185,000. Whites possessed 153,000 acres, valued at $1.1 million. When the value of buildings and town lots was figured in, black

63

county residents possessed a quarter-million dollars worth of real estate, a rate of approximately $55 per capita. Whites in the county, who made up 42 percent of the population, owned real estate assessed at $1.5 million, six times that owned by blacks.

Five years after that assessment, Boisseau Bailey was born into a county rich in history and natural resources, famed for its native sons and contributions to the creation of the nation, scarred by slavery and prejudice, and locked into some traditions and customs that would require decades to replace. As he matured through childhood, adolescence and early adulthood, he would, almost inevitably, be affected—and infected— by the good and the bad of Prince George.

CHAPTER SEVEN

WELCOME TO NEW GUINEA

Australia in the fall of 1943 (springtime below the Equator) was only a stop-over for Boisseau, who was soon to be delivered to Oro Bay, New Guinea. Code-named "Penumbra" during the war, Oro Bay is located close to the eastern tip of the second-largest island in the world (Greenland is first).

M.W. Stirling, in "The Native Peoples of New Guinea," writes that the island "sprawls like a gigantic turtle, with its head facing to the west. Lying barely south of the Equator, it is separated from Cape York, Australia, by the narrow, island-dotted Torres Strait." In his assessment of one of the battles fought on the island, Dr. Edward J. Drea captures the massiveness of New Guinea:

> If New Guinea were superimposed over the United States, Milne Bay would be south of Norfolk, Virginia, Lae at Pittsburgh, the major Japanese base of Wewak at Detroit, Biak Island at Minneapolis, and the westward extension of Dutch New Guinea would extend well into the state of South Dakota.... The north coastline is about 2,400 kilometers long, and the island, at its widest point, is 645 kilometers wide, approximately the distance from Washington, DC., to Cincinnati, Ohio.

In his history of the war in the Pacific, Samuel Eliot Morison was more succinct, calling New Guinea "one of the least known and least wanted parts of the world." But the Japanese wanted it badly for strategic reasons. In early 1942, just months after Pearl Harbor and well aware of the island's significance to both themselves and the Allies as a shield lying above Australia, a country they needed to neutralize, the Japanese began their conquest of New Guinea. In his entry in "The Dictionary of the U.S. Army," John R. Kennedy writes, "In 1942, New Guinea was strategically valuable as both a blocking position and a springboard between the Allies in Australia and the Japanese in the Philippines."

Within weeks of their surge against the island, the Japanese forces would be stalled by two outside forces—the unwelcoming geography and stalwart Australians—as well as by something internal: the nature of the Empire's own military. Barrie Pitt, a journalist, enumerated the natural barriers:

> *To the Japanese [taking the island] was to have been almost a routine operation.... Several factors conspired to make it the reverse of easy. There were the difficulties of the overland route across the Owen Stanley Range, the only practical approach to [their ultimate goal of] Port Moresby. For most of its length, originally a one man wide trail, it successively burrowed through steaming jungle, scaled mountains and dived into ravines. Maintaining supplies over such a road presents problems. Then the appalling climate which, among other trials, often turned the track into a muddy torrent.... Thirdly the climate's associated pests, parasites and diseases, which weakened and debilitated, turning fit fighting men into shaky shadows in a few days.*

In "The Pacific Campaign," author Dan van der Vat asserts that the Japanese assessment of New Guinea was based on "a misapprehension. The....command believed that there was a 'road' from Buna across the Owen Stanley range and also seriously underestimated the treacherous horrors of the terrain."

Facing those inhuman foes was one problem. Another was the Australian troops that had been rushed into New Guinea to counter Japanese aggression. Pitt named the Aussies' pluses as "dogged persistence and courage in resolutely denying the Japanese advance, and more, pushing them back." Meanwhile, according to "New Guinea: The Tide Is Stemmed," written by John Vader, U.S. reinforcements were hurrying to SWPA—the South West Pacific Area. By June 1942, nearly 40,000 Americans were in the region to bolster the 100,000 Australian regulars and 200,000 militiamen who were striving to repel the invaders.

In the late fall of 1942, a photo was taken of three dead U.S. soldiers along a beach on the island. For nearly a year, the picture was unseen by Americans. Then, in a breakthrough approved by the War Department,

Life magazine printed the image in its September 20, 1943, issue, along with these words:

> *Why print this picture…of three American boys, dead on*
> *an alien shore?… The reason is that words are never enough.*
> *The eye sees. The mind knows. The heart feels. But the words*
> *do not exist to make us see, or know, or feel what it is like, what*
> *actually happens…. This is the reality that lies behind the names*
> *that come to rest at last on monuments in the leafy squares of*
> *busy American towns.*

While united in pain and death, Australian and American troops could sometimes have a contentious relationship. The men from the States were occasionally derided as "over-paid, over-sexed and over here." Additionally, the U.S. military leadership had the attitude of "move over and let the big boys run things." As van der Vat puts it:

> *Australia played broadly the same role in the war in the Far*
> *East as Canada did in the struggle against Germany. Each was*
> *a geographically vast, demographically small, and strategically*
> *important dominion, an independent British commonwealth*
> *nation…. Each loyally declared war when Britain did;…each*
> *had to see its armed forces serve, often far from home, under*
> *first British and later American commanders-in-chief. Like*
> *Canada's…. Australia's steadfast and usually unglamorous*
> *contribution to ultimate victory has been consistently undervalued.*

In "The Long Green Shore," his novel about Australian troops in New Guinea, John Hepworth, an Aussie veteran, writes:

> *The Yanks always seems to have too much of everything—*
> *compared to us—and they always seem to leave half their gear*
> *behind them when they go…. They are all right—they fight well,*
> *when they can throw a couple of hundred tons of high explosives*
> *into a position. They live too well—compared with us, that is. They*
> *get too much money—compared with us. They talk as though no*
> *one else was fighting the war. They take our girls.*

Lieutenant Commander Morris D. Coppersmith, born in Eastern Europe and raised in Illinois, pled guilty to the charges in a letter home from Australia (www.topshot.com/dh/Victory.html):

> *The Australian soldier is jealous of the American serviceman and has begun to resent him. You can hardly blame him. He is given the equivalent of about $1.00 a day to spend when he is in town. That would be about enough to buy his food. He has no money left with which to take out girls.... It's impossible for them to compete. As for the girls—they love the American boys. The Aussie hasn't a chance.... I'm sure if the situation were reversed and if the Aussie would take over in our country as we have here, the resentment would run much higher.*

But, under assault by the Empire of Japan, the Australian troops, nicknamed Diggers, were relieved and happy to see the GIs, as witnessed in a song, "Mr. Doughboy," that celebrated unity among British, Australian and U.S. soldiers:

> *Mister Doughboy, off we go boy;*
> *We've taken it, but we can give it too.*
> *Tommies, Diggers and now the Doughboys,*
> *All for one and one for all,*
> *The Eagle, the Lion and the Kangaroo.*

As a result of the predominance of American officers, troops and equipment, as well as the preponderance of U.S. post-war historians, Australians have been given little notice for their role in liberating New Guinea. A notable exception was the Academy Award given to "Kokoda Front Line!" a 1942 Australian documentary about Aussie troops battling the Japanese.

In addition to the doggedly persistent Allies and the forbidding nature of New Guinea itself, another factor was working against the Japanese. In "Fire in the Sky: The Air War in the South Pacific," Eric M. Bergerud outlines how the Japanese might have been their own worst enemies:

When pressed, the Japanese command did not just make errors; it wallowed in confusion and indecision. Japan's operational planners had done a splendid job of designing the initial blitzkrieg [against New Guinea]. However, in retrospect, serious disagreements between the army and navy as well as between factions within the navy had been covered over by the press of events and the cavalcade of victories. Worse still, the Japanese had not evolved an effective mechanism for developing a coherent response to an unexpected situation. Allied leaders feuded continually, yet at some point a decision was made.

The precise date of Sergeant James Boisseau Bailey's arrival on the island isn't known, but his first surviving letter from New Guinea is dated January 11, 1944. In it, he speaks of not enjoying Christmas and working as usual on that holiday. That implies that he arrived on the island at the same time as the 2nd Cavalry Brigade, which left Strathpine, Australia, on December 19, 1943, bound for Oro Bay. They were coming to a site that had been active for exactly a year. By December 20, 1942, the deep-water port of Oro Bay had become an advanced base for the U.S. military. Five months later, it was formally designated as "Advanced Sub-Base B."

The location became the repeated target of fierce Japanese air attacks in the spring of 1943. According to the website of the Australian War Memorial, "On 8 March 1943, [a ship named] s'Jacob was sunk off Oro Bay by Japanese bombers; Bantam fell victim to a similar attack later in the month, and was run aground as it was about to sink. Van Heemskirk was also sunk by aircraft at Oro Bay in April, and several other ships were seriously damaged by bombs." In May, a newspaper for servicemen ran the headline, "Enemy Air Force Active in N.G." The accompanying article listed the attacks as including "a raid by the Japanese on Wau, a strike by enemy dive-bombers against our forward troops,...and a raid on Moresby." Port Moresby is located across the slice of New Guinea that holds Oro Bay. Wau lies northwest of the port.

Boisseau's new home remained a danger zone as late as mid-October 1943, when 26 Japanese dive bombers and 45 Zeroes and other fighter planes blasted ships resting in the bay. U.S. airmen fended off the sorties, downing dozens of enemy aircraft. The danger of attack was so constant that orders were issued that all cargo, whether troops or supplies, was to be off-loaded only at night, beginning at 11 p.m. Whether or not the discharging was finished, the work was to cease at 4 a.m. so that the ships could scatter and not become sitting ducks for dawn patrols.

A 1943 military map of Oro Bay shows that it pokes into the island like a finger pressed against an elongated balloon, leaving a C-shaped indentation. Wharves and a pontoon bridge lined the edges of the bay. During his nearly two years there, Boisseau would have become familiar with nearby place names identified on maps by meandering stripes and hash marks: Pritchards Point, Chinaman Ridge, Beamu Creek, Leggs Lookout, Clarks Crossing, Crebers Road and Swamp Lake. Roads, Jeep tracks and footpaths traced throughout the area like veins. The bay itself—headed by the disconcertingly named Cemetery Point, which indeed featured a graveyard—rises from a depth of nine fathoms to two nearer the shore.

In his book, "The GI War: 1941-1945," Ralph G. Martin captured the many drawbacks of New Guinea:

> It was a fever country, a nightmare country, a country
> of torrential rains, tropical ulcers, and a steaming, sucking
> heat.... Somebody called the war in New Guinea a war of mud,
> mountains, malaria, mosquitoes and monotony.

Private Amico, the Connecticut teenager who belonged to the 481st Air Service Squadron, based in Nadzab, near Oro Bay, needed only five words to sum up the island: "blazing hot and always wet." His camp lay just a football field away from the jungle. "It was right there," he recalled. "The screeching of the birds scared you."

Joseph J. Martinelli Sr., a soldier from Brooklyn, was equally jumpy, as he told in an oral history collected by Rutgers University:

> You don't go deep into the jungle, because it gets dark in
> the jungles maybe by two o'clock in the afternoon, three o'clock,
> and, [if] you get lost in there, forget it.... Oh, the crocodiles and
> snakes and the bats; you used to hear them at nighttime. They'd

chip away…at the coconuts and you can hear them coming down,
"Boom, boom," and you don't know who the heck did it, you know.
Well, like I say, in the nighttime there, [with] all the noise, you
couldn't hardly sleep. You didn't want to sleep anyway.

In a WAC-published newsletter, a very-much-tongue-in-cheek article
sang the praises of New Guinea, noting:

Bring your golf clubs and tour the unmatched fairways of
the Buna Foxhole Club. Here the traps have frustrated the very
best Japanese professionals. The nights—ah—the nights…. The
soothing coo of the vampire bat is heard in the distance…. What
can be livelier than driving home through the ack-ack-spangled
night, watching the lazy searchlights in their slow probings…. The
elfin drone of the mosquitoes urge you gently down the slope of utter
peace. Tune your ears to the [creek] as it wanders toward the sea,
chuckling contentedly through the eye sockets of Jap skulls…. Yes,
come to New Guinea—and bring your straight jacket.

The conditions at Oro Bay, very crude to begin with, were slow to
improve despite military efforts. In an oral history, Edward Ferreri, a
dentist from Cleveland, Ohio, said that, in 1942, "the hospital facility
was primitive. The ward was a slab of concrete, 200 feet by 30 feet. It was
supported by posts. It had a tin roof, no sides. The surgery suite was like
a MASH unit. When I got there, we had no electricity to run the dental
drill. I had to have a man operate a foot treadle while I worked."

A soldier who passed through in early 1943 said it was "just a small
native village, tucked under some coconut trees, indistinguishable from
a dozen other native villages strung along that…coastline." It had a few
tents surrounding a field hospital. Writing on April 4, 1943, to his wife in
New York City, Major Grant Levin depicted his surroundings in Oro Bay,
where he had just arrived to staff the 1st Evacuation Hospital:

My house is again the ubiquitous small…tent…. The floor is
mud—not deep but squishy…. I have no furniture but my card
table…. There is nothing of which to make furniture but palm leafs

71

and saplings which are spongy and bleed sap when bruised....
We are close enough to the air strip now to be able to draw fresh
fruit, vegetables, meat occasionally for our rations since these
commodities are flown in, space permitting.

In the fall of 1943, the site, said one soldier, "looked like what we had been led to believe 'a South Sea tropical paradise' looked like, but the humidity and musty smell spoiled it all." So did the mosquitoes, bats and tarantulas. Levin told his wife that the "insects are rather troublesome and in unbelievable variety. There are 20 (at least) kinds of flies, most of them in beautiful iridescent colors, gnats, moths, butterflies, beetles, etc. The mosquitoes are the largest I have ever seen.... We also boast spiders in great number and variety, including tarantulas."

In "An Artist at War," his wartime journal, Private John Gaitha Browning, Mississippi-born and Texas-raised, described—in both frank and poetic language—coming to Oro Bay on October 26, 1943, just prior to Boisseau's arrival:

The beach...was a grayish black color from the volcanic soil. To
add to the unlovely look of the beach, the army camps have built a
mile-long string of latrines down the shore, each one a long walk of
poles extending out ninety feet into the ocean with a small canvas-
covered structure on the end. As the altitude is the terrific height of
from one to three feet above the sea level, no holes can be dug for the
latrines.... Every bug, bird, butterfly, tree, and weed is stranger here.

Levin told his wife, whom he addressed as "Jane darlingest," that "I wish you could see the night sky down here, with the Southern Cross. Nowhere else have I seen such brilliance. And when the moon is full, it is so light that only the brightest stars are visible. Some day we will see them together." But romantic images could not conceal the grim realities of Oro Bay. In "Proceed Without Delay," his memoir of the war, Thomas R. St. George described what he saw on arriving there:

From five miles at sea Oro Bay had all the romantic requisites
of a South Sea Island postcard—a dazzling sweep of white beach

backed by slim graceful palm trees and fronted by a foaming line of surf. Closer inspection revealed that the American Army had pretty effectively shattered the postcard possibilities by building latrines at frequent intervals along the beach.

When General Douglas MacArthur, commander of forces in the Southwest Pacific Area (SWPA), visited in mid-1943, he was dismayed by the state of the base and ordered it to be improved. It didn't happen swiftly. On December 18, 1943, Private Sy M. Kahn, a 19-year-old New Yorker and a member of the 244th Port Company, 495th Battalion of the Army Transportation Corps, landed at Oro Bay. In his wartime diary, published under the title "Between Tedium and Terror," Kahn recorded:

When we arrived [at Oro Bay], it was a discouraging sight.... The camp is a huge mud hole. Tents were up. Ground very wet, huge puddles and swamps about. Some of the tents couldn't be used, filled with water. Everything looks dilapidated and rickety. Conditions crude. Water is heavily chlorinated so that it puckers your mouth when you drink it. It must rain a great deal here. Directly to my left there is a small swamp with frogs. They make a continual racket, really an amazing amount of noises—which continued all night and, more surprisingly, all day.

MacArthur had handed the task of bringing the base up to speed to General Walter Krueger, who commanded the Sixth Army. In "From Down Under to Nippon," his account of the war in the Pacific, Krueger explained the obstacles that had to be overcome, while also fighting a war:

The difficulties were very great, especially since speed was of the essence. Extensive jungle areas had to be cleared, swamps drained, many miles of road built where not even trails had existed before... shelter and hospitals erected, and numerous other facilities provided.

Months after Kahn's assessment, a soldier still complained about "a reeking clutch of pit privies" that were "located within thirty feet of pumps providing the depot's drinking water." But the port was constantly, if tardily, being upgraded as more and more troops, male and female, arrived. Evidence of that is found in a letter written on June 18, 1944, by Corporal Vincent H. McLaughlin, a native of Rhode Island:

This present station is a much more pleasant base than our previous one.... Our tents are only a few yards from a beautiful beach and I average at least one swim a day usually just before dinner. The sun shines almost every day and the heat is abated by a cooling breeze from the sea.

Repairs to the facility and leisurely activities took place between repelling attacks—and dodging friendly fire. Lieutenant John R. Probert, a Pennsylvanian, got to Oro Bay in early 1943. For a time, he was transferred into Boisseau's 343rd QM Depot Company Supply. In an interview for this book, he described watching a battle of 300 to 400 planes above his head that was successful for the Allies and reduced the enemy bombings to scattered nighttime raids. Troops also had to be cautious about being wounded or killed by their own anti-aircraft fire. "The Australians would shoot straight up at planes," he explained, "and shrapnel would come down on you. You had to make sure you were wearing a helmet and in a foxhole."

The purpose of the port at Oro Bay was to provide all sorts of services to shipping, including ammunition supply, food provisioning, fueling and fresh water. One author described the bay as "badly congested with American shipping," leading the Australians to shift their own port to Buna, farther north. Probert recalls that the bay "could take sizable freighters," not to mention the off-shore barge on which officers built their own club. Dodging sharks, they would swim to and from it.

Roger Sykes, a New Yorker stationed at Oro Bay with the 491st Port Battalion, described the area for the website, www.pacificwrecks.org:

I remember the hot, humid, weather. I remember the constant traffic on the beach road. I think at that time perhaps two dozen ships were in harbor. Oro Bay was just a place to receive cargo and ship it to the forward areas. We were assigned to an area on Chinaman Ridge Road.... It was at a height we could see all the whole bay area.

In an interview for this book, Sykes elaborated, "I spent three years in Oro Bay. It was quite an active center. It was a tropical place—nice, quiet, with nice local people. The English and Australians manned all the facilities, like the electricity, which was iffy—meaning they gave it to us if they wanted to." He remembers Boisseau's quartermaster camp with "all kinds of facilities and shops. If you wanted something, you ordered it, and it would come in on a ship. I remember the Liberty ships in the bay. It was a fantastic sight."

The QM camp's role is described in the Army Field Manual covering Boisseau's unit:

> *The quartermaster depot company, supply, functions as a*
> *"pumping stations" along the supply line which…extends from the*
> *base section of the communications zone to the extreme forward*
> *areas. It is the joint mission of all installations along this supply*
> *line to push supplies forward within reach of troops in front.*

In April 1943, Yank magazine carried an article headlined "When an Outfit Moves up in New Guinea, They Always Tell the Quartermaster First." It describes a depot supply unit that, if it wasn't the one at Oro Bay, must have matched how Boisseau labored in terms of activity. "Sprawled across several hundred yards of muddy tropical shoreline is a GI supermarket that overcame all sorts of natural and enemy-made difficulties here to get food, clothing and equipment to the American soldiers," said the reporter. "Officially called the Quartermaster Supply Depot, it stands as one of the unsung achievements of the war in the southwest Pacific." The article lauded the QM unit for staying in touch with the locations of units in the field, providing necessities for survival and serving "units as small as 15 and as large as 6,000."

What it was like for Boisseau to be at the Oro Bay depot can be found in letters from other soldiers stationed there. For instance, TEC3 Ernest Carlson, a native of Washington State who was in the Signal Corps, told a college professor in a letter:

> *If you would like a GI's eye view of New Guinea, it would be*
> *an unending succession of steamy jungle, sunny bathing beaches,*

mess kits flashing in the sun, chow lines, beer lines, mosquitoes,
bugs, birds loud in both color and voice, gum wrappers and empty
beer bottles under bunks, black fuzzy-headed natives laughing
at the primitive methods GI's use to open coconuts, blazing hot
days, sudden violent downpours, muddy roads, hitchhikers, second
lieutenants, soldiers dodging falling coconuts, outdoor movies
where you bring your own box to sit on, heat rash, insect bites,
and last but most important, mail from the states. The weather
is always hot and humid and sticky.... It rains a lot, from light
drizzles to downpours where the water comes down hard enough
to drive nails. But this doesn't serve to cool it off much, as soon as
the sun comes out again it gets too hot to wear even an expression.

Still, said Carlson, "all in all, it isn't a bad life. We have quite a bit of work to do, but we get plenty of time for ball games and swimming. On a Sunday afternoon the beaches look like Coney Island, as all the boys and girls go to cool off." Boisseau told his mother in an August 1944 letter, "Am going swimming this after noon in the ocean."

A WAC who served in Oro Bay, Private Jennie Clark, began a V-mail home with a description of her new residence. "With the ocean on our front door & the jungle at the back," she said, "we are comfortably settled. It is a beautiful setting really—banana leaves, cocoanut palms, banyan trees—long stretches of beautiful beach." A month earlier, one of the women hitting that beach was Private Leatha Walker, a 29-year-old WAC from Ohio, who came to New Guinea to serve in Cape Sudest, about 15 miles north of Oro Bay. She was a stenographer in the Judge Advocate General's office there.

WACs were late in reaching New Guinea, partly because the ships needed to deliver them were crammed with combat and other military personnel. "The Oro Bay area proved generally suitable for women, with WAC camps, carved from the jungle, lying along the seashore, with beaches for front yards and palm trees for shade," wrote Mattie E. Treadwell in "The Women's Army Corps," a post-war analysis. "Swimming was permissible under certain conditions. Barracks were made of wood and screens, with a large recreation hall and mess hall already built nearby.... Since Oro Bay was principally a major supply base, much of the WACs' duties concerned the stock record reports and other paper work necessary to get materiel forwarded to combat troops. The Distribution Office was almost entirely staffed by WACs, who kept track of the ships and supplies in New Guinea."

Private First Class (and sometime Corporal) Robert Kopplin, an Illinois infantryman in New Guinea, described to his wife how the Army women were cordoned off from the men:

> *If you want a date with a WAC, you have to meet one outside somewhere & then have her put your name on the list, so you can get into camp, as they have a M.P. by the gate; also a fence around their camp, covered with canvas. The same with their tents; are screened in & got cement floors with electric lights. Now darling, the reason I know this, is we go past it to the movie. As I gave you my promise, I'll never cheat on you.*

Concerned about the mixing of male and female personnel, the Army was overly protective of the women, according to Treadwell:

> *Barbed wire was put up around the Oro Bay WAC area, and the women were forbidden to leave "any area at any time" without armed guards, even being marched to approved movies in formation under guard.... Off-duty activities were limited to approved unit parties and other mass entertainment to which women could be taken under guard, and even for these a woman's date had to be named twenty-four hours in advance, subject to disapproval by the senior WAC officer.*

Walker and other WACs were delivered first to Oro Bay by a cruise ship that had been refitted as a troop transport. In the third person, she wrote of the experience, one Boisseau most likely experienced when he disembarked:

> *On the last morning of the voyage, she came up on deck to see that the ship was anchored in a harbor and for the first time her wondering gaze fell on the island of New Guinea. The harbor looked out toward green hills, black masses of mountain in the*

background, their tops obscured by wisps of fog, and a thick grove
of tall slender cocoanut palms growing down to the beach. In spite
of all the training on cargo nets, [the WACs] walked from an open
hatchway in the side of the ship to a floating platform and there
were packed standing in amphibious jeeps to be taken ashore.

In an interview for this book, Walker described Cape Sudest as "a major base right on the ocean. You could see it from our office. A dirt road led from our office to our barracks, which were made out of plywood and screens. The men lived in tents in the opposite direction from us. We very rarely got away from the base. Once, I went on a truck to a cape east of us. The jungle was dense; you couldn't see much of anything. We also went to a battlefield. The trees were all scorched."

The scarred site was probably Buna, which lies northwest of Oro Bay. It was dubbed "Bloody Buna" after a ferocious battle was fought there in 1942-1943 as part of early efforts to re-take New Guinea from the Japanese. A report of the brutal warfare in Life magazine described a jungle "which looks like a Gaugin painting, sounds like a good-sized earthquake and smells like a charnel house.… As a general, who himself was using a tommy gun to pick off snipers from the treetops, said,… 'Damned war's gone old-fashioned on us up here.'" The reference was to World War I's trench fighting that increased both body counts and brutality. "One Jap was strangled to death by the bare hands of a big corporal from Chicago," said the Life author, who added, "Nowhere in the world today are the American soldiers engaged in fighting so desperate, so merciless, so bitter, so bloody.… It's kill or be killed."

In "MacArthur," author Sydney L. Mayer notes of Buna that "two weeks of fighting in November and a four-pronged Allied offensive had been stopped dead. Malaria and dysentery affected the Americans and the Japanese defenses were tough to crack." Frustrated and angry, MacArthur replaced the commanding officer, and it would be late January 1943 before victory was seized. Mayer estimates than 13,000 of the 20,000 Japanese forces died in the assault, with some of the survivors attempting to escape by swimming away from one of the battles.

In his official report on the Battle of Buna, Lieutenant General Robert L. Eichelberger, the substitute commander, stated as simply as possible the great significance of the event: "It was the first victorious operation of American Army ground forces against the Japanese." In his comments, he credited the supply efforts, including those "by water from Oro Bay."

However, an appendix to that assessment presented "The Quartermaster Report," which declared flatly that "logistically the campaign was a nightmare" and that "ineptitude played as big a part in the supply difficulties as did the physical conditions encountered." The fault, said the QM report, lay with the Engineers, who had been given the job of delivering supplies and were judged to be "inadequate for the job…. This instance is pointed out to emphasize that Quartermaster supply is specialized and that no one or no establishment can accomplish it properly except trained Quartermaster personnel."

Meanwhile, continued the assessment, QMs had been pressed into other duties, including delivering mail. "It is obvious," said the report, "that insofar as time and energy…was required in these duties, that personnel was handicapped in the performance of its own functional duties."

An infantryman, Private E.J. Kahn, later wrote about the conflict in "G.I. Jungle" and credited the quartermasters for their heroic efforts:

> Trawlers loaded with supplies for our advance elements would sneak up the northeastern coast of New Guinea under the cover of darkness and anchor several hundred yards off shore. It would then devolve upon the quartermasters to unload the cargoes and to do it quickly, …making dozens of exhausting trips without rest in order to get the vulnerable trawlers on their way again before daylight.

When Japanese planes appeared, he continued, "most of the soldiers would prudently run for foxholes. One quartermaster lieutenant, however,…would grab a tommy gun, rush out on the beach, and…yell angrily at the Zeroes trying to harm his nest of boxes."

But all of that was two years in the past when Private Walker visited the battlefield. Following Buna, the U.S. forces succeeded in defeating the Japanese in an array of land and sea battles. United Press summed them up in a round-up that ran in newspapers in early 1944, shortly after Boisseau's appearance in New Guinea:

Winning the Coral and Bismarck Sea battles by the slenderest
of margins, General MacArthur's men have defeated the Japanese
at Milne Bay, Papua, Wau, Lae, Salamaua, Finschhafen.
Markham and Ramu valleys, Arawe, Cape Gloucester and Saidor.

New Guinea was exotic in more ways than place names, including the native population. In his in-depth analysis of the island campaign, "MacArthur's Jungle War," Stephen R. Taaffe comments on the "hundreds of separate tribes" who

dotted the big island, from headhunters and cannibals in the
interior to more docile groups who had been exposed to European
culture and rule. Almost everything about them was alien to the
Americans. Most of the men dressed in loincloth.... The women...
wore grass skirts and nothing else.... The GIs called them "Fuzzy
Wuzzies," after their hair, and communicated with them in
pidgin English.

An article in The New Yorker termed pidgin English "a vastly confusing tongue" and quoted a language expert as saying that it was a mélange of English, German, Portuguese and Melanesian. Probert complimented the ingenuity of the native men, who were recruited to help build warehouses and tent platforms for Boisseau's unit. "They were handy with construction," he noted. "They made the warehouses for us, using native timbers with palm-frond roofs that were woven like shingles."

At some point, on the Pacific or in Australia, Boisseau was handed a copy of "A Pocket Guide to New Guinea and the Solomons." One soldier in an Engineers Battalion who served on the island said that he got his copy "on the way over." The pamphlet warned that it was "for use of Military Personnel only."

The cover featured the silhouette of a dancing male native, wielding a lance and clad only in a grass skirt and an elaborate headdress. Opposite the table of contents, a cartoon shows a terrified soldier fleeing natives, two of whom swing from the trees. One of them has clonked the soldier on the helmet with a thrown coconut. Looking on are two wiser military men, one of whom says, "I told him to read his Pocket Guide, but he said he knew how to make friends!"

"You don't need to be told," the introduction to the small booklet admits, "that campaigning in these islands is no picnic—you're often steamy and sweaty and muddy; in fact conditions are about as bad as on any battlefront in the world. But the islands are not all bad by any means.... An important part of your military assignment in these islands is to get along with the local people."

The locals, the brochure assures readers, were not likely to be headhunters or cannibals, who were to be discovered farther inland, but Christian converts. Nonetheless, it warns military personnel to make sure they stay out of sacred sites, Christian or pagan. As for clothing, what was Boisseau's reaction to reading that he would learn to "spot the home locality of a man by his type of loincloth or his penis covering of shell, gourd, or bark, and of a woman by the cut of her grass skirt or kilt"?

He was also admonished that "natives...are likely to resent outsiders interfering with their women.... Gonorrhea is very common; so is a venereal disease known as yaws." The women were usually clad only in skirts. In January 1944, Sergeant Robert D. Tuttle, an Ohioan stationed there with an Engineers unit, told his girl back home, "Hope you are fine and enjoying that nice cold Ohio weather. I am tired of seeing half naked women. I want to see something in a fur coat."

Sergeant William Alexander, a Mississippian working in a medical unit in New Guinea, was more complementary to the natives, describing in letters how the women skillfully caught fish and how boys worked with the sick at a native hospital run by the Australians:

> Last night the Aussie [from the hospital] came to the picture
> show and brought with him 3 of his young doctor boys (oldest
> was 12, then 8, then 7) who help with some of the tending to the
> patients' wants. These kids are fairly intelligent, can read and
> print as they went to German mission school. The youngest named
> Carleboo wanted to stay and help me.... The oldest named Awoo

was very intelligent and could sing some American songs such as
"Springtime in the Rockies" and "Are You Lonesome Tonight?" and
lots of our religious songs.

Alexander would also tell how deeply he was touched when he visited the native hospital:

I saw many sick women whose little children slept alongside
of them on the ground and tried best they could to help their needs
and to somewhat understand their pain. I saw several women who
would not weather through and I silently say a prayer for them
and [their] children. Tears could easily flow if I permitted for my
heart and soul was touched by their suffering.... As long as I live
I'll remember the native mothers and their babies alongside them
in their suffering. May they rest in peace with God.

Boisseau was probably also given a copy of "Getting About in New Guinea," produced by the Allied Geographical Section in the South West Pacific Area and "published for the information of all concerned by command of General MacArthur." The pocket-sized, soft-cover, 30-page publication was a guidebook for surviving in the jungle, and it strongly recommended reliance on the native population:

[The native] can live in the tropics, and not because he
has brown skin. It is partly because he has developed some
immunities, but mostly because he has learnt how to live there....
Remember that your great ally is the native. He knows his country
backwards—what to do and what not to do. You will do well to
make him your friend and rely on him.

The New Guineans would prove to be valuable assets in other ways, such as litter-bearers for the wounded, scouts, guides and laborers. One Ohio lieutenant told his wife:

The [native] men have been godsends to the troops in this area.
They have been tireless & uncomplaining workers. As stretcher-
bearers, they are unequaled. As builders of grass & palm-leaf

*huts, they have done a fine job. They are willing workers, & you
couldn't lose them in the jungles if you tried. They have carried food
& ammunition to the men in the front lines, & brought back the
wounded. As road builders & mosquito control workers, they are to
be thanked.*

E.J. Kahn Jr. sent dispatches from New Guinea to his former employer,
The New Yorker magazine. In one of them, he admitted that "the better
we American soldiers have come to know the permanent residents of this
island, the more we've appreciated them. At times they have been our sole
supply lines, as valuable as a railroad and somewhat surer." An Aussie soldier
penned an ode in tribute to the natives who carried wounded servicemen.
A couplet runs:

> *May the mothers in Australia, when they offer up a prayer,*
> *Mention these impromptu angels with the fuzzy-wuzzy hair.*

"Jungle Warfare," a publication of the War Department, credited
native peoples for their many "invaluable" pluses, including "scouting,
raiding, and harassing enemy communications," and "their familiarity
with the terrain and knowledge of the people and the language."
On the other hand, the manual warned that native peoples "usually
have very little sense of humor and do not understand American joking
and 'kidding.'"

All of that is not to say that the indigenous population was 100 percent
on the Allied side. Many natives worked for the Japanese forces and
retained fond memories of doing so when asked about their experiences
years later. Philip Strong, the Episcopal bishop of New Guinea, was not
shocked, as he noted in his wartime diary:

> *The fact that some natives in the Buna area went over to
> the enemy does not seem to me surprising. ... In similar
> circumstances of an overwhelming invasion—and the flight
> of all organized personnel, it would have happened in. ...
> Australia, and those cooperating with the enemy would have
> been white.*

As an article in The New York Times reported, a lieutenant in New Guinea said a native told him, "Jap come, we friend him; white man come, we friend him."

The War Department's introductory booklet about New Guinea encapsulated the political and religious makeup of the island, its history and climate, its customs and foods, its people and manners. As kindly as it treated the New Guinea population, the pocket publication was jammed with dire warnings about mosquitoes, dengue fever, poisonous water, snakes, hookworm and sunstroke. The War Department listed the many diseases troops encountered:

> *Water supplies are grossly contaminated, and there are no modern water supply systems. . . . There are no sewerage systems and natives are unwilling to use latrines. . . . Mosquitoes capable of transmitting malaria, elephantiasis (filariasis), break-bone fever (dengue fever), and yellow fever are found in large numbers. Flies are abundant and are important mechanical carriers of intestinal diseases and yaws. Mites are numerous, and lice and fleas are found. Blood-sucking leeches are extremely common. Chiggers may be carriers of "scrub typhus". . . . Other pests are ants, centipedes, cockroaches, scorpions, and rats. Poisonous snakes and crocodiles are the principal dangerous animals present.*

Probert, who contracted a mild case of malaria himself, said that the Army fought a constant battle against the disease. One reason was the soldiers' reluctance to take atabrine to block it. "They came down with malaria in droves," he said, "because they thought the atabrine would make them sterile." He and other officers in the South Pacific found the solution by insisting that the troops swallow the distasteful, yellow tablets in front of a witness before being allowed in the mess hall for chow. "That shut off the malaria very fast," he said.

The slogan, "Be Wise, Atabrinise," appeared in one Army Air Corps newspaper to remind soldiers to take their medicine. Kopplin said to his wife, "We still get those little yellow pills called adabrene, and they have a very bitter terrible taste. Got to drink water with them, and no one gets sick from them any more."

Atabrine was developed in the 1930s by German chemists as a synthetic option for quinine. Ironically, those scientists thus undercut their WWII allies, the Japanese, who had cornered the quinine market through their early successes in the Pacific, particularly in the Netherlands Indies, which accounted for 90 percent of the world's sources of cinchona bark, from which quinine was produced.

The U.S., aware of what the Japanese might do, had secured half-a-million ounces of quinine, but it was lost at sea, according to The New York Times. In March 1942, Sterling Products announced it was increasing its production of atabrine by 8,000 percent. In December, Rear Admiral Charles E. Stephenson, director of the U.S. Typhus Commission, said that the increase in atabrine had nullified Japan's monopoly on quinine. Production of the drug rose to 800 million tablets annually and then to one billion by May 1943. Between January 1942 and August 1945, nearly five billion tablets were manufactured. One study found that atabrine helped to reduce annual malaria admission rates to hospitals in New Guinea from 740 per 1,000 soldiers to 26.

Although it didn't sterilize troops, atabrine was not without its side-effects, both minor and major. Some military personnel reported that their skin turned color as a result of the medication. Sergeant Thomas, the Ohioan, said simply, "I was yellow." In a letter to her husband, Lieutenant Irvin Michelson, with the 262nd Medical Battalion in Australia and, later, New Guinea, Jo Michelson assured him:

> I don't know anything about this atabrine you're going to
> start taking but you know damn well I'll love you if you come home
> yellow, purple or even Kelley green just so you come back to me in the
> shortest time possible.

Coloring was a minor side-effect, compared to another outcome. Medical personnel found that two in a thousand patients developed "psychotic reactions" to the drug. Convulsions were also reported in patients.

Malaria was only one drawback to Boisseau's new home. Private Raymond L. Porter, a quartermaster from New Jersey who was a year older than Boisseau and also stationed in New Guinea, described the island in a V-mail as "nothing but jungles and mud. There isn't even one town of any sort on the entire island." Shapiro, the poet who ended up on the island, wrote that the rain was "a rain that no one had ever before imagined existed and couldn't be called rain. It was more like a shipment of solid water with no space between the drops."

One private stationed in New Guinea, in a letter home to his father, described a particularly nasty insect. "Did you ever have any experience with the so-called banana bug in your Army life in this part of the world?" he asked. "It is a black bug about an inch long and as one soldier said pinches you with one end, raising a lump, turns around and bites the lump off. It hurts.... I have had experiences."

A West Point professor and brigadier general labeled the island as "a hot and humid mixture of jungle and swamp, infested with insects and leeches. Scrub typhus, malaria, dengue fever, dysentery and skin infections were endemic."

Much to his regret, skin ailments would be an affliction Boisseau was about to learn a lot about.

CHAPTER EIGHT

THE LATE WAR

The Second World War was not the first conflict to impinge on the lives of people of Prince George County. Visitors who deploy the expression "the war" had better be more specific about which one they mean because not all Southerners have let go of the Civil War.

Days after the fighting began with the bombardment of Fort Sumter in South Carolina in April 1861, Virginians held a convention to decide the question of formal secession. When the roll of delegates was called, Timothy Rives, the representative from Prince George, where 60 percent of the population was enslaved, replied, "The Government being already overthrown by revolution, I vote 'aye'." The final vote was 88 to 55 to leave the Union, an action that would have a powerful impact on Rives' home county. The Richmond Daily Dispatch, for example, reported in August 1864 that "we are informed that the Masonic Lodge at Prince George Courthouse, and other houses, have been pulled to pieces, and the timber used in the construction of Yankee hospitals."

Explaining 150 years later why so many historic documents are missing from the county's courthouse, a Prince George County woman said, "We had 'The Burning Time.' That's when..." She paused and looked at the New York man seated on the other side of the table. "That's when the,..." she trailed off again. Finally, summoning as much politeness as she could, she said, "That's when *your people* pulled everything out of the courthouse and burned it."

The New York visitor asked, "Do you want to say 'damn Yankees'?" She nodded gratefully. Told about the conversation, a man from the vicinity of Richmond confirmed, "Some of us are still fighting that war." For many Southerners who had been invaded and soundly defeated, blind anger and deep resentment would be passed down through generations, along with stories of Yankee depredations. As one Virginian said in the 21st century, "My family always talked about how my grandma's grandma was—I won't say 'raped'—but bothered by a Yankee soldier."

In its August 8, 1864, issue, The New York Times told readers that "St. [sic] George court-house was wantonly set fire to and destroyed this morning by some soldiers." In 1886, an article in The New York Times reconfirmed the wartime arsons, lit by both sides of the conflict:

> *Destruction of public property, authorized and unauthorized,*
> *is a certain accompaniment of civil war, and the records of many*
> *a county at the South were made useful in kindling a fire beneath*
> *the Union soldier's coffee kettle.... Neither side can properly claim*
> *any virtue over the other in this respect.*

The reporter then revealed that he had personal possession of "writs issued out of the County Court to the Sheriff of Prince George County," given to him by the descendants of a Union soldier. Two of those documents were written in 1745 and 1774, dates attesting to their historic value. The thefts and arson rightly outrage people 150 years later, and enmity against the Northerners who stole them still burns in some as hotly as the fires that consumed the papers.

Sometimes, however, that heat could be transferred to people from the North who had nothing to do with the destruction. In 1901, for instance, when William B. Wemple, the deputy clerk of Prince George County, was arrested for "having attempted an assault upon Mrs. Hoggard," the Richmond newspaper made sure to include the information that he was "of northern birth." The obvious implication was that a southern gentleman would do no such thing. It turned out that the inebriated clerk had merely put his hands on her shoulders to ask for 80 cents.

As he grew up, Boisseau would have breathed in tales connected to the "late unpleasantness," as more courtly Southerners termed the Civil War. His great-uncle, Sheriff Boisseau, was 11 when the battle of Gettysburg was waged and 13 when Abraham Lincoln was assassinated. Returning Confederate troops were no doubt passing by his front door and coming inside as kin looking to resume their civilian lives. His daughter Marywood, whom Boisseau affectionately called Aunt Macy or Sis Mary, was born only 20 years after the hostilities ended in a farmhouse in Appomattox, another courthouse town 85 miles to the west. She, too, would have listened as her elders swapped tales of the war and passed them on to a red-headed boy born on the 50th anniversary of the end of the war.

Boisseau also grew up in an atmosphere of racial prejudice that was so common it wasn't noticed. In a V-mail, he did not hesitate to call a black man who worked at the town gas station "Old Coon" Jones. A search for the word "nigger" in Petersburg newspapers between 1865 and 1900 turned up 86 examples, such as this one in 1868 in The Petersburg Index: "A nigger woman delivered a lecture at Farmville on Monday evening. Subject 'The Beauties of Radicalism!'"

Beyond such insults, there were racially motivated lynchings in the county, where a black man accused of attempted rape of a white woman was killed in 1889. However, the hangings did not always involve whites executing blacks outside the law. In January 1904, a rare instance of black-on-black mob violence occurred when outraged black men hanged Elmore Mosley, a "colored person" or "negro" in the vocabulary of the time. Due to insufficient evidence, Mosely had been acquitted of killing Alexander Fields, yet another black person, and the mob was enraged that Mosely had literally gotten away with murder. Mosley protested his innocence even as the rope was draped around his neck. The deed was "quietly and quickly done," complimented The Alexandria Gazette.

There was also another side to Virginia life. In Farmville, in Prince Edward County to the west, authorities learned around midnight on April 4, 1903, that a mob planned to attack the jail. Irate over the murder of a railroad conductor, the lynchers plotted to forcibly remove Alexander Davis, the accused black man, for some swift, moonlit justice. Two white men—the county court judge and the mayor—consulted about what to do. At 2 a.m., they determined to spirit Davis out of the jail and conceal him somewhere until the crowd simmered down. "Saved A Negro's Neck" headlined the report in The Washington Post. In that instance, upholding the law trumped hanging the black man.

In a reverse instance that occurred in 1889, a black man attempted but failed to save a white from being hanged. Robert Bland, 21, was arrested for attempted sexual assault on a 16-year-old and placed in the Prince George County jail. A lynch mob of about 40 men seized Henry King, "the negro jailer," and demanded the keys. Despite a rope that was placed around his own neck, he refused to surrender them. The crowd found them in his pocket, however, and pulled Bland from his cell. A newspaper report said that Bland was strung up about 75 yards from the jail. As he choked to death, his body became target practice for the mob.

In 1897, Charles O'Ferrall, the outgoing governor of Virginia, issued a message to the legislature about several pressing matters, including health, farming and industry. Then his message came to a new and dramatic heading: "Preservation of Law. Lynching." He proudly noted that three illegal hangings had occurred during the four years of his administration and contrasted that figure with the average of nearly four per year that had been carried out over the prior 18 years. One of the three was particularly dismaying, he said, because it happened with the deliberate neglect, if not approbation, of the public authorities of the city of Alexandria:

There may be no doubt the prisoner was guilty of a most heinous crime, committed under the most diabolical circumstances, and deserved death, but he was in the custody of the law officers, safely confined, and yet a mob was permitted in a city of 18,000 population, with a strong military force at the command of the Mayor, to bid defiance to the law and trample down the authority of the Commonwealth. There can be no possible excuse offered for the success of the mob. . . . The spirit of lynching will never be fully eradicated in any State until there are stringent laws against it, so enacted as to be enforcable, and then behind the law stands a warm, living, sustaining public sentiment, and this sentiment will never assert itself until the people fully realize that "where law ends, tyranny begins," and the public press no longer caters to the spirit and condones the crime of lynching as some of the papers in Virginia, be it said to their shame, have done recently.

Virginia would not pass anti-lynching legislation until 1928.

The hanging of blacks was one of the few ways in which Virginia newspapers took note of them in the years after the Civil War. An analysis of The Richmond Times-Dispatch during one random week in June 1910 found little notice of black people at all and almost none that was positive. Page after page of the issues can be turned without any attention being given to anyone who wasn't white.

On the occasions when black people were reported on, it was almost universally because they were criminals. In more than 40 small news items, the journal told of "colored" people who had stolen, picked pockets, assaulted, murdered and gone to prison. Black-on-black crime was often relayed, such as the man who clubbed his friend with the handle of a pick-axe or a "negro" shot at by another black man. Lengthier articles rarely strayed from negative portrayals of black men and women, like a female nurse who tried to poison a white child and a ruling by the Supreme Court of the District of Columbia that a single drop of "negro blood" rendered the person black. The Richmond paper termed the decision "hard, but sound policy" because a drop "fixes on him forever the stamp of inferiority."

Even articles that seem, on the surface, to be positive about black people turn out not to be. For instance, the newspaper urged immediate U.S. Senate confirmation of President Taft's appointment of Dr. W.D. Crum of Charleston, South Carolina, as ambassador to Liberia, but only because he "is a very good negro." It noted that he had earlier been named collector of the Charleston port "not because of any special fitness for it but because of the color of his skin.... He represents one of the most disgraceful incidents in American politics." In Africa, on the other hand, he would be the absolutely right person in the very right place.

The single obituary of a black person in the week's worth of news was for a "colored cook" who "followed howitzers in war." In what war did he fight? The War Between the States. On what side did he fight? The Confederacy. The obit lauded him for being "one of the few remaining colored men who followed the fortunes of their white friends.... He shared the discomforts of camp life, the hardships of the march and often the dangers of the battle in his faithful service to the hungry soldiers."

In 1962, a century after the Civil War, Attorney General Robert F. Kennedy's Justice Department filed suit to end racial discrimination in schools that got federal assistance. The target was Prince George County, which had received more than $2.5 million in aid, half for construction of schools and half for maintenance. In its September 28, 1962, issue, Time magazine summed up the case this way:

If they work on U.S. bases in the South, Negro civilians and servicemen must send their children to the generally inferior Negro schools. Yet they pay federal taxes to support such segregation: the Government gives some $75 million a year to help schools in the South's "impacted" areas—those whose local taxes are insufficient to provide schools for an influx of federal workers' children. Is this fair to U.S. employed Negroes?

Emphatically no, said the Justice Department last week in a significant federal suit involving the Government for the first time as original plaintiff in a school desegregation case. The target: Virginia's Prince George County, site of Fort Lee, which houses the Army Quartermaster School. While getting hefty impact aid, Prince George last year assigned 117 of Fort Lee's Negro children to Negro schools. The Justice Department goal is not to cut off the aid, but to force an end to segregation. Ultimate aim: the same for about 70 other impacted school districts throughout the South.

A Prince George school board member retorted that the federal authorities were "trying to cram [Negroes] down our throats—in the white schools—whether we have room for them or not and we don't have the room."

CHAPTER NINE

'I GOT YOUR V-MAIL LETTER YESTERDAY'

On his sleeve when formally uniformed, Boisseau sported a patch with the traditional eagle, and crossed sword and key over a wheel of the Quartermaster Corps, along with a T4 insignia on his arm and QM collar insignia. He wore his rank of TEC 4 proudly enough that he made a point of telling his mother in late August 1944 that Mrs. Zikes of Prince George was still addressing her letters to "P.F.C. James Bailey," a rank the sergeant hadn't held in months.

While there is nothing overtly emotional about that remark, it hints at his hurt pride. In his letters, his feelings are mostly muted, the biggest exception being another August letter in which he vehemently—and uncharacteristically—vents his deep disgust and lets loose his buried anger. Still, an undercurrent runs in the other letters that betrays such feelings as profound longing for home, solicitous and constant love for his mother (and not just in his rote farewells), and an evolving affection for a special woman named Jane that traces a whipsaw course from hoping for more letters from her to anger that she apparently does not share his eager plans to marry her as soon as the war ended.

In the summer of '44, Boisseau stood about 5'10" and weighed between 150 and 160 pounds. He was red-headed and had hazel eyes. A black-and-white photo of him outside what could be his shared tent in New Guinea shows a man in his late twenties, dressed in fatigues and topped by a round-brimmed cloth hat. In the picture, Boisseau holds a cigarette in his left hand, wears a watch on his left wrist and sports an ID bracelet on his right. Far from displaying the lost look seen in a high school portrait of him, he flashes eyes that are bright above a sweet grin. The middle finger on his right hand is bandaged, a small sign of the nagging injuries he would write about.

In the 1940s, there was nothing unusual about an American man smoking, and a U.S. soldier overseas was no different. In their letters home, servicemen often begged their families to mail them cartons of smokes to supplement the packs the Army rationed in PXs. Sergeant Hollis M. Alger, an Oregonian stationed in England with a bomb squadron, told his girlfriend in a letter:

> I was able to sweat out the P.X. [post exchange] line and buy my weekly rations which were pretty good; Camel cigarettes (we can buy seven pkgs for the week), and four good candy bars, among other things. Also a non-smoker presented me with seven more packages of Camels.

Boisseau Bailey weighed the pros and cons of cigarettes in the humid atmosphere of New Guinea. On September 3, 1944, he informed his mother:

> I got the cigarettes...yesterday. Thanks a million for them but, don't send anymore cigarettes. They don't have celaphane and therefore they don't keep so well. Send all the...cigars that you can. They will keep.

The means of communication he used was his only connection to home. Once in New Guinea, telephone and radio communication were uncertain at best and reserved for emergencies. Soldiers had little chance of going home on furlough because the distance was too great and the need for troops, too keen. Since they were on the island for the duration, any kind of mail took on an extra depth of meaning for soldiers.

Except for two letters to his sister Charlotte, all of Boisseau's extant missives are V-mails, a clever device that saved space and weight at a time when both were precious on board cargo ships. V-mails—"V" for victory— went from military personnel to their loved ones back home and vice versa, and worked efficiently at both ends of the system.

The writer of a V-mail confined his or her remarks to a prescribed space on half-sized paper, which then folded into an envelope for mailing. The letters were collected, censored if necessary, photographed en masse and reduced to the size of thumbnails. The miniature photos could be processed at the rate of 2,500 per hour and then collected on reels of microfilm that were brought to central locations. There, they were blown back up to half the size of an ordinary sheet of paper and delivered to their destinations.

One soldier dubbed them "Wee Mail," while another exclaimed to his wife, "I wonder how you read the damned things."

No longer on typing or onion-skin paper, the V-mails ended up on photographic sheets that were slick to the touch. The Army and Navy were responsible for transporting the letters overseas, while the Post Office Department delivered them in the U.S. For civilians, the cost of a stamp was three cents, six for air mail; servicemen and women paid nothing. Although the V-mail process originated in England, it was invented by an American, Charles Case, whose father took a job in England and moved his family there. The elder Case died when the Titanic sank in 1912, the year his son began working for Eastman Kodak. He came up with the idea of using microfilm to reduce newspapers to a storable size for archival purposes.

The War Advertising Council worked with the Office of War Information to produce "Our Plea on Behalf of V-Mail," a brochure that encouraged businesses to help promote the use of the new communications method:

> *The Armed Forces ask the support of advertisers who can*
> *co-operate in this important campaign by devoting space to the*
> *V-Mail story. A series of suggested advertisements dramatizing the*
> *V-Mail story is shown in the following pages. You may pick up the*
> *copy from these ads 'as is' or adapt the message to your*
> *own requirements.*

The document also sang the praises of V-Mail, lauding its speed, its space-saving and its confidentiality. The National Postal Museum, an arm of the Smithsonian Institute, notes:

> *V-mail ensured that thousands of tons of shipping space could*
> *be reserved for war materials. The 37 mail bags required to carry*
> *150,000 one-page letters could be replaced by a single mail sack.*
> *The weight of that same amount of mail was reduced dramatically*
> *from 2,575 pounds to a mere 45.*

The system transported enormous amounts of mail. "Between June 15, 1942, and April 1, 1945, 556,513,795 pieces of V-mail were sent from the U.S. to military post offices and more than 510 million pieces were received from military personnel abroad," according to the museum. However, military personnel abroad and their relatives back home still penned regular letters. The postal museum said that, in 1944, "Navy personnel received 38 million pieces of V-mail, but over 272 million pieces of regular first class mail."

V-mail was formally inaugurated in June 1942, when President Franklin D. Roosevelt received two letters from England that had been sent to the White House by the U.S. ambassador there and the commanding officer of U.S. forces in the United Kingdom. The use of the system was formally begun in the Pacific via an August 1, 1943, letter sent from Admiral Chester Nimitz to Colonel Frank Knox, Secretary of the Navy:

> *It is a great pleasure and satisfaction that by this letter I am able to initiate the first "V-Mail" letter to you from the Pacific Fleet. I believe that the delivery of official and personal mail by means of the microfilm process will solve our mail difficulties. It is also hoped and anticipated that this mail service will eliminate the congestion now present in our greatly overtaxed postal system.*

Most V-mails were blank sheets on which soldiers could write, but some prepared forms did the writing for them, including Christmas, Easter and Mother's Day cards that came with appropriate illustrations and verses. For example, this holiday V-card was mailed by a Signal Corpsman in Oro Bay:

> *A cheery greeting across the miles—*
> *(At Christmas, you seem so near!)*
> *May joy and happiness*
> *fill your heart*
> *Each day of the coming year!*

There were also generic V-mails with word options on them that could be checked off to create a letter. One soldier writing from Corsica was given many choices for a salutation that ranged from "Dear Mother... Dad...Wife...Sweetheart" to "Sis...Brother...Friend." When he was done making his selections, his letter read:

> *Dear Mother, Dad, How are you? I am well. Doing lots of day dreaming. Hope you have everything you want. Corsica is*

smelly. The food is strictly GI. Are you missing me? My job is going
well. Will be thinking of you. I have seen interesting places. Yours
with love.

To describe Corsica, he comically opted for "smelly" over sunny, beautiful, hot, picturesque and out of this world.

Combat medic Keith Winston of Pennsylvania wrote his wife about the limitations of the service: "Of course, you can't enclose anything with V-Mail, and must use the prescribed envelope. Also, it takes extra time to photograph V-Mail. So the consensus [among soldiers] is that airmail is faster." In 1943, Jo Michelson sent a V-mail to her husband in Australia as he waited to be shipped to New Guinea:

Everyone keeps telling me these letters come out so small you
can hardly read them so I'm trying to write a little larger. Also I
have so much to tell you I could only scratch the surface here so I'm
going to write an air mail letter, too and see which arrives first.

Soldiers were well aware that their letters, regardless of how intimate, would be read first by censors. Putting his tongue firmly in cheek, Private First Class Russell Cobb of New York, an infantryman in Europe, told a friend, "There's a lot I could tell you but the censor suggests that I save it for that post-war bull session that may run into a matter of weeks." However, none of Boisseau's letters was edited. Each one was stamped "Passed" by Army Examiner No. 16324.

The censors—supposedly officers but often chaplains when the former didn't judge it to be an important task or had more imperative duties to perform—were on the look-out for information that would aid the enemy and signals of sinking morale. A soldier in New Guinea described to his wife the censorship process in his unit:

The censor is the platoon leader. That is, I mean, the Lt. as each
Lt. has a platoon, and there is also a base censor which may open
one occasionally and you can tell when they open them as they open
the envelope up then seal it, whereas we don't seal them when they
go to the censor in our Co., and they seal them.... As a rule if you

have something written in a letter that isn't up to par, [the censor] will call you in on it, and rewrite it. As yet, I haven't been called in. You also can write on your envelope blue mail, then you seal it and the base censor will censor it. That is personal matters.

Probert, who commanded Boisseau's unit for a time, does not recall censoring its mail, but he was responsible for screening letters sent by his original outfit, the 222nd Quartermaster Salvage Company. "I was the chief censor," he said. "There were 100 men in the platoon, but they didn't all write every day," so the task was do-able as part of his routine responsibilities. "I looked for particular words and phrases," he said, explaining his approach to censorship. "It got so you could give a letter a quick look" and spot offending material.

The use of V-mail made his task easier because its small size limited how much soldiers could say. He was also alert for any references to the location of the writer or his unit size. He didn't pay attention to the content of the letters beyond that information. Although he blacked out places and unit details, he added, "I don't think the Japanese were under any misapprehension as to who was where and the size of the units. I wasn't overly scrupulous about censorship; I had other things to do. My only concern was to prevent the transmittal of information that might be militarily significant. Most men understood that."

Soldiers were given a War Department Pamphlet titled "When You Are Overseas These Facts Are Vital." Under the heading "Writing Home," ten commandments were handed down, including:

1. Don't write military information of Army units—their location, strength, materiel, or equipment.
2. Don't write of military installations.
3. Don't write of transportation facilities.
4. Don't tell of any casualty until released by proper authority.
5. Don't give your location in any way except as authorized by proper authority. Be sure nothing you write about discloses a more specific location than the one authorized.

Locations were often blacked out or even scissored from letters, leaving behind rectangular slits. Winston wrote his wife in September 1944, "As you are probably aware, things are happening—and fast. We have moved, but I can't tell you where although I think it permissible to say [censored]." Sergeant Tuttle wrote from New Guinea, "This afternoon we took another ride out to the [censored] and got to examine some mighty fine [censored]."

A year earlier, Jo Michelson told her husband, who arrived in Oro Bay on July 31, 1943:

> You asked me to tell you how many of your letters are censored.... Well, all of them are.... The only trouble is the most interesting words have been cut out.... You evidently mentioned where you are and that has been cut out.... Then in one letter you say you saw something through binoculars[;] all that was cut out.

Private James Clarkson, a Michigander who was a cook in the Army, wrote his parents a V-mail and identified his location only as "somewhere in England." He wanted to describe where he had met with relatives (he had been born in England) but couldn't. "Mom, while I was there, I went to every place you would have wanted me too," he said. "I never walked so much in my life, one day we walked a good 14 miles. I left it up to them to tell you about it as it would be censored if I wrote & told you." The censor also forbade him to send a photo of a church he went to since it could be identified and reveal where he was.

Corporal Elbert Thompson, a 23-year-old Engineer in Lae, New Guinea, who signed his mail "Jack," had a clever solution to problems with his censor. His parents wrote him letters with numbered questions, and he replied:

> I hope the censor will approve of me answering this way. Your second, fifth, tenth, eleventh, thirteenth and fifteenth questions can be answered with yes. Your third, fourth, eighth, ninth, fourteenth, sixteenth and eighteenth questions can be answered with no and your first, seventh, twelfth and seventeenth questions can be answered with OK and the sixth question I cannot answer.

Officers who felt they had more urgent things to do were not averse to shrugging off the censorship process. In "Company Commander," his account of leading an infantry unit in Europe, Captain Charles B. MacDonald told how he approached letters while holed up in a pillbox in Germany:

> *I began to sign my name to the bottom left corner of envelopes which comprised the day's mail from the men in the company. Except for the official censorship stamp that would be imprinted on the envelope later by the mail orderly, ...the letters would not be censored further.*

Since none of Boisseau's letters was altered, anyone who read them knew exactly where he was. "I have just finished writing [Billy Burrow] all about New Guinea," he told his mother on June 17, 1944. On August 3, he would joke, "I also read [in the newspaper], that I am in New Guinea. Is that true?"

While in U.S. training facilities or even before being drafted, many wily servicemen devised complicated code systems to let their loved ones know where they were sent overseas. Lieutenant Avery told his parents that the ship he was leaving San Francisco on was "docked about 200 feet from where Frank works." He also revealed his destination with a pre-arranged code. "Remember," he counseled, "the map squares are the last two numbers of a Spring Rd address." One soldier told his girlfriend that his location would be concealed in the words he used to sign off. Before he shipped out, he gave her six possibilities. For instance, if he wrote "Regards," she would know he was in Australia. But if he wrote "regards" with a lower-case "r," he would be near, not in Australia.

When WACs arrived at Oro Bay, in part to assist with the handling and censoring of mail, they proved especially adept at spotting such shenanigans. According to one assessment,

> *I don't know what there is about women that makes them so sharp-eyed in reading letters, but the ones I have here possess an uncanny knack for picking up hidden security breaches, such as tricky codes a soldier may devise to tell his wife where he is.*

100

Letters were a soldier's last link to home and a precious gift to be savored. Many V-mails from both theatres of war began with soldiers recounting what correspondence they had received, charting how long it took to arrive and hoping for more. In a letter from his time in a stateside camp, Ben Courtright, the airplane mechanic from Kansas, told his wife:

Every time I get a letter from you and read it my throat gets a lump in it about the size of a grapefruit. And tears run down my face—I feel just like a big baby. I guess I am but I can't help it.

Writing in 1945 from Leyte in the Philippines, First Lieutenant Jacob J. Zillich of El Paso, Texas, informed his wife, Emily, "Tomorrow I intend to reread all your letters, not only to see if there are any unanswered questions but reading them again makes me feel that you are so very much close to me."

Private Joseph Barrington from Rensselaer, New York, was sent overseas on Thanksgiving 1944. On his 19th birthday the following January, he wrote his sister, "It sure was swell to hear from you! No kidding, you can't imagine how much a letter means to a fellow. I didn't realize it until I came over here, but you live the whole day for mail call at nite." A few weeks later, as he trekked across the continent, he enthused to his parents from "somewhere in Belgium," "Today I am just about the happiest guy in the army, I think. The reason for it is that the mail came.... Boy, oh, boy, you just can't imagine the joy created by such an event."

When mail didn't come, a soldier's morale fell, and he might feel by turns nostalgic, sad and forgotten. Clinton Thomas, a Pennsylvanian who served briefly in New Guinea with the Army Air Corps, remembers that "a mail call that didn't have as least one letter was a real let-down. The guy who... walked away with a handful of mail was the envy of the whole squadron."

In a September 1944 letter, Boisseau complained about not getting mail from his girlfriend and told his mother, "Boy, my morale is way below a thousand tonight." Writing from Oro Bay, Sergeant Tuttle told his girlfriend,

Well my dear we had mail call today but I was one of the unlucky ones. I didn't get any, I will probly have better luck next

*time.... It is pretty lonely here right now. I am all alone in the
tent just me[,] two candles burning and my thoughts of the past
and hoping what the future will be.*

Private Berrien J. Hull, a Signal Corpsman from Missouri, was stationed
"somewhere in New Guinea," as he labeled each of his V-mails. Actually, he
was just south of Oro Bay. In a V-mail to his father, he said, "I had a very
good mail call on February 15th so my morale is up where it should be."

Mail to and from Virginia took two to four weeks to reach its destinations.
The earliest of Boisseau's surviving letters is a V-mail to his sister Charlotte,
dated January 11, 1944, when he was still a private:

*What's the matter? I haven't heard from you in a long time.
You haven't forgotten me, have you? I have a heck of a time with
my mail lately. For two weeks I didn't get any. Maybe it was the
Christmas rush or something of the sort. I know I certainly missed
it. Did you and Phil get home for Christmas. Mom said she was
looking forward to your coming home. Hope you all had a swell
time. Xmas was just another day for us. We worked just as hard
as ever but didn't mind it. Will do anything to get this damn war
over and to get back home. Va wrote and said that they had a
wonderful time in New York. She told me I should try married life
and that's exactly what I'm going to do when I get home. Going to
get in my car and go straight to Judge Binford and tell him here
we are and to do the deed as soon as possible. Maybe we will get as
far as N.N. That will be far enough for me. I know I will be plenty
"tired." I am feeling lots better now. My ears don't bother me so
much lately. They sure did give me plenty of hell for a while and
I hope that they never will again. The other trouble hasn't come
back on me either. Charlotte, see if you can't get Mama down N.N.
for a few days. Make her get her teeth fixed. I will pay the bill. I
know she really need[s] a rest. Well, gal, so long until next time.
PLEASE WRITE.*

 Love,
 Boisseau

The letter contains some major themes that appear frequently in his writing, such as pouty complaints when he doesn't get enough mail, great joy when he does, depressed worry that he has been forgotten (he would even wonder at one point if he had been reported killed in action), everyday comments that connect him to home, offhanded remarks on his health and attentive concern for his mother.

The initial letter also hints at a theme that would run like the refrain of a romantic song throughout his mail, namely that he was thinking about marriage and family life after the war. This time, he does so without naming anyone specifically, but presumably he was referring to Jane. (The letter also includes elements that need to be explained: Phil is his sister Charlotte's husband, Philip Branch; Va is Virginia, his other sister; N.N. is Newport News; Judge Binford is the town traffic court justice. As for his mother's teeth, they would form an odd leitmotiv of their own throughout the summer.)

While he might have written many V-mails between January and the last days of May, the next one that survives is dated May 30, 1944. It is the first still-existing one to his mother, and he is now a sergeant:

> *Dearest Mother,*
>
> *It is really getting hard to find something to write about these days. We are not getting hardly any mail now. When you get mail, at least there are a few questions asked and that gives you something to write about. Maybe we will get better service in a few days, being as that the W.A.C.'s are going to take over the postal jobs. I didn't mention the above to Jane. Afraid she would get sorta peeved about it. I will still stick to what I said. That I wouldn't date any women in uniform, so if she reads this letter, that should make her feel better. Mama, we are working harder than ever. I have worked overtime for three nights. It's a pity we don't get paid time and a half. I would mop up if that were the case. I am feeling fine, except for being tired. Maybe I [can] catch up on my rest some of these days. I hope it will be at home and not too long off. The news certainly sounds encouraging now but I'm afraid the end is a long way off. What has happened to Mr.*

103

Lawrence? I haven't heard from him in a long time. Also I haven't heard from the two sisters. Get them on the ball, please. Well, Ma, don't work to hard and take care of yourself. Love to all.

Love,

Boisseau

The flavor, style and flow of the letters are now settling into a pattern. He begins by reporting on how much or how little mail he has received, he talks about friends in Prince George, he updates his health (often expressed in terms of exhaustion resulting from how hard he is working), and he closes with an expression of love for Rella.

The salutation, "Dearest Mother," would change as the summer wore on, a subtle evolution that makes for a tantalizing psychological micro-study. "Dearest Mother" in May becomes "Dearest Mama" in June, with a child-like "Dearest Ma" making an appearance. He reverts to the more formal address of May only once, and that was at the start of his angry August V-mail.

The spelling in Boisseau's letters—while sometimes slangy—is almost 100-percent correct, although (as above) he habitually uses "to" when he means "too." Given his circumstances, the punctuation would generally please a lenient English teacher, except for his penchant for omitting question marks and putting a comma after "but" instead of ahead of it. The comma thus acts almost as a breath he takes before proceeding. He is also cavalier about apostrophes, with "its" filling in for "it's." As for his vocabulary, he is not shy about being coarse while writing to his dearest mother. "Just think of us poor bastards working like hell," he says at one point. At another, he writes, "Just think about the bitching I have done about rain."

The weather in New Guinea didn't please Boisseau at all, to say the least. He could be as fevered as the temperatures, labeling them "hotter than the hinges of hell" and "hotter than seven hells." In addition to the high temperatures, the weather was made miserable by monsoons that constantly dumped torrential rains that sagged palm fronds and collected into muddy streamlets. As a sergeant in a field hospital said, "It sure is hot here[;] it rains at nite and the sun roast[s] you all day."

In a July 1944 letter, Boisseau notes:

It has just started to rain and I mean its pouring down. That will give us some relief at best for tonight but, you can bet your boots by ten in the morning it will be 120 in the shade and we don't have any to much of that.

In his interview for this book, Lieutenant Probert said that the rains in Oro Bay were frequent, long lasting, heavy and occasionally dangerous. "The mountains around us were of sufficient elevation that the Oro River would rise ten feet in a short time" during a storm, he recollected. "One company lost five or six men who drowned in a flood. The water would pound down the stream after a heavy rain."

In his next letter, June 3, 1944, Boisseau puts many of his themes together:

Dearest Mother,

The streak has finally broken. We got some mail yesterday. A letter from Jane, Charlotte, Eleanor, J.J. Temple, second Presbyterian Church and your card. Gosh, it certainly made me feel lots better. I didn't answer any of them last night but I expect to soon. We got so everlastingly busy now. Work all day and prepare for inspection all night. We all are just about whipped. Working day and night will get the best of the best man. Especially in this climate. We were off tonight and I took advantage of it. We went to the fights and enjoyed them a lot. Charlotte wrote and said how much she enjoyed have all of you down there. I wish I could have been there with you but this to will pass away. I hope so and damn quick with it. She also said that Phil had been sick. Guess he is worked to death also. Mama, you haven't written anything about Papa Joe lately. You are not mad with him are you? Don't let that happen because you will need a long rest on a nice farm after this is over. It would beat the P.O. racket. You will have to carry Sis Macy along to keep house I imagine. Well, Mama, take care of yourself and keep writing. Love to all.

Love,

Boisseau

The on-off relationship between Boisseau and Jane is matched throughout the summer of 1944 by his comments on the growing link between Rella and "Papa Joe," as Joseph Burrow was known. In Broadway musicals of the time, a younger couple would often act as a counterpoint to the main lovers. In this case, the oldsters were the background performers to the main show of "Boisseau and Jane."

Papa Joe was an available older man, a farmer and the county highway superintendent—with 11 children. Like Boisseau, Burrow enjoyed dancing and going to the movies. His first wife had died, and his second had left him. Family lore holds that wife number two thought she was marrying a rich man with two sources of income and soon found out he was only "Papa Joe," not "Sugar Daddy."

With his mother having been a widow for nearly 15 years, the faraway son encouraged her to make a match with the man who worked at the highway department adjacent to the Bailey house. "Bet 'Papa Joe' really looked 'sporty' in that car of mine," he wrote in July. "What did he have to say about it?" In late July, her son would be even blunter, saying, "Yes I do believe that you are in love with Papa Joe." On August 24, he declared, "So you and Papa Joe are still going steady, eh? I still think he is the grandest man that I have ever met and I have met a hell of a lot of those 'critters.' Hold him if you can."

In September, he would react to something she said by writing, "Love in Bloom! Boy, I really believe you have it bad. Get him if you can. I don't blame you a bit. Although with all of those step grandchildren you will have your hands full." He was apparently teasing her about how Burrow's 11 children would produce dozens of kids of their own.

How the relationship with Joe Burrow would resolve itself is hinted at in the single surviving letter from Rella herself, written to Charlotte in the spring of 1945. That letter also provides a touching insight into how she mothered her three children.

CHAPTER TEN

LIFE AND DEATH IN PRINCE GEORGE

Letters kept servicemen and women in touch with the gravitational centers of their lives. Their families and their hometowns were firmly fixed points in an insane world. Between those two points, men and women "over there" could hang the hammock of their memories, dreaming about the past and hoping for the future.

For Boisseau, the steamy New Guinea nights, noisy with the buzz of insects and screams of night birds, must have been filled with cozy—and sometimes sad—memories of the little town and the big family he had left behind. The geography and sociology of his first quarter-century of life—along with his family, education and the other factors that form an individual—had contributed greatly to who he had become: a Virginian born into a history of rebellion against the British and the North, a white man with an inbred sense of superiority to minorities, a small-town boy with a tragic background thrust into a global conflict, a son of town government officials in thrall to the federal government "for the duration" and a rural kid and kidder now living as an adult in a jungle.

In 1916, when Boisseau was a one-year-old, the adult male citizens of Prince George County made their way to the polls to vote for president. They chose Woodrow Wilson, a Virginian, over Charles Evans Hughes, a New Yorker, 258-72. One unknown maverick bravely cast a ballot for Allan Benson of Michigan, the Socialist Party candidate.

In that same year, the Norfolk and Western Railway Company published an "Industrial and Shippers Guide" that described the county as consisting of "generally level soil, sandy loam and clay subsoil, generally thin, though there are extensive tracts of valuable alluvial lands on the rivers." The railroad report catalogued the crops grown on the flat soil: "corn, cotton, peanuts, tobacco, wheat, oats and the grasses. ... The lands are well adapted to pears, peaches, plums, quinces and grapes, and berries, both wild and cultivated, are abundant. ... Livestock of all kinds do well." Rising skyward throughout the countryside, the guide continued, were "pine, poplar, oak, walnut, gum, persimmon and other" trees.

Earlier, "A Handbook of Virginia" recorded that "saw, grist and flour mills" could be found throughout the county, along with "cotton gins, peanut factory [and] brick kilns."

Eugene P. Lyle Jr., a minor writer of pulp western novels and magazine articles, bought a farm called Jamescrest and shared with The New York Times in August 1908 what it was like to till Prince George's land:

> I am farming all right, all right; from sunrise to sunset, and
> then till bedtime. Between my window here and the river is my
> first crop, oats I planted last Fall, ready for the reaper at the rate of
> fifty to the acre. Then lower down on the bank are seven hundred
> peach trees That I set out this Spring, and behind the course is
> a field of alfalfa two feet high, ready for the mower this week.
> And further back are fields plowed last Winter, to go into corn,
> peanuts, ...cow peas, &c.... Then almost every week there is some
> new living creature on the ranch, pigs and calves and turkeys and
> dogs and kittens, and even a coal black little pickaninny. We are
> prolific, all right.... Let me tell you that farming is an endless
> hurdle race, until you take the last one into the Beyond....

Such was the rural—and almost unconsciously racist—atmosphere of Boisseau's childhood. An early 1920s' photo of him, taken when he was about five or six, shows him in what must have been a typical pose. Wearing the air of a boy prince, he is surrounded by friends and relatives, including his younger sister Charlotte. His hands shoved in the pockets of his short pants, he glows with a huge grin. During those years, he probably joined other kids and families in celebrating Virginia's special days, such as National Apple Week and Fire Prevention Day. On January 19, the commonwealth marked Robert E. Lee's birthday, but it ignored Abraham Lincoln's on February 12.

As he grew, the red-headed Bailey boy fell in love with baseball and would play it on sandlots with his schoolmates. One person remembers the kid called "Red" as a particularly adept centerfielder. He became a fan of the New York Yankees. Attracting devotion in a neighborhood so far away from and foreign to the Bronx that it might as well have been Egypt was due to its string of World Series victories. Everyone loves a winner.

Frances Sebera, who married Joe Jr., recalls something even more telling, "He was always getting into mischief."

> *Boisseau was quite a character in the county. He was a great*
> *friend of my husband's. Joe considered the Baileys to be sort of his*
> *family, too. He and [Boisseau's sister] Virginia were really close,*
> *like adopted siblings. They grew up together. One Christmas, Joe's*
> *father bought him a used bike and fixed it up and painted it.*
> *Virginia and Charlotte stole it while he was in church. Joe said*
> *he could have killed them. They would tell stories of the old times*
> *when they got together. About the parties in what they called*
> *"the big house," where the Baileys lived. It seemed sometimes like*
> *it [shook so much with laughter that it] would roll down the*
> *hill. Rella was very popular in the county. Boisseau was always*
> *carrying on with foolishness. Most of the time, he was upbeat,*
> *kidded around. His personality was just to have fun.*

Declared a relative of the Baileys, "That family was something! Everybody liked them." Indeed, many of Boisseau's playmates were kin, such as Tommy Munt, a cousin who was one of his closest companions. Tommy's mother was Rella's sister, Annie Munt, who lost two of her four children to early deaths and suffered under an abusive husband. Because she spent much of her adult life in a mental hospital, her kids latched on to surrogate parents. Tommy fell in with the Baileys, becoming almost a brother to Boisseau.

As years of winter schooling and summer playtime rolled on, the small town of Prince George Courthouse went about its daily business. And it was a very small place. "One time, we interviewed a candidate to be the new minister at our church," an elderly woman recounted. "I asked him, 'How do you like our town?' He said, 'Well, where is it?' I said, 'You're in the middle of it!'" She laughed and continued, "I like to say I live downtown because my house is between the only two traffic lights."

Naturally, the courthouse itself was the dominant landmark. The British burned the first one during the Revolution. A second rose in 1810, only to be set on fire during the Civil War by Union forces. An attempt at repairing it failed to please anyone, so, for a time, court sessions were held in a private home. In 1884, a new courthouse was constructed, with an arcade added in 1929 to fancy up the front. About ten years later, an observer gathering information about Virginia for the Federal Writers' Project passed through and described a town "with its few houses and stores that are supported by court days and court business. Compactly set within the courthouse square are the county buildings, facing an obelisk of roughhewn stone, the monument to the Confederate dead."

The same author focused his attention on the courthouse itself, describing "a two-story red brick building with gabled roof and arcaded porch [that] is flanked by two single-story buildings, one separate and the other connected by a continuation of the arcade." Inside, in the words of an application for its designation as an historic site, the first floor had "a central hallway with two fourteen-by-twenty-by-ten commonwealth's attorney offices, two twelve-by-fourteen-by ten trial judge offices and a small courtroom located in the rear of the building. The county's circuit courtroom was on the second floor."

In the late 1920s, when Boisseau was in high school, the memorial to fallen Confederates mentioned in the federal writer's report was dedicated. The granite obelisk was "erected....to the memory of Confederate soldiers of Prince George County that their heroic deeds, sublime sacrifice and undying devotion to duty and country may never be forgotten."

Directly across the street—which has been variously called the Old Stage Road, Courthouse Road and State Route 106—was one of the stores mentioned in the Depression-era description. Located there since the Civil War era, it was at one time owned by William D. Temple and Brothers. They sold it in 1927 to James Thomas Williams. When he died, the store went to his heirs, including a daughter, Eleanor Buren, and her husband, Francis. They ran the store from 1942 to 1984. The now vacant building still bears their surname on its fading sign: Buren Store. In the 19th and 20th centuries, the general store was packed with everything from grain and feed to harnesses, from candy to nails, from sacks of corn to long underwear.

A little walk down the street from the store, just beyond Joe Sebera's filling station, rested the Bailey house with its inviting porch. Rella's post office, where V-mails from New Guinea would one day arrive, was just a small shed to the right of the home, only a few steps away from her front door. It contained little more than a stove for heat and shelves of pigeon holes into which the mail was placed. The lone mail carrier would stop in to help sort the letters, gossip a bit and then leave to make his deliveries.

Completing the courthouse circle, the home of ever-watchful Sheriff Boisseau, her Uncle Willie, lay on the other side of the street.

If Impressionist painter Mary Cassatt had turned to photography, she might have taken a photo of Rella that captures her in a pose of quiet maternity. In the 1920s picture of a plump woman with short hair, Rella wears a plaid shirtwaist dress and holds Charlotte in front of her by both hands. The anonymous finger on the camera button might have belonged to Ben. His wife, her eyes cast down, looks older than her age, which would have been her mid-twenties. Her expression is glum, with no touch of the loving gaze of a mother. But, as in a Cassatt portrait, the absence of facial emotion is deceptive, and the action—looking at her child, holding her hand—is all. Her lone remaining letter will attest to that.

Most of the men in Prince George—white and black, Protestant and Catholic, Anglo-Saxon, Scotch-Irish and Bohemian—farmed, worked for the county or labored in the three huge plants that sprawled up the road in Hopewell, the company town that DuPont constructed where City Point once stood. Hopewell was created to house workers for a dynamite factory. The boom exploded the price of town lots from $40 to $3,000. The plant was soon re-tooled into a guncotton factory to meet the needs of World War I.

A 1921 article in The Literary Digest described Hopewell as springing "into existence almost overnight in a section of Virginia which was virtually a wilderness. At one time during the war it had a population of more than 30,000. It was a complete modern town, with huge factory buildings, paved streets, hotels, and theaters of permanent construction."

The town had expanded so rapidly that it had sprouted into the southern equivalent of a Wild West town. Vice and crime moved in with the rapidly expanding population. The front page of the August 5, 1915, issue of the Harrisonburg [Virginia] Daily News Record screamed:

BRIBERY, GRAFT AND LAWLESSNESS
RAMPANT IN CITY OF HOPEWELL

CHIEF OF POLICE IS CHARGED
WIITH EXTORTING BRIBES
IN DU PONT POWDER
PLANT TOWN

ENTIRE POLICE FORCE IS
FIRED BY JUDGE WEST

In the summer of 1915, just as Boisseau was being born, the crisis came to a head when a grand jury began examining the town's dark side. Sheriff Boisseau was dragged into the probe, and his ethics and drinking habits both came into question, as reported by the Harrisonburg paper on September 11:

It was asserted that the grand jury had been told [by the coroner] that the chief had drunk intoxicants at the Hopewell Hotel on at least one occasion during the month of July, and that the drinks were paid for by the agent for a Baltimore brewery, who had his headquarters in Hopewell. Sheriff Boisseau denounced the statements which, he said, had been made by the coroner as absolutely false and in plain words told Dr. Hargrave that he was a "liar".... The sheriff handed his pistol to a friend and afterward remarked that he had invited the coroner to meet him "in the woods" or any other place the latter might name and they would settle the matter.

The grand jury returned 240 indictments for illegal sales of liquor, and W.D. Henderson, chief of police in Hopewell, was removed from office, pleaded guilty to liquor trafficking, paid a fine of $200 and spent 15 days in Sheriff Boisseau's jail.

The town's rocket rise wouldn't last. After the war ended in 1918, the factory was abandoned, almost literally overnight, and the town went from Hopewell to seemingly hopeless. A magazine reported that

> its great factories were closed down and boarded up; workmen,
> storekeepers, and population left. There lay Hopewell, a small
> city of more than 2,000 residences, with its churches, clubhouses,
> restaurants, its wharfs and docks on the James River, its roads
> and railroads, condemned to be torn down, ripped into pieces, and
> auctioned off to the highest bidders as scrap.

While DuPont had slated it for demolition, Hunter Grubb, the man the company sent to oversee the coup de grace, had a far different vision and found a way to spin gold from the dross:

> In his mind's eye he pictured Hopewell as it should be, with
> merchants in its stores, preachers in its churches, men, women,
> and children upon its streets, the mighty forces of industry and
> production whirling the wheels of its factories.

Within a few years, 23 new industries had debuted in the town. In 1920, for example, the Tubize Artificial Silk Company, a Belgian firm, put 1,000 men to work on building a mammoth plant on the site to produce rayon. The construction crews did their work so expertly that they got raises of as much as ten percent. Meanwhile, mail-order Sears houses went up for the new workers and their families. The reporter sent by the Federal Writers Project captured the feel of Hopewell by writing:

> Factories stretch far and wide within and beyond its corporate
> limits, and the air is filled with both profitable odors and sulphuric
> smoke. Several huge mills produce kraft and synthetic textiles,
> and an enormous plant lives off air, using the synthetic ammonia
> process for the fixation of the inactive nitrogen in the atmosphere.
> Other products of Hopewell pottery, car liners and doors, insect
> sprays, sheet metal, machine equipment, and building supplies.

The mention of nitrogen referred to The Atmospheric Nitrogen Corporation, which founded its plant in Hopewell in 1928. In 1935, when a 20-year-old Boisseau might have been weighing his options for getting a job in Hopewell, a newspaper recorded that "a Japanese freighter is docked at the Atmospheric Nitrogen Co.'s plant, taking on nitrates." In a few years, Japanese freighters would definitely not be floating in the James.

In the 1930s, as the Great Depression settled over the world, Civilian Conservation Corps workers and Social Security came to the county. In 1935, the Tubize plant temporarily closed, throwing hundreds of employees off the payroll. In her novel, "To Kill A Mockingbird," Harper Lee described an Alabama courthouse town during this time, a depiction that could have applied to Prince George:

Economic ruin forced the town to grow. It grew inward. New people so rarely settled there, the same families married the same families until the members of the community looked faintly alike.

On April 2, 1930, when a census-taker came to the Bailey home, he counted "J. Ben, Rella B., J. Boisseau, Charlotte W. and Virginia W." They were five of the 10,311 people in the 259 square-mile county. The value of their home was estimated at $5,000, and it contained a radio, an idiosyncratic census question intended to determine how quickly the new-fangled device was spreading throughout America as well as how affluent the homeowners were.

Asked by the census-taker how old she was when she got married, Rella opted for the truth. She had been 16. After three children and many years of marriage, the Cupid Special ruse of 1914 didn't matter anymore.

The up-and-coming family with the radio sent their teenage son to Petersburg High School, which was out of the county and therefore had to be paid for. It was another sign of their status that they had the income from Ben's county job to afford the luxury of placing Boisseau among the 40 or 50 students in his class.

However, the privilege would not last. The weight of the Depression bowed the family down. Ben's income as commissioner of revenue depended on collecting taxes from people in the county, but many of those people had less and less to tax. The losses brought Boisseau back to Prince George County and to Disputanta High School for the final two years of his secondary education.

As the economic slump deepened even more, a much more personal time of bottomless sorrow draped itself like dark bunting over the Bailey house. Three deaths in two Februarys were coming and would leave harsh consequences the teenaged Rella never imagined during her wedding ceremony.

The first death struck most closely. On February 3, 1931, James Benjamin Bailey died at 46. His perfunctory obituary in The Bee, a newspaper in Danville, Virginia, may have been a sign of the level of the family's penury. The obit, which cost little more than a dollar, was hidden among the classified ads, legal notices and comics on the second-last page. Little Orphan Annie carried on just below this brief announcement:

> *James Benjamin Bailey, 46, for a number of years,*
> *commissioner of the revenue of Prince George county and one of the*
> *leading men in this part of the state, died early today at his home*
> *at Prince George after a brief illness from pneumonia.*

He received more attention in The Washington Post, which called him "James Ben Bailey." The paper added the names of his parents—James Thomas and Annie Hobbs Bailey—as well as those of his siblings, who were Boisseau's three aunts and his Uncle Karl. Rella, Charlotte and Virginia were named, as was the deceased's son, listed as Boisseau, not James.

The Bee and The Post both said that pneumonia took Ben, but some friends wondered if his drinking finally got him. Family lore tells of how, when he would visit relatives, his Aunt Annie's daughter Louise would play the piano for him as he grew steadily drunker. In his cups, he always requested "The Old Rugged Cross," a 1913 hymn with its refrain:

> *So I'll cherish the old rugged cross,*
> *Till my trophies at last I lay down;*
> *I will cling to the old rugged cross,*
> *And exchange it some day for a crown.*

One day, puzzling over his frequent drinking, Louise asked, "Uncle Ben, why do you do like you do?" He shot back, "Lulu, why do you do like you do do?"

On Ben's gravestone were carved four words: "His memory is blessed."

His widow, Rella, so young when they eloped, was only 32 when he died. Boisseau was 15; his sisters, even younger. In his 1931 Disputanta High photo, "Red" Bailey assumes a very serious pose. His long face with its long nose—both very much like his father's features—rises from his shirt, its collars draped over a sweater. The picture does not capture an eager scholar or a hope-filled teenager. It shows a devastated child. What is most striking about the image are his eyes, which seem to belong to someone who is at once lost, yearning and empty.

Husbandless, Rella had to assume the care of three children and find a way to earn money. To her rescue came members of the courthouse oligarchy. She received immediate income when Judge Marshall R. Peterson of the Prince George Circuit Court generously appointed her to fill out her husband's unexpired term as commissioner of revenue. She was named his successor within 48 hours of his demise. It might not have been much, but it was something. The February 5, 1931, issue of The Washington Post took notice of the appointment, saying that Rella "will take office immediately.... Her term will end December 31 of this year."

It may have been at this time that Rella began taking in boarders, many of them teachers in county schools.

The second death of the Depression years would occur on February 2, 1933, when Mollie, the sheriff's wife, passed away. She had been postmistress in Prince George Courthouse, and her demise allowed the courthouse ring to once more take care of their kind. On February 10, eight days after Mollie's death, Rella was appointed the U.S. postmistress for Prince George. She also cooked for people that Boisseau would refer to as those "across the road," meaning the prisoners kept in the small jail beside the sheriff's house. It was probably a task that Mollie had done for years.

Rella's appointment must have seemed to her like a welcome turn to good fortune, even if it did result from tragedy. But more sorrow would come less than two weeks after her postal appointment. That's when the third February death occurred. At 12:30 p.m. on February 23, 1933, just a few months shy of his 80th birthday and precisely three weeks after Mollie passed away, Sheriff Boisseau died.

His obituary claimed that he had never drawn his pistol from his holster, much less fired it, over the course of four decades of police work. Termed "one of the county's most beloved citizens," the uncle who had played a large role in the lives of the Bailey clan was gone.

In the span of two years, Rella lost her husband, her aunt and the uncle who had done so much for her through the years. The Bailey kids attended funeral services for their father and two relatives who lived across the road. Boisseau, in his mid-teens, had to adjust to the sudden and shocking removal from his life of his dad, Aunt Mollie and a surrogate grandpa. The devastation on all of the Baileys can only be imagined. One death weakens people's knees and shatters their lives. A second one drops them to the ground, perhaps to pray, perhaps to pound the earth in anger. The third might lead them to believe that nothing good will ever happen again, that God does not exist or, worse, that God exists and despises them.

Rella was once the vibrant teen eloping to Washington with her older beau…the carefree young mother-to-be spotted riding a motorcycle shortly before her son was born…the beloved wife whose husband once flew over their house in a rickety plane in an ill-conceived attempt to drop her a letter, only to have the plane drop instead as her husband walked wobbly away. Now, she grew mature-looking for her years, overweight ("rotund" was the adjective chosen by someone who knew her) and constantly tired from her many duties. She would too soon lose all of her teeth. And then her life.

Watching those changes in his mother was Boisseau. In his adolescent analysis of the world, did he see the effects of his father's drinking? Did he suspect it contributed to his dad's loss of income as much—or more—than the Depression did? In the evenings, did he hear his mother weeping over her husband's alcohol abuse? Did he think his world was doomed to more misery? Was his mother the next one to die?

Was he?

In his letters from World War II, filled with such deep affection and solicitous concern for his mother, Boisseau never mentions his father.

CHAPTER ELEVEN

THE SIMPLE THINGS OF LIFE

Boisseau's car, mentioned in his comment about Papa Joe, would be a summer-long topic in 1944—as well as a connection to Jane and the Sebera family. Joseph Sebera Sr. operated a gas station a brief stroll from the Bailey house along the main road in Prince George Courthouse. His son, Joe Jr.,—the kid on the hurricane camping trip—was also in the service (aboard a Navy mapping ship) and would later run the family business. (It is now in the hands of his son, Dennis, the third generation at the spot and now the owner of the Bailey homestead.)

In his V-mails, Boisseau never names the make and model of his car, but someone who knew him recalls a 1938 tan Plymouth convertible with a rumble seat, a long-nosed "waterfall grill" and running boards. It cost under $800, which was do-able for a man who had been salaried since 1936 and living with his mother, perhaps for free. It's certain that he resided there because, in his letters, he worries about an ailing relative taking over his room, which he wants left as is so he can reoccupy it after the war. On July 16, 1944, he pleaded with his mother, "If you have to take care of her, please don't let her get married to my room. I want that for myself when I return." His use of the word "married" discloses what was on his mind.

His car needed serious repair work, and the soldier, who hadn't seen it in nearly a year, fixated on the process throughout the summer of 1944, with characteristically mixed feelings as he shifted back and forth on whether it should be sold:

> • *June 16: I am glad Joe has started to work on my car. Tell him to put it in first class condition and I'll pay him shortly. All he will have to do is to send me the bill. I really played hell with it, didn't I. I usually do a good job at everything and that wasn't an exception.*

> • *July 3: What have you ever done about my car? Hope it has been sold and you got a good price for it.*

- *July 13:* This is when the sergeant mentions Papa Joe driving his car, which indicates it has been made road-worthy.

- *July 16: You said you enclosed Joe's bill in the letter but, it wasn't in there. Tell Jane to write him a check for the full amount if you haven't sold the car. He was nice enough to fix it, so please don't let him wait so long for the money. I also hate to see it sold if you haven't, don't.*

- *July 18: I hope that you took Joe Sebera's advice about selling my car. That motor is in a terrible condition, I know. $500 will be a good price for it. Am very anxious to know the outcome. I'm glad it was fixed so Elise could use it.*

- *July 21: Am still anxious to know about my car. Haven't heard anything about it lately.*

- *August 4: About that automobile business. Call the whole thing off. Keep it. Let Jane pay Joe Sebera with a check. You can use it around home but, please don't let anyone borrow it. It's a lot of money tied up in that wreck. I imagine automobiles will be hard to get for awhile after the war.*

- *August 13: What did you do about the car? Hope you sold it.*

- *August 27: How did the auto sale turn out or did it?*

- *September 3: PS Has Joe S been paid?*

The frequent mention of money in his V-mails—paying for his mother's dental work, for instance, and making arrangements for the car repair—hints that he was careful with his finances. Many a soldier wrote home asking for money, rather than offering it to pay family bills. An example is a V-mail sent two days after Christmas 1944 by Private Charles Smith of

California, a member of an anti-aircraft artillery battalion. "I'm somewhere in New Guinea," he informed his mother in Los Angeles. After admitting that he was broke and wouldn't be paid until February, he begged, "How about sending me $50?"

While Boisseau's relationship with his car mirrors the one with Jane—confused, on-again, off-again, love and then rejection—it also betrays that Jane was more than a passing dalliance. The proof is that he relied on her to pay his bill to Joe Sebera Sr., a trust that indicates something deeper between them—at least on his part—than a simple dating connection.

One might expect that his V-mails would be filled with deep and insightful thoughts on war and peace, declarations of firm patriotism, and vows of an undying (or, perhaps, dying) commitment to the cause, rather than repeated references to a wrecked coupe. With only a few exceptions, however, the mundane triumphs over the special in Boisseau's remarks. The letters zero in on minor issues, everyday occurrences and the shallow stuff of life, all of which keep him connected to what most deeply matters. Those include Prince George Courthouse in general, his family more specifically and his mother most especially. Portions of his June 5, 1944, V-mail provide an example:

> Dearest Mama,
>
> We are still having trouble with the Mail situation and its awful not hearing from you and Jane. I hope that you are having better luck than we are. If you're not I know exactly how you feel. We haven't gotten our one and only newspaper in four days. So we have nothing at all to read. The only thing to do is bitch and that doesn't seem to help matters at all. . . . I am feeling fine and gaining some weight. I should because I really have an appetite. Well, Ma, take care of yourself and give my love to all.
>
> I Love You,
>
> Boisseau

Those contents, read without context, could have appeared in a letter home from a child at camp (minus the "bitch") or a teen away at college. The letter basically says: "I am homesick." His mood is considerably brighter five days later because of what happened in the interim:

> *Today I have a different story. Somebody got the "Pony Express" started again and I got twenty-one letters out of the deal. Boy, I surely feel relieved now. I was beginning to think that everybody had forgotten me.... I went to the fights again tonight and really enjoyed them. That's about the only time that I leave camp now. I was supposed to work last night but, didn't. I slept with my clothes on all night waiting to be called and you can imagine how I have been feeling all day.... Please call Jane and tell her that I heard from Flora Dora & forgot to tell her and I know that I will catch hell about it but Never-the-less I'm going to answer it soon. The rest of the mail was from you and My Only Jane. It took about two hours to read them but, didn't mind it at all.... Love to all*
>
> *Boisseau*

While the identity of Flora Dora, undoubtedly a nickname, has been lost to time, the emotional content of the letter is readily apparent. Boisseau is ebullient because he has been re-connected to his town, mother and girlfriend through their trans-Pacific messages.

One subject that gets repeated attention in the letters is so commonplace that it is almost stunning to find it a matter of discussion at all, much less an ongoing one: Rella's teeth. In her mid-forties, she was confronting what was literally a face-changing decision that came with a great deal of pain: whether to have all of her teeth pulled and supplanted by dentures. In his January letter to his sister Charlotte, Boisseau was already on the subject, and he would continue to dwell on it:

> • *June 10: Have all your teeth fixed at my expense.*

> • *July 11: Have you gotten your false teeth yet and how do you like them if you have? You and 'Papa Joe' should have a wonderful time 'sopping' soup together. No teeth will mean the chickens last longer, I guess.*

122

• *July 16: Am glad to know you are still having your teeth worked on. Why of course you are worth all of the gold in the world but, I don't think you can get that much in your mouth. Hope you don't look like Rachel Eppes when it's all finished.*

• *July 21: Have you gotten your teeth yet? I know that will make you feel lots better. I hope so anyway.*

• *July 31: Have you had all of your teeth pulled? Bet you are really a soup hound if you have. I know you will feel lots better now.*

• *August 3, repeating himself: Have you had all of your teeth pulled? Bet you are really a soup hound if you have. I know you will feel lots better now. Poor kid.*

Sometime, probably in mid-to late-July, Rella drew a picture of her store-bought teeth and mailed it to her son. He responded on August 4: "That was a beautiful set of false teeth that you drew. I know they will be becoming. Have you gotten them yet?" Four days later, he joked, "I thought that picture that you drew was of Mrs. Tojo. Really got a kick out of it." The reference to the wife of Tojo, the Japanese military leader, reflects wartime racist depictions of "Japs" as buck-toothed. Nine days later, Boisseau turned to humor again, "You haven't swallowed your new teeth have you? Better be careful with them." On August 17, he told his mother that Jane had complimented "your store teeth."

So much space devoted to teeth extractions and their replacement conveys a meaning deeper than the wisecracks. It shows that Boisseau had matured to the level of becoming a parent to his parent, even though she is 45. He has taken on the role of caregiver by relieving Rella of money worries over her teeth, encouraging her to proceed with the dentistry, inquiring about the progress as well as her feelings and making light of the whole state of affairs, as if to say, "It's no big deal. Don't worry. You'll be fine."

The dental discussion is symbolic of the constant (in two senses) care he lavishes on his mother from 9,000 miles away. He ends almost every letter with "Ma, take care of yourself and give my love to all," or some variation of it. Within the bodies of the V-mails, he often inquires about her health, which always seems delicate. That she was losing her teeth and overworking were not good signs to her son. He saw the roomers she took in as a burden she didn't need. "Why can't you get rid of the boarders," he penned in a June 29 letter. The lack of a question mark makes the sentence less of an inquiry and more of an order. He continued:

If I were you and really wanted to get them out, I would kick them out. Hard-hearted me. Just don't go to any trouble about feeding them. I would cook exactly what would suit my appetite and they could eat it or else. I wouldn't worry about them.

Almost a month later, he scolds his mother:

Mama, if you don't get in a better spirit and get to feeling better and stop working so hard I am certainly going to give you a spanking when I return. Its no sense in it.

He was also concerned about what he saw as a tendency for people, especially relatives, to take advantage of her. In late June, he learned that Aunt Macy, who was actually Rella's cousin, was experiencing health problems.

At first, he jests that Macy's stomachaches are the result of eating her own cooking, and she seems to be recovering. But it soon becomes clear that the ailment is far more serious (she would die within a few months). In his July 16 V-mail, he writes, "Hate to hear Aunt Macy will be an invalid. Mama, how in the hell can she be an invalid any more than she has been?"

Aunt Macy, aka Sis Macy, who was about 60, soon moved in with Rella for a period of recuperation in order to grow strong enough to travel to Texas, where her daughter Elise had gone with her family. On August 26, he tells his mother:

I will be so glad when Sis Macy will be able to go to Texas and I know you will be also. She must be an awful patient. Mama, if I was you I just wouldn't feed all of her company.

Just wish I could be there to tell them off. I don't believe in imposing anymore.

In early September, Macy had improved. "I am glad to know that she is so much better," he tells his mother, "and I know you are."

CHAPTER TWELVE

HEALTH CHECK-UP

The status of Rella's dental and Macy's overall health was not the only physical report Boisseau wrote about in his letters. He also shared his own shifting conditions, even in his first extant letter, in which he mentions trouble with his ears. As he told his sister Charlotte, "My ears don't bother me so much lately. They sure did give me plenty of hell for a while and I hope that they never will again."

The nature of his specific problem is not known, but soldiers who swam in the New Guinea streams and lakes risked fungal infections that "could eat away the eardrum," according to Stephen R. Taaffe in his in-depth analysis of the island campaign, "MacArthur's Jungle War."

In "Jungle Fighters," his book about New Guinea during WWII, Jules Archer recounts:

> We took advantage of dry days to dam a portion of the stream
> to make a swimming hole....Unfortunately, we failed to realize
> that the water was downstream from a native village and was
> polluted. I was one of the unfortunate who developed a case of
> what was called jungle rot, a skin infection of spreading
> pus-filled blisters.

One soldier who couldn't swim reported that he kept his head above water and found that, "in a few weeks, some of those [who] had gotten a little water in their ears had fungus infections." He didn't.

Lieutenant Avery, who was with a Naval unit assigned to malaria and epidemic control in New Guinea, told his parents, "Our greatest annoyance is fungus diseases of the skin, ears, etc....The fungus spores of middle-ear infection are in the water." By that, he meant the water in lakes and streams as well as the water in which men showered. He recommended thorough drying, with special attention to the ears, to cut down on the infections.

Boisseau also had at least two bouts of ringworm as well as a broken thumb. And he found it deucedly difficult to keep his skin from splitting open. In the first letter to his sister, he also makes a mysterious reference to "the other trouble [that] hasn't come back on me." It was, obviously, something Charlotte already knew about, and she was a nurse, so why was he being circumspect? Was it just another case of ringworm, something more gruesome or something so personal that he didn't want the Army censors to know about it? One possibility is that it was dysentery. "Bacillary dysentery had been the most frequently encountered disease transmitted by infected food and polluted water," Brigadier N. Hamilton Fairley, a British officer, wrote in a 1945 paper for the Royal Society of Medicine. "Human carriers and flies are important factors in the dissemination of this disease."

Another possibility is that Boisseau was referencing malaria, a recurring disease that plagued veterans for decades after the war. One of his friends remembers Boisseau saying, in the late 1940s, that he had contracted malaria. By another Virginia soldier's count of his own woes, he had the disease in Australia, New Guinea and back in the U.S. more than two dozen times. In February 1943, Lieutenant Charles L. Wooster, an Ohioan stationed at Port Moresby, New Guinea, wrote to his wife:

> I'm still confined to the hospital and expect to be out in another week or ten days. It's malaria, and believe me I had a couple of mighty sick days. Temperatures of 104 .2[degrees] and 105.8 That is really hot. … It's the malignant type. They say that anyone up here for four months or more will come out with malaria. I'm still pretty weak.

In June, he would return to the topic, telling her, "In and out of the hospital.… Here's hoping I don't get it again. Twice in four months is enough." In all, he would contract malaria four times.

Ringworm, which Boisseau definitely had, is a fungal infection that thrives in warm, moist areas like New Guinea and causes itchy rashes. It is also highly contagious. Boisseau reported his ringworm and skin problems as separate concerns, but they could have been the same affliction because untreated ringworm (so named because of the circular rash that comes with it) can lead to blisters that erupt.

"I have been feeling fine except for my hand," he notified his mother in an August 8 V-mail. "I have a terrible time with it. Keep on knocking the skin off of it and its sore as hell. Its nothing serious." But the ailment proved stubbornly persistent, as he noted less than a week later:

> My hands are still sore as can be. Still have the bandage on them. A person can really get scratched and cut more here than any other place in the world and it takes forever for them to heal.

And the next day:

> Im still feeling fine and my hands are just about well. I am determined not to let them get in that shape again. Will wear gloves from now on. Even when I'm eating. I imagine the trouble is, the perspiration make[s] your skin so tender. All you have to do is look at the skin and it breaks open.

Time magazine noted during the war that "American troops in New Guinea are generally in good health. Scratches don't heal easily as they do in better climates, sometimes linger as little sores for weeks, then turn into ulcers. The Medical Corps thanks its stars for sulfanilamide powder," an anti-bacterial. Private Martin Norberg, an Idahoan in New Guinea, wrote home about "a lot of trouble with a lot of boils." He counted 16 of them on his forehead, cheek, neck, hips, nose and even an eyelid.

"Getting About in New Guinea," the Army handbook that soldiers received, warned:

> Broken skin means trouble in the tropics unless dealt with immediately. A small scratch may turn into a sore that takes months to heal. It may even cause your death.... Dry the scratch thoroughly, then use iodine, Friar's balsam, or other disinfectant, right on the spot. Plaster or bandage.

Boisseau might have been suffering from what soldiers bluntly nicknamed "jungle rot," "New Guinea crud" and "the creeping crud." A year after he wrote about it, Time listed those terms in an article about how to treat the tropical disease, including applying silver nitrate and avoiding sweating, the last advice bolstering Boisseau's diagnosis of one of the causes. The "crud" could have been any number of ailments, such as poison ivy-like rashes, impetigo and scabies. "All the eruptions go away in time, but some hang on for months," Time reported. ("Crud" was American military slang that debuted during World War II as a variation of "curd.")

Ironically, the cause of his skin ailment could have been the atabrine he was taking to stave off malaria. The Associated Press said, in September 1945, that "army doctors in the southwest Pacific place some blame on atabrine…for a type of noncontagious skin diseases—a variety of 'jungle rot.'… The disease apparently becomes active partly because of unusual sensitivity of certain individuals to atabrine, army medical reports indicate."

As much as his skin troubled him, Boisseau's most common complaint was utter fatigue. Anemia could have been a cause. Two other aspects of his life certainly were: where he was and what he did. A War Department publication titled "Jungle Warfare" explained:

> The hardships of jungle operations demand physical fitness and acclimation of individuals. The loss of body fluids by perspiration, the increased concentration of the blood plasma and urine, the elevation of body temperature because of physical exertion at high external temperatures, and the effects of the sun all tend to lower the resistance of the body. The outstanding effect of jungle operations on the troops is fatigue.

As for the impact of his location on Boisseau's fatigue, Corporal Milton "Dewey" Thompson, a Missourian who trained at Camp Lee, wound up stationed on Okinawa. He wrote to his parents about soldiers who had been transferred to the island from Europe and provided a glimpse into what being stuck on a god-forsaken island was like:

> I was talking to some fellows from over there that came here, and they said [Okinawa] is to much like hell. There is not any towns or any thing here, and they said you could go places over there, but you are on one little island and you can see it all in a day. And then you are through and have not seen any thing. These fellows were asking us how we could stay in a place like this

without go[ing] nuts. We just told them you will get used to it in time, if you don't go nuts first. We had three boys or as I should say, men that went nuts here in our Sq[uad]. Boy, I can see why it is too. I know at times I believe a man would be better off that way.

Most of all, Boisseau's Army duties as a Supply NCO led to his exhaustion. The Army Field Manual for "Quartermaster Base Depot Supply and Sales Company," issued in mid-1945, outlines the mission of such a company as being "to furnish food, clothing, gasoline, quartermaster supplies and equipment, transportation and labor for the personnel of the installation to which it is assigned." The company was "designed to operate at base general depots, branch depots or ports of debarkation which serve troops with strength in excess of 100,000."

In 1955, Major General Albert C. Smith, Chief of Military History, said:

In the Pacific, as elsewhere, Quartermaster supply responsibilities included the determination of requirements, the procurement of the items needed both from the United States and from local producers, and the storage and distribution of items after they had been received. Quartermaster troops also furnished numerous services, including the collection or repair of worn-out and discarded articles, the provision of bath and laundry facilities, and the identification and burial of the dead.

Boisseau's own separation papers from the Army describe his duties this way, possibly transcribing his own words:

Worked with army supply depot supervising receipt and issuance of all supplies needed by various army groups and divisions. Kept record on all supplies received and issued and checked all requisitions to make sure that supplies went to the proper authorities. Supervised 25 to 50 men on detail and was assisted by four permanent warehousemen.

It was grueling work that occupied him for many hours at a time, exertions that were appreciated by soldiers like Clinton Thomas, the air corpsman stationed in New Guinea. "The role of quartermasters was important," he said in an interview for this book. "It was nice to be able to draw a fresh and clean pair of socks, but far more important was replacement equipment, spare parts, expendable supplies, not to mention rations for the mess hall. The abundance of spare parts for everything, including our aircraft, was an important part of winning the war."

Possibly adding to Boisseau's chronic exhaustion was behavior he inherited from his father. As personable as he was as a teenager, as attentive as he was as a son and as intensively hard-working as he was in his military role, one aspect of Boisseau wasn't so appealing. Like his father, he drank way too much and far too often.

"That's why my father wouldn't let me date Boisseau," recalls a woman who went to high school with him. Even in those early years, she said, "he had shaky hands" from the amount of liquor he downed. Perhaps the car he worried about all summer had been wrecked because he was driving under the influence. As he put it in a V-mail, "I really played hell with it." A story still told around the courthouse neighborhood involves how he once came to a traffic roundabout in nearby Surry County and drove straight through it, rather than follow its circular course.

When he reached New Guinea, however, Boisseau began two years away from easy access to alcohol, which he alludes to only four times in his surviving V-mails. On June 26, 1944, he told his mother, "The only thing that we can't get is fresh milk and I miss that along with beer. We will get beer in August. Six bottles per week. Not bad, eh?" On July 2, he commented, "Is Elise [Aunt Macy's daughter] enjoying her vacation? Bet she finds things pretty dull around the 'old burg' this year. Hope she can at least get a few bottles of beer to help keep her in good spirits."

A day later, he discussed "Possum" Jones, a black man who did odd jobs around town, including gardening at the Bailey house. Boisseau noted, "Wish I could be there to help him drink some of that good liquor." Two weeks later, Boisseau remarked, "Gosh, when [Elise] told me what you had for supper my mouth started watering. Especially when she mentioned rum cokes. As bad as I dislike that I would like very much to have a few of them right now. We will be issued six bottles of beer per week beginning August 1st."

While he previews the brews of August two times, he does not remark on them again in letters written later that month or in September. No joy over the bottles' delivery, and no sadness if they were cancelled, which could have been what happened. Taaffe notes that beer was ordered for New Guinea, "but other materials had higher priority." The concern over beer rations reached the highest military levels. General Walter Krueger, who directed the Sixth Army in the Pacific, was annoyed that the Navy issued beer to its men, while the Army did not. "My men not only wanted beer," he recalled sympathetically, "but felt that it was unfair to deprive them of something that the men of the sister service received."

Even if the requisitioned beers never showed up, Boisseau had unauthorized ways of getting a drink. A veteran of the Italy campaign in World War II recalled that liquor could be scrounged up by enterprising soldiers. While "liberating" wine from basements in Italy had no equivalent on the Pacific island, Navy ships arriving in port might have had spirits aboard. As a Supply NCO, Boisseau could have wielded heavy influence in negotiations for the destination of recorded or smuggled alcohol. Some of what was intended for the brass could be "lost" en route. In a 1943 diary entry, Private Browning, the Texas artist stationed in New Guinea, revealed:

Last night four bottles of the officers' gin disappeared from their tent. They get a regular supply of it.... They were very mad, but also very helpless, for no one could be turned in...for taking liquor that really isn't supposed to be here anyway. I have no sympathy for the officers in their loss, for they should not have liquor any more than the men. For those men who drink, it is a slap in the face to see the stuff brought in right under their noses when they can't have it.

Malcolm E. Anderson, an associate editor of The New Yorker who served with the 431st Fighter Squadron in New Guinea, complained of an Army policy that allowed officers to "import liquor from Australia [but] did not give any such privilege to the enlisted men, who are officially expected to drink chlorinated water, G.I. coffee (which, being made with chlorinated water, merely substituted two bad tastes for one), and a fearful lemonade which came in bottles and had to be diluted with water—chlorinated water, naturally."

Another reliable source of alcohol, said the veteran of the Italy campaign, was pilots, "who always found ways to stow a bottle or two in their planes." Ben Courtright, the airplane mechanic in France, told his wife that "my pilot…gave me a bottle of scotch. It is really good stuff." In his Rutgers oral history, Martinelli, the Brooklynite stationed in New Guinea, said:

> A friend of mine…used to guard General MacArthur…and
> he used to go on our B-24s to go to Australia. [They were] supposed
> to get milk, but the guys were loading up whiskey and mostly beer.

At Oro Bay, Boisseau was near airfields, and he might have acquired a small supply of scotch or bourbon from a friendly Army Air Corps pilot. Anderson offered still another source of alcohol:

> Men in outfits stationed in or near Moresby, Buna, Oro Bay,
> or some such port were occasionally able to bribe an Australian
> dock worker to smuggle in a bottle of raw Australian gin or
> Australian navy rum in return for a few cartons of American
> cigarettes…. Also, sometimes an American sailor on shore
> leave could be persuaded to part with a bottle he'd picked up in
> Australia. The sailors were never interested in barter, though; they
> always demanded cash.

If he was really desperate, Taaffe explains, a soldier like Boisseau could have linked up with others in need of a drink to ferment "coconuts, canned blackberries and peaches, or vanilla extract…. Some [soldiers] even poured rubbing alcohol through bread until the loaf took on a shiny waxy texture, then they rung it out and drank the liquid straight or mixed with grapefruit juice." The results were nicknamed "jungle juice" by servicemen. According to one soldier, the idea for it came from the natives of New Guinea. They "tell me they make a small hole in the nut, add sugar, then bury it for a time," he recalled. "Later, they say, 'It is some fun time.' This fermentation process makes like a moonshiner's

'White Lightning.'" A Navy lieutenant in New Guinea wrote to a nurse in Australia to say you can

> drink [it] or drop [it] on the Japs for bombs. It's truly rough,
> positively guarunteed to curl toe nails, straighten curley hair and
> curl straight, all the effect of T.N.T. with a dynamite detonation.
> In other words, ROUGH.

An Ohio dentist who served in a field hospital in New Guinea recalled that "there were times when I could smell the GIs cooking up some jungle juice." Private Walker recorded in her New Guinea diary that she visited a makeshift "night club" in June 1944. The "Quivering Quail" was operated by a Signal Corps unit. "We sat there and had some beer and then some jungle juice which was quite strong, or it seemed so to me," she wrote. "I didn't like it much but I drank some anyway."

Regardless of the number of sources around him, in his July 18, 1944, letter, Boisseau implies that he has been a teetotaler. "Guess the first bottle [of beer] will knock me sky-high as I haven't had any in such a long time," he said. Was he telling the truth or simply reassuring his mother, who was sadly familiar with her husband's alcoholism and must have been worried about her son's drinking from the time he was a teen?

In one of his letters to his parents from Camp Lee, Fox addressed the issue of drinking while in the service.

> If I were only home I would get dam good and drunk. I think
> it would do me good. You don't have to worry about me getting
> drunk or raising hell here, because I am always thinking of you
> folks...and I want you all to be proud of me someday, and I
> promise you will be.

There is evidence that Boisseau, perhaps thinking of his mother, dreaming of Jane and imagining a future different from his father's, might have felt exactly the same way, evidence that would be found in his demobilization papers.

CHAPTER THIRTEEN

BOISSEAU IN UNIFORM

Although his letters center mainly on everyday matters, Boisseau did occasionally touch on Army life and the ongoing war. Like many of his uniformed peers, he was given to griping and grouching, justifiably, about the conditions in which he lived. The New Guinea weather and mosquitoes certainly irritated him. A joke circulating on the island told of two insects contemplating a soldier. "Shall we eat him here, or take him with us?" asked the smaller of the two. "Let's eat him here," replied the other one. "If we take him back to the swamp, the big ones will take him from us."

In addition to the torrential rains, oppressive heat and bloodthirsty bugs, military life vexed Boisseau. Stuck in a jungle half-a-world from home, he was given CQ (Charge of Quarters) duty, which entailed 24 hours of activity, including cleaning barracks and answering phones. He declared it to be "very dull." During CQ, he also was responsible for handing out passes to soldiers, a requirement he found ridiculous. "All of us have to have passes when we leave camp," he told his mother on July 3, 1944. "I don't know what we will have to do next. Imagine having to have a pass in a place like this. It looks like they do everything in the world to make life miserable for us."

Taaffe notes in his book on New Guinea that "there was nowhere to go but the jungle, which, for all its charms, was unlikely to attract many homesick Americans," a situation which all but eliminated desertion, AWOLs—and the need for passes. In a letter to a friend, a doctor posted to Milne Bay, New Guinea, complained:

> This stuff sure gets old fast. There isn't any recreation of any type, no place to go as it isn't too safe to venture far out. There have been no AWOLs since we hit the islands for obvious reasons.

Boisseau and the physician were deploying an age-old military exercise: griping. The word "gripe," in both its noun and verb forms, was new to

American English in the 1930s, while the verb "bitch" debuted about the same time. The duo were put in wide and frequent use during the 1940s as men were uprooted from their hometowns and families, sent over two oceans, ordered to do what they were told with no questions asked, and placed in circumstances that threatened their health and lives.

Journalist H.L. Mencken observed that "World War II, though it threw off an enormous number of what…appeared to be neologisms, actually produced few that were really new, and not many of them have stuck." He explained that what seemed to be new coinages—dog tag and commando, for example—had appeared during the Civil War and South African War, respectively. Mencken continued:

The actual soldier…limited his argot to a series of derisive names for the things he had to do and endure, and the ancient stock of profanity and obscenity.… A few four-letter words were put to excessively heavy service. One of them, beginning with f, became an almost universal verb, and with the –ing added, a universal adjective; another, beginning with s, ran a close second to it. The former penetrated to the highest levels, and was the essence of one of the few really good coinages of the war, to wit, snafu.

The f-word and the s-word rarely made it into letters home for two reasons: the scissoring power of censors and a soldier's own unwillingness to offend family members. As a result, "snafu" posed a major problem, namely, how to explain what the "f" stood for. The New York Times blushed when using it in a 1943 article and gave this translation, "Situation normal; all finagled up." The Oakland Tribune lifted its skirts even higher when a columnist informed his readers that "everything's snafu means everything's normal—gummed up, as usual." TEC5 John G. Burk, with an Engineers unit in Milne Bay, New Guinea, ventured a version of snafu in a letter to his wife in St. Louis, Missouri: "Situation normal, all futzed up. That's the way it goes."

The Oxford English Dictionary, citing the word's first use as occurring in 1941, defined the acronym as "an expression conveying the common soldier's laconic acceptance of the disorder of war and the ineptitude of his superiors." The word quickly entered wide use in military and civilian life. It became the name of a swing number ("Snafu Jump") recorded by Glenn Miller and of a cartoon character, Private Snafu, a doofus who got entangled in wacky circumstances that often ended in his demise. The cartoons, produced by Warner Bros., were voiced by Mel Blanc, who also did Bugs Bunny and Porky Pig, and were occasionally written by Theodore Geisel, who became Dr. Seuss. The cartoons were cautionary training films on such subjects as mail censorship, booby-traps and malaria prevention (they can be viewed at www.youtube.com).

Servicemen used the word "bitch" in their mail, as in a July 1944 letter from an Army captain to his wife:

> *Remember back in Texas [where he trained] about the guys*
> *who were so crazy to come overseas? You'd oughta see them now,*
> *honey. Do I ever get a kick out of listening to them bitch.*

One soldier put it very succinctly in a letter home, "Practically all I can do is bitch, and I'm getting tired of doing that, but it's almost become a habit." In other words, he was griping about bitching. In a similar vein, Boisseau used the word in a letter home, orating that "the only thing to do is bitch and that doesn't seem to help matters at all."

In "My War," his book of letters and drawings, Tracy Sugarman, who was in the Navy, includes a letter he wrote to his wife while on Utah Beach in Normandy after the invasion of France. In it, he rhapsodizes about bitching:

> *Without bitching, this whole setup would be impossible. After*
> *all, bitching is just rebellious impatience at the status quo. And*
> *the world's greatest bitchers are those who, having known the best*
> *before, are discontent[ed] until it's theirs again. I choose to include*
> *myself in this category.*

In New Guinea, Boisseau had a female compatriot in griping. In February 1945, Private Walker, a WAC, let loose a string of complaints in her diary. The powers-that-be, she complained as she warmed up, "have so many restrictions now that it's like being jailed."

139

*In fact it's godawful. They have the beach floodlighted which
makes it nice and cozy to talk or kiss in, the light in your eyes, and
the feeling of a gold fish. And they still blow the curfew at 10 in
spite of the fact that the time is different.... I hate it all.... I feel
completely cooped up, bottled up, and horribly depressed. All life is
is work and heat and movies.... I guess I might as well complete
my gripes. I detest that sergeant in our office, such a stupid silly
idiot, and Captain Fairgrave makes me sick.*

Boisseau complained about the shower system when it broke down. In mid-July, he moaned, "We are in a terrible fix. We don't have water to shower with. Something has happened to the pump that pumps water into the camp. Boy, I really smell like a man now."

Griping wasn't a 24-hour activity. Soldiers could find some small pleasures to distract them, even in their difficult circumstances and surroundings. Boisseau, for instance, found great pleasure in boxing matches, writing on June 3, 1944, "We were off tonight and I took advantage of it. We went to the fights and enjoyed them a lot." Exactly a week later, he reported, "I went to the fights again tonight and really enjoyed them. That's about the only time that I leave camp now." A month later, he told his mother, "I didn't write to anyone last night, went to the fights instead. Enjoyed them a lot."

His ardor for prize fighting may have been sparked at Camp Lee, where light-heavyweight champ Billy Conn was boxing instructor during Boisseau's time there. Yank Down Under magazine reported in its April 21, 1944, issue on "The All-New Guinea Joe E. Brown Boxing Tournament," a series of matches in various weight categories that were sponsored by the touring comedian. Trophies were paid for by several Hollywood stars, including Betty Grable, Cary Grant, James Cagney, Dorothy Lamour and Alice Faye.

Boisseau also delighted in going to the rifle range, "except for one thing," he wrote on July 8:

*We had to clean our rifles. They were really filthy. I cleaned
mine for three hours and haven't finished yet. Had an awful time
putting it together again. First I put a piece in backwards and*

then a piece fell out and went through the floor of my tent. Had to
crawl under the tent to get it out.

At Camp Lee, Boisseau had qualified as a marksman with the 1903 Springfield rifle, a five-shot weapon used in World War I and still employed in training and warfare. Soldiers tended to think of it as irreplaceable. In "From Here to Eternity," his novel about Pearl Harbor, James Jones described it as "long, sleek,…very slim but with the potent bulges all in the just exactly right places." The 42-inch rifle weighed nearly nine pounds.

In 1943, George C. Marshall, the four-star general who was chief of staff of the Army (and who would become Secretary of State after the war), ordered that scientific surveys be taken of soldiers in the Pacific and other theaters of war to determine the status of their morale. The results were published in a series of publications, "What the Soldier Thinks: Monthly Digest of War Department Studies on the Attitudes of American Troops."

The very first issue, dated December 1943, contained an article with a long title, "Leisure-Time Activities in New Guinea: Even in an active theater, men find time for recreation and entertainment." The survey was taken among "a cross-section of enlisted men in all types of installations in New Guinea." From the results, it is clear that Boisseau was not alone in finding letters to be his number-one occupation. The article begins:

In New Guinea, as elsewhere, soldiers report that letter
writing is the most frequent off-duty activity. Three-quarters of
the men on this battle-torn island report that they wrote one or
more letters on a typical day—most of them more than one.

If Boisseau was like the majority of soldiers in New Guinea, he also flipped through magazines, watched movies, played cards, listened to music and comedians on the radio, read books, participated in sports, and took part in group singing. Memories of the Bailey house regularly rocking with piano music (some of it pounded out by his sister Charlotte) and boisterous voices hint that he might have joined in. If he did, he could have crooned "We're the Gang that Keeps Things Moving," aka "The Quartermaster Song," penned in 1941. The refrain goes:

We're the gang that keeps things moving,
At the front and post to post,
When a soldier has tough going,
We're the guys he needs the most.

From the day he joins the Army
'Til the day he's home once more,
If he should have to shoot or ride
The buddies fighting by his side
Will be from the Quartermaster Corps.

In 1942, three musicians composed "The Fighting Quartermaster Corps." One of them was bandleader Fred Waring, who put his name on a succession of service songs, including "Roll Tanks Roll," "The Men of the Merchant Marine" and "Look Out Below," for parachute troops. His QM song, penned with E.W. Tyler Jr. and Pat Ballard, was set to an unmemorable melody and included lyrics that said:

From the shell-fire of the battleground
to the sheltered shores of home,
From the peaceful blue of sunny skies
to the depths of Davy Jones,
We're the boys who help the fighting
Yanks sink the flag of freedom's foes.
And when the bugles blow
and we've won the whole damn show,
Thank the Fighting Quartermaster Corps.

Hollywood and Broadway songwriter Frank Loesser, assigned by the Army to write such tunes, doubted that any member of any unit wanted to hear his efforts, much less sing them:

Every week or so I get a request from some general for a good
marching song. "My men want a rousing march," he says, but I bet
you twenty-five cents they don't. When a fellow's been marching
all day, he wants to come in and sing a marching song? When he's

142

*been digging latrines all day, he wants John Philip Sousa? Mostly,
he just wants to gripe at his officers.*

But singing around a battered piano in a PX or a cappella in a tent could improve morale, insisted the Music Branch of Army Service Forces, which invented "Hit Kits" in 1943. The New York Times described them as "collections of popular songs published in magazine form," and 70,000 of them were printed monthly. Each kit contained the lyrics to eight songs with simplified music so that even amateur ivory-ticklers could accompany servicemen and women. The tunes in a 1944 "Hit Kit," with a cover that showed a pair of embarrassed soldiers atop a tank with four glamour girls, included two Judy Garland standards, "Over the Rainbow" and "The Trolley Song."

A committee of musicians chose the songs for their sing-ability, selecting old-time hits like "I Can't Give You Anything But Love," "Put on Your Old Gray Bonnet" and "Margie." The committee numbered among its members bandleaders Waring and Guy Lombardo, singers Kate Smith and Bing Crosby, trumpeter Harry James and clarinetist Benny Goodman. The Times noted that "their judgment [of brand-new songs] has to be good because the songs they pick go into the Hit Kit, printed six weeks after they get the ballot, and it doesn't reach the troops on the other side of the world until a month later."

That delay doomed the project. As early as August 1943, The New Yorker wondered how the kits would ever reach soldiers in a timely manner. In October 1943, Life magazine reported that a survey of front-line soldiers and war correspondents found that the Hit Kits had "not yet been widely enough circulated in battle zones to have a pronounced effect." The effort ended in the summer of 1944, a year before the war's conclusion.

The military had more success in shipping another form of entertainment: motion pictures. Marshall's statistical report on New Guinea noted that "three out of every five [soldiers] had seen two or more" films in the previous week. As to what sort of movies men like Boisseau enjoyed, the answer is surprising. "By an overwhelming margin, [they] expressed a preference for two types of films," said the report. "Pictures with singing and dancing and pictures with clever comedy and light romance were named by three-fifths of the man as one of their two favorite types."

In December 1943, Private Kopplin wrote his wife about seeing a musical while stationed in Hawaii and awaiting transfer to New Guinea:

> *I can't begin to tell you how blue I was this evening as you see*
> *I went to the show and saw Hello Frisco Hello with Alice Fay,*
> *John Payne and Jack Oakie and Honey she reminded me so much of*
> *you[:] her hair, skin, and those wonderful Love scenes really got me*
> *down.... Did you see that picture[?] It was really good and when*
> *they sang that song ["You'll Never Know Just How Much I Love*
> *You"] my heart really began to pound and my stomach felt empty.*

What the troops didn't want to see was so pronounced that it was printed in italics in the Army survey results: *"Only one man in twelve named movies with war stories as one of his favorite types."* They wanted to escape from their surroundings, not watch he-man action hero John Wayne stuck in the same dank jungle that surrounded them. The Wing-Ding, a unit newspaper printed in New Guinea, editorialized in 1944:

> *We went to see Donald O'Connor in "Top Man" the other*
> *night, thinking to ourselves that surely...there will be no flags*
> *here, only good, wholesome movie entertainment. But no, this time*
> *they snuck an aircraft factory in on us...and naturally, Donald*
> *had to boost the production way high. Any movie mogul who says*
> *that the movie industry shouldn't film escapist movies is strictly*
> *off the beam. We already know that there's a war on, and so do*
> *millions of war workers and blood donors and mothers and on*
> *down the list.... Our one desire is to get this cussed war over.*

Arty films were rejected, too. After viewing "The Picture of Dorian Gray," one droll G.I. quipped, "Give us more Betty Grable and less Oscar Wilde."

At Oro Bay, according to one soldier, films were projected on Tuesdays, Thursdays and Saturdays. Private Walker said that the movies were shown outdoors in her part of New Guinea on a fixed, sizable screen. If the log benches were filled, "you brought a chair to sit on and watched it even in the rain," she remembered. "I would sit up front so I could feel I was in the movie." She especially enjoyed "Rhapsody in Blue," a biopic about composer George Gershwin. "I was one of the few to sit in the pouring rain to watch it," she admitted.

In a letter home, she declared an Errol Flynn movie, "Objective Burma," the "most realistic war picture I have ever seen" and told her parents to "be sure to go. It's really terrific." An infantryman recuperating in a French hospital agreed, writing, "I enjoyed it very much. Many of the scenes were very similar to some of my experiences." Members of an Engineers unit in New Guinea decided to review movies in their mimeo'd newspaper. Written by two servicemen who called themselves "a Pair of Jacks," the authors were not enthused about the Flynn flick. "Although the director gets the last drop of vivid melodrama and suspense out of this undertaking, the picture is over-extended and tends to become repetitive," they said.

Rating the movies for August 1944, the duo gave top marks to "Lady in the Dark," "See Here, Private Hargrove" and "Standing Room Only," describing the last named as full of laughs and therefore "the type of show preferred by GIs." Sergeant Tuttle attended the showing of "Hargrove" and wrote that "it was more like the army than any picture I have seen yet."

The following month, the two Jacks recommended "Double Indemnity," a film noir directed by Billy Wilder with atmospheric music by Miklos Rozsa, saying it "restored...our faith in Hollywood" and was "a neat bit of entertainment." (After the war, Rozsa received a letter from the father of a soldier. While in training, his son had seen the movie but would never do so again because he had been blinded overseas. Back from the war, the son expressed a wish for a recording of the score so he could recapture, through sound, a happier time.)

Films were not the only diversion on the island. Performers arrived in person to sing, dance, joke or just chat with servicemen. A month after Boisseau reached Oro Bay, actors Gary Cooper and Una Merkel showed up in person to entertain the troops on an outdoor stage. Her godfather was commander of the 491st Port Battalion there. Lieutenant Wooster, on duty in the Oro Bay hospital, reported to his wife in Ohio about the famous visitors:

Cooper is just as natural off the screen as he is on....
They all went through the wards to see the sicker patients and
those who couldn't get over to see their show. [Merkel] cried most
of the time she was going through the wards....Gary was all
choked up and wasn't ashamed to admit it. They seemed to be
honestly impressed and sincere in helping the boys with
their entertainment.

Cooper, known for playing characters who were men of few words and fewer lyrics, uncharacteristically sang a novelty song, "Lay That Pistol Down, Ma." He also recited Lou Gehrig's farewell speech at Yankee Stadium. In 1942, Cooper had played the dying baseball star in "The Pride of the Yankees."

A year later, baseball-crazy Boisseau might have seen Al Schacht perform at Oro Bay. Known as "the Clown Prince of Baseball," Schacht had a brief playing career with the Washington Senators. He then turned to coaching and clowning, eventually entertaining at minor- and major-league games with impressions of players and outlandish pranks performed while wearing a battered top hat and worn swallowtail coat over filthy baseball pants. In 1944, he brought his shenanigans to Oro Bay's hospitals and his familiar act to baseball games played by the 38th Infantry Division, 1st Training Center, 278th Quartermaster Corps and 5th Replacement Depot.

Men drafted into the service from roughneck jobs in Texas oil fields, West Virginia coal mines, Kansas farms and Pennsylvania steel mills brought with them a facile familiarity with four-letter words loudly employed. Philip Strong, the Episcopal bishop of New Guinea, had no time for the foul language that often accompanied ballgames. In his diary, he recorded that he happened on a game among U.S. soldiers:

[Someone] told me of the bad language and blasphemy that
went on during the base ball which vexed me very much.... So I
walked straight out and told some of the Americans standing by
that they must ask their comrades to cease using that blasphemy or
else they must cease to play.

In April 1944, an Army Special Services show titled "Stars and Gripes" moved around New Guinea. "The men really appreciate our efforts," Private Al Checco, one of the performers, remarked in a letter to his hometown newspaper, the Pittsburgh Post Gazette, "and we're working all the time. We will tour New Guinea and all the neighboring islands, and then play Australia.... Naturally, the show runs into many difficulties, but we carry on as best we can. One night we did a show with flashlights as our only means of lighting the stage! This is a wonderful experience—show business in the raw!!!" Checco would go on to appear in scores of movies and TV shows.

Also in the cast was comic actor Don Knotts, who would achieve national TV fame on "The Andy Griffith Show" in the 1960s. In a reminiscence about his time on the island, Knotts recalled seeing Jack Benny, sitting in a Jeep "outside, back of the stage. This was in New Guinea, it was raining and everything, and I just couldn't believe it, seeing him sitting there." Benny, whose radio and television series were popular for decades, arrived in New Guinea in 1944 for a tour that lasted more than three weeks. Asked about the island, he told an Army newspaper there was "nothing over here...no cities...nothing." Billboard magazine reported on his appearance at a base hospital with the comedian beginning with a simple "Hi ya, fellas" that prompted a standing ovation. After adlibbing with the audience, he began the formal show, joking about actor Errol Flynn, radio star Fred Allen and FDR. He fiddled with his violin while harmonica virtuoso Larry Adler comically refused to accompany him, and swapped one-liners with actress Carole Landis.

Landis made an effort to visit sick and wounded men in hospitals throughout the island. A soldier wrote his sister to say that the actress "spent all of her time with the wounded, speaking to each patient individually. Not just saying hello and passing on but stopping and sitting on the edge of each patient's bed and chatting for some time." He reported that she returned the next day to spend six hours in the wards. Her efforts exhausted her so much that she eventually ended up in a New Guinea hospital herself, suffering from pneumonia.

A grateful soldier who saw the Benny show spoke to him in absentia, "Some G.I.s who came to New Guinea didn't get a chance to see you, Jack;

some others who did may never go back to tell the folks at home about it, but none of us will ever forget you, trouper."

Given the soldiers' preference for humor and escapism, it is no wonder Bob Hope—who sang, danced and joked—was such a mega-star at the time and attracted tens of thousands to his traveling USO shows. He made it to New Guinea with a gang of performers that included eccentric comedian-singer Jerry Colonna, with his pop eyes and bushy mustache, and leggy songstress Frances Langford. A snapshot of the entertainers, taken by a soldier, shows them on the island in pith helmets and GI clothing. In a laudatory article about the comedian, novelist John Steinbeck said:

> When the time for recognition of service to the nation
> in wartime comes to be considered, Bob Hope should be high
> on the list. . . . He gets laughter wherever he goes from men
> who need laughter.

The same could have been uttered about Joe E. Brown, who appeared in "Hollywood Canteen" and who would, in 1959's "Some Like It Hot," utter one of the most famous final lines in cinema history. In a 1945 profile of him, The New Yorker tabbed him as "one of the two or three most-travelled war-zone entertainers" and estimated his mileage at 100,000. He eventually came to New Guinea, which he described as being the "next-door neighbor to hell."

A correspondent for The Chicago Daily News credited him for turning up where other entertainers wouldn't. "Our favorite amusement here," said the reporter, "is killing rats trapped in slit trenches. There are no movies here. But this Joe E. Brown fellow goes where even the [the service newspaper] arrives only rarely." The comedian rattled off jokes about endless rain and mobs of mosquitoes that invariably induced vociferous laughter. Before cheering crowds of soldiers, he related how things had changed back home:

> Remember those physicals you fellas took to get in? Well, you
> can get in much easier now. All they do—a doctor looks in each
> ear, and if they can't see each other...pfft...you're in. If they can...
> you're an M.P.

In "Your Kids and Mine," Brown's 1944 book of his experiences at the fronts, he wrote about Oro Bay, Boisseau's location

>*in the roughest jungle country imaginable. They have roads, but the best way to describe them is to tell you that it took us two hours and forty minutes to travel fourteen miles. When the boys knew we were coming they built a platform for us. After thirty-five minutes of our show a tornado struck. . . . There was a wind that blew the very fillings out of your teeth, and a rain that sent a million needles through your clothes and soaked your bones. . . . We went on with the show, and every one of the seventeen hundred of us was wet to the marrow.*

Probert remembers John Wayne coming through Oro Bay with a USO troupe. "He was a good sight to see," he recalled, adding that the iconic actor ambled away from the officers and mingled with the enlisted men. "He fancied himself a good bridge player, but he stumbled into a hornet's nest of excellent players. He lost a considerable amount of money. Maybe it was his way of contributing to the war effort. We all liked him." Private Hull, the Signal Corpsman in New Guinea, also liked what the actor brought with him. In a letter to his father, he wrote, "The John Wayne troupe was showing last night and in the cast are two girls, a very rare thing in these parts."

Late in 1944, composer/lyricist Irving Berlin docked at Oro Bay with a huge traveling cast that included a 24-piece orchestra. They lived on a boat, going ashore to put on their show. In his biography of the composer, "As Thousands Cheer," Laurence Bergreen describes how the troupe of performers struggled against such hardships as

>*overcrowding aboard decrepit ships, inferior food, isolation, constant danger. . . . During their year-end stand in New Guinea. . . the men received vaccinations hours before they were to give a show, and by the time the curtain went up, they were already suffering symptoms. . . . The conductor felt his knees buckle. . . . Musicians tried blowing on their instruments, but were too weak to produce any sound. . . . The show stumbled to a conclusion, and the next day's performance was canceled while the men recovered.*

On January 26, Walker attended the Berlin show with her boyfriend. "It sure was something," she recorded in her diary. "Everybody mobbed the roped off theatre about 4:30 waiting until 5:00 when it was a free-for-all to get seats…. The music was good, and Irving Berlin came out and sang some of his songs, and we enjoyed it very much."

The performance ended with Berlin calling for the houselights to be dimmed and inviting the audience members to hold up flashlights or lighters as they all sang his hymn, "God Bless America."

Sgt. James Boisseau Bailey—"Boisseau," to all who knew him—in Oro Bay, New Guinea, where he spent nearly two years during World War II. The photo, in the cardboard frame shown here, was discovered by the author during research for this book.

The Boisseau-Bailey family of Virginia (clockwise): a teenage Boisseau in high school in 1931… a portrait of his father, J. Benjamin Bailey…his sister Charlotte… Boisseau as a youngster, at left in row of playmates. *(School photo courtesy of Christine Belsches; childhood photo and portrait of J. Benjamin courtesy of Dorothy Stansell)*

Boisseau's mother, Rella, with toddler
Charlotte, in the early 1920s… Rella's final
surviving letter, written in 1945… Charlotte
with an unidentified man…a portrait of
Sheriff W.E. Boisseau, who watched over the
Bailey family from his home across the street.
(Rella photo courtesy of Dorothy Stansell)

Boisseau's final surviving letter, mailed from New Guinea in 1945 to Charlotte, his sister...Joe Sebera Jr., a sailor who was a close friend of Boisseau's, and his father at their gas station in the 1940s... Rella's tiny Post Office, located next to the Bailey home. *(Sebera photo courtesy of Dennis Sebera; home and post office photo by the author)*

Prince George Courthouse in the 1950s and today…the Bailey home in the 1940s… the "yearbook" of Boisseau's 10th Training Regiment at Camp Lee, Virginia, containing his "graduation photo" *(Bailey house photo courtesy of Dennis Sebera; modern courthouse photo by the author)*

V-mails were advertised widely to encourage their use. Microfilmed for easy shipment overseas, they were then enlarged, sorted and delivered to eagerly waiting soldiers, such as an unidentified recipient in New Guinea, who shows off a clutch of his latest communications from home. *(New Guinea photos throughout from author's collection)*

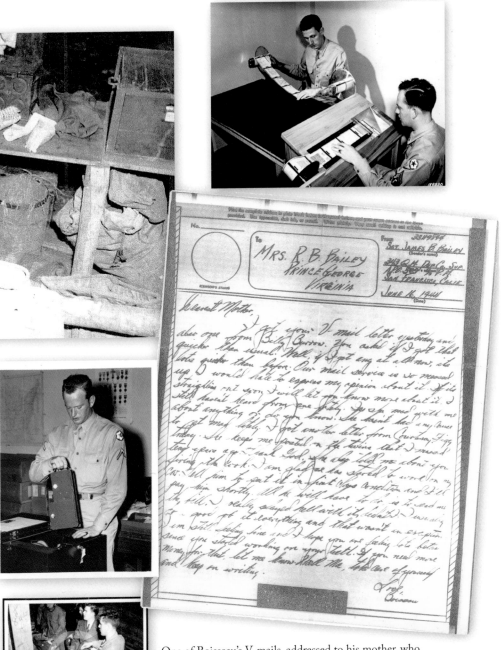

One of Boisseau's V-mails, addressed to his mother, who received his letters in the Prince George Post Office, where she was postmistress. The upper right of the V-mail reveals his name, service number, rank, unit and location: APO 503, which was Oro Bay, New Guinea.

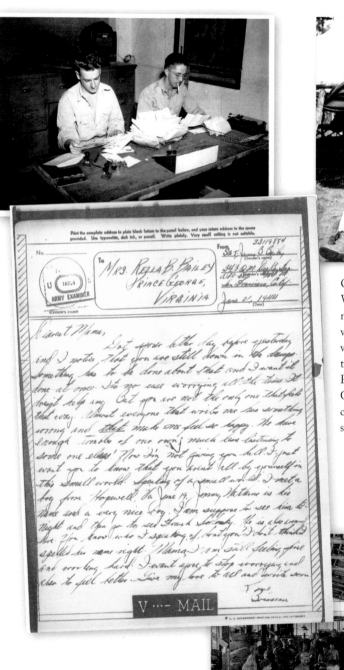

One of Boisseau's surviving V-mails, written to his mother in 1944, when it was summer in Virginia and winter on the Pacific island that lies below the Equator. Photos of life in New Guinea show letters being censored, sorted and read by servicemen.

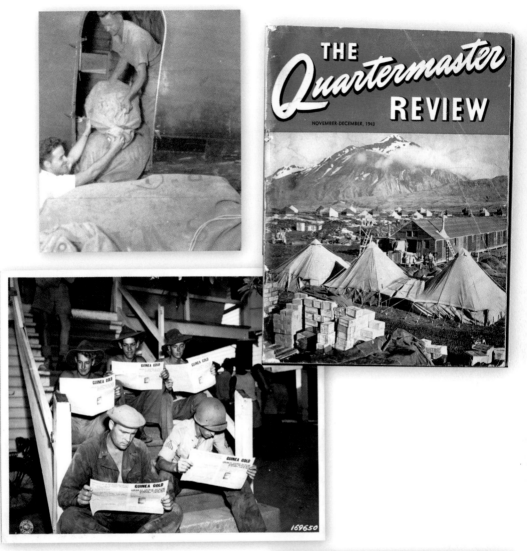

Besides reading mail, servicemen, including Quartermasters, devoured copies of Guinea Gold, a newspaper for the military that was published in Australian and American editions. In a posed publicity shot, five men from different branches of the service look over the latest copies of the daily. Receiving mail was a major part of a soldier's day. Those who walked away from mail call with letters were connected to home and happy to hear about everyday life. Those who left with no letters felt forgotten.

Homemade newsletters, like the one at left for an Engineers' outfit stationed in New Guinea, were published by thousands of units around the world to boost morale and share information about one another. Above, V-mails are processed. Below, a well-stocked warehouse in New Guinea, such as the one Boisseau oversaw.

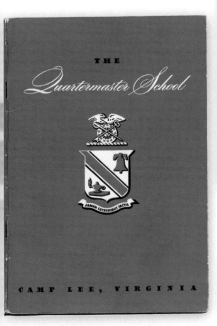

When WACs arrived in New Guinea, right, Boisseau the Quartermaster was careful to tell his mother that he would never date a woman in uniform, a message he wanted her to share with the woman he called "My Only Jane."

Life in New Guinea was brightened by visits from USO performers who entertained in open-air theaters. Gary Cooper, John Wayne, Frances Langford, Bob Hope, Irving Berlin and Joe E. Brown were among those who came to the island. Right, Yank Magazine included an article praising the essential role of Quartermaster units on the island, such as the one Boisseau was part of. Servicemen regularly posed for group shots to remember their brothers in arms. No photo of Boisseau's unit has been found.

No. 419 OBSTACLE COURSE QUARTERMASTER TRAINING CENTER—CAMP LEE, VA.

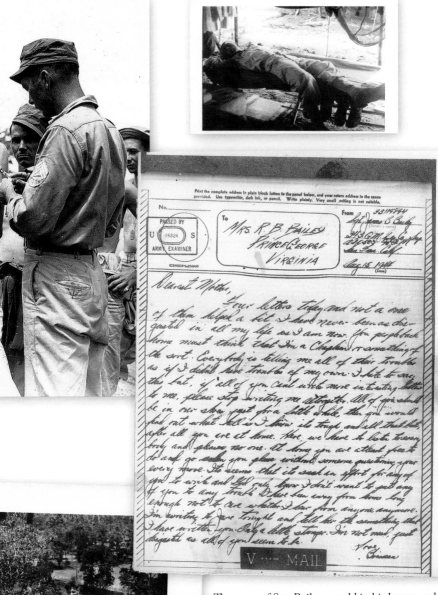

The story of Sgt. Bailey, as told in his letters and expanded through research into his life, includes training at Camp Lee, getting inoculated against dreaded diseases, living in a tent that was pelted by the island's frequent and powerful rains, and complete exhaustion from endless work related to Gen. Douglas MacArthur's campaigns in New Guinea and the Philippines.

Pictures mailed home by servicemen recall everyday life in war-time New Guinea, which Boisseau experienced from around December 1943 to late summer 1945. Guinea Gold offered encouraging news about the progress of the war. Boisseau's marker in Blandford Cemetery, near Petersburg, Virginia, marks his final resting place. *(Marker photo by Nancy Crowell)*

CHAPTER FOURTEEN

HOLIDAYS DURING WARTIME

In the Army, the rotation of holidays through the year was nothing to write home about, but Boisseau did anyway. Saturday, December 25, 1943, was most likely the first Christmas the 28-year-old had spent outside of Prince George Courthouse. In his earliest surviving letter from New Guinea, written in January 1944, he tells his sister Charlotte that "Xmas was just another day for us. We worked just as hard as ever."

As a quartermaster, he may have been occupied with preparations for an upcoming assault. Supplies were no doubt pouring into his warehouse for what would happen in a few weeks. As described in "The Army Air Forces in World War II," a major battle would occur at the end of February 1944:

> The attack group [on the Admiralties] was composed of three destroyer-transports with immediate escort provided by three other destroyers. A supporting group of six destroyers followed the attack group out.

Boisseau's dismissive opinion of the holiday was echoed by another soldier on the island, Private Browning, who noted in his journal, "There was little thought of Christmas anywhere today." Stationed in Oro Bay, Sergeant Robert Tuttle wrote his Ohio girlfriend in December 1943, "I can think of a lot better places to spend Christmas than here."

The island Christmas all three were referring to was described by Vincent Tubbs in The Afro American, a Baltimore newspaper. Dubbed "AFRO War Correspondent with U.S. Troops in the S.W. Pacific," the journalist said the day was rainy with the temperature peaking at 103 (it being summertime south of the Equator). The rain and heat were two elements, in addition to the war itself, that made it difficult for soldiers to be merry and bright. At one service, Tubbs reported, they sang carols like "Silent Night" and "Joy to the World," an Alabama sergeant read the Nativity story from the Bible, a corporal from Pennsylvania soloed on the sax, and the base chaplain recited a prayer. At an integrated midnight service, Tubbs continued:

Each man held a tiny white lighted candle in his hand. . . . The scene was the sort that makes cold chills dance up your spine, your flesh tingle, and your heart glad, for here. . . . was true Christian Democracy in action. . . . By signal, the candles were doused. Only the moon cast a ray into the pitch black night in this place.

With dawn, some of the men, Boisseau among them, chose to work through the day. A few found presents in the woolen socks they had hung in their tents, but Tubbs noted that "the best collective gift anyone could have given these men" was the arrival of women earlier in the week. The long-awaited WACs had shown up.

The Christmas 1944 issue of The Rigel Morning Star, a daily newspaper printed aboard the U.S.S. Rigel, a destroyer tender in the southwest Pacific, included an editorial about the holiday:

All members of the armed services are giving—giving to the entire world and on a scale much too vast to be encompassed here. . . . Today, though we cannot give the gifts of former years, we can give freely of the love, consideration, and spirit of good will that had prompted the giving of those gifts. In our letters we can give the cheerful reassurance of the love and confidence the folks back home so sorely need. In our conduct toward our shipmates we can give the consideration and cooperation that means so much. . . . Instead of being meager, our simple expressions of the true Christmas spirit this year can become a priceless gift—far outweighing the material things of other years.

That same Christmas, WACs stationed in Hollandia, New Guinea, assembled the elements of a party for themselves. Each woman brought "a tiny gift," wrapped in holiday style, for Santa to hand out in the mess hall. Writing from an unidentified Pacific location after Christmas 1943, Private John C. Coleman told his mother:

We had a pretty cool Xmas. They gave us [one-eighth] of a pint of brandy, 2 cans of beer, some gum, cocoa, and 2 candy

bars. I went to church on Xmas, and we sang Xmas carols.
The guy who said there are no Atheists in a fox hole sure was
on the beam.

T/Sergeant James F. Barrington, a brother to Private Joe Barrington, the combat soldier in Europe, was serving in New Guinea in 1944. He described his holiday in a letter to Bill Barrington, a third brother in the military who was stationed in Texas. "We had as nice a Christmas as you could expect so far from home," Jim opined. "Had a nice dinner all the fixings and was able to get hold of a few spirits to top it off on Christmas Day. I attended Midnight Mass which was very nice."

In England, awaiting transfer into the European theatre, Joe Barrington penned a quick note to the same third brother on Christmas Eve to say he was about to head off to Midnight Mass.

In upstate New York, the trio's mother wrote Bill to say, "We had a very nice Christmas quiet but pleasant.... I went to midnight Mass & Holy Communion & I went to 8 o'clock Mass Xmas day & before I came back I had been to 4 masses." A few days earlier, she had admitted to him that

Xmas really is not going to mean much this year. I would like
to get up a little pep for the girls sake, but I really don't seem to be
able to. I wish the Holidays were over with & maybe next year
might have a different outlook.

A week before that letter, she had sent Bill a clipping from the local newspaper. A photo showed a mother from their town standing stoically at the bedside of her hospitalized son who had had his leg amputated as a result of wounds he received during the invasion of Peleliu in the South Pacific. "Twice-Wounded Youth Cheered by Mother," the headline announced above a story about their hope for an artificial leg.

Linked by a religious service held in the four corners of the world as midnight moved through the time zones, the Barrington family connected to one another and God.

In a letter penned on Christmas Eve to his wife, Liz, at home in Kansas, Private Courtright, stationed in California, used an expression that, unknown to him, linked him to the mother and son in the photo:

> *I would gladly give my right arm to be with you this evening.*
> *We could all set around the Xmas tree and open our presents to*
> *each other. I can just see Jimmie [their one-year-old] going wild*
> *about things. Boy I sure wish I were home tonight. I would be*
> *there if I had to walk every step of the way.*

On Christmas Day, he tried to phone his wife but couldn't get a long-distance operator. When he tried to send a telegram, he was told the wires were jammed. "I just about cried because I couldn't talk to you," he said in a letter. "That hurts and I am not kidding.... I could just imagine you and Jimmie with me. You setting across from me and Jimmie in his high chair really having a good time. But a day dream makes you feel bad. I never was so homesick in my life.... I don't think I will ever get over it."

On the next Christmas, Courtright was stranded in Waycross, Georgia, because an airplane he was aboard had to make an emergency landing. Marking time until parts arrived that he needed as a mechanic to repair the engine, he wandered into the local USO and wrote a plaintive message to his wife on its stationery:

> *I am thinking of you. I am spending a hell of a Christmas*
> *here.... I sure am blue and homesick for you and Jimmie. I suppose*
> *you and Jimmie are up to your folks house eating a big turkey*
> *dinner. I can just see Jimmie going for the white meat and saying*
> *Mmmm or what ever it is he says. And I can see the table pulled*
> *out real long, covered with a white dinner table cloth, And of corse*
> *two white candles one at each end—all the white shinny plates*
> *set just so-so. And Jimmie's high chair sitting next to your place.*
> *I can see all this in my mind[;] it is almost like I was there.... I*
> *guess when you are all alone you feel extra blue on Christmas....*
> *When the horrible mess is over we will have many more happy*
> *Christmas to spend together.*

Corporal Wallace Hunt of New Mexico, stationed at an ordinance depot in New Guinea, wrote this poignant message on December 22, 1944:

*Don't feel bad about your son taking a mud bath in a foxhole
instead of being in a room by a fireplace looking at the tree piled
high with packages, then looking out the window at the snow....
A couple or three Christmases in the jungle is a small price to pay
for the millions of peaceful Christmases we will return to.*

Throughout the year, soldiers received packages crammed with cigarettes, candy, magazines, and such personal-care items as combs and brushes. Watches seemed to be an especially desirable present to servicemen. Regardless of the month, the boxes were a treat to receive, but getting presents around Christmas was a particularly warm experience. In a December 1, 1941, letter home from Camp Lee, Private Behrmann ticked off what he was hoping for:

*Things I can use: fig newton bars, assorted mints, Beechies, and
other cookies occasionally.... Western Auto ad in news showed a
swivel head flashlight that looked pretty good. Night duty makes
one handy. Pen light is swell for going to bed after dark, though.
Paper drinking cups—like half-envelopes, you know.*

A soldier in New Guinea mailed home an extensive shopping list that included "Betty Crocker soup,...those little fruit cakes,... any candy bars,...a couple of smoking pipes."

Opening holiday gift boxes was a special experience in itself, as movingly described by Corporal Hunt:

*When you get a package from home, you set the package in
front of you, look at it, get a lump in your throat and feel like
crying—when your hands get shaky, your heart full of happiness as
you wrestle with a package which seems like [it takes] ages to open.
Then you bring out the items—everything from nuts to a wrist
watch.... One Sunday, everyone in here rated a couple of packages,
[it was a] mad house and [we] act[ed] like a bunch of kids
bumping into a guy in the middle of the room who was bringing
eats over for me to sample. We acted crazy but it was the craziest
happiness we have had for a year.*

During the war years, companies designed special Christmas cards for soldiers. Private Lynn J. Knapp of Gloversville, New York, a quartermaster who had trained at Camp Lee, was in England when he was the recipient of many cards. From his mother came "Christmas Greetings to you, son, in the service." The words appeared above a white eagle perched on the Liberty Bell and backed by an American flag. Inside, a poem declared:

> And if you're here or miles away,
> Please keep this thought in mind;
> You're always close in every heart
> Of those you left behind.

Knapp's sister mailed him a card, decorated with crossed trumpets over an evergreen sprig and bearing the message, "Christmas Greeting to You in the Army." A red-white-and-blue Uncle Sam with white, fuzzy whiskers that protruded from the card was sent across the Atlantic by another sister and her family. It included doggerel:

> Uncle Sam gives you the orders
> 'bout your drills an' your salutes…
> 'bout your answering the bugle…
> an' the way you shine your boots…
> Uncle Sam gives you those orders
> But the order I send through…
> Is: "Have the kind of Christmas
> That is just as swell as you."

Knapp's son Billy signed a card that showed a rifle-toting Santa, sporting a helmet decorated with mistletoe and spearing a message on his bayonet. "Here's a Merry Christmas Greeting bringing loads of wishes, too, because I think of you so much," it read.

In a 1943 editorial titled "We Fight For Christmas, Too," The New York Times wrote:

> There is much evidence in this war-tortured world of
> compassion and unselfishness. There is the love of families and
> friends for those who are absent and in danger. How much of this

has been carried in the V-mail and the Christmas cargoes these
many weeks past!... If the artillery must thunder,...is it not done
for the dignity and sanctity of the humblest human lives....Some
Christmas Day the soldier will be home, to go to war no more. Isn't
this what we fight for? And need we be ashamed to fight for it on
Christmas Day?

On December 25, 1943, General MacArthur, commander in chief of the Southwest Pacific Area (SWPA), issued this message to his forces, which now included Boisseau: "On this Christmas Day, the anniversary of the birth of our Lord, Jesus Christ, I pray that a merciful God may preserve and bless each one of you."

Despite special cards, warm editorials and military messages, Christmas didn't seem like a holiday to Boisseau. Six months later, another holiday would hold just as little excitement for him. Just before the Fourth of July, he informed his mother:

I will be....off the 4th of July. I can truthfully say, that is the
first holiday I have ever been off in my life and look where I had to
be. A million miles from nowhere.... I will...sleep all day I hope.
Have seen all of this place that I want to see.

His wish to see no more was no doubt prompted by what was going on in New Guinea. Back in the States, the July 4, 1944, issue of The New York Times was packed with war news, especially from Europe as the push that had begun on D-Day a few weeks earlier continued to press German troops backwards. But an editorial in the July 4, 1944, issue of the Times, also mentioned the region Boisseau was living in:

At the end of the first year of war against us Japan had seized
every inch of land in the Pacific,...with the exception of Australia
and the Hawaiian islands. The ocean map looked like a Japanese lake
dotted with enemy strongholds. But if the map had been animated
we would have seen two giant American arms reaching...across the
Pacific to clutch island fortress after fortress.... It is pretty clear that
General MacArthur will not be turned back from the Philippines.

157

Frazier Hunt, a war correspondent who wrote "MacArthur and the War Against Japan," mixed his metaphors in describing "the first general offensive in the Southwest Pacific area.... It was a great double envelopment with the two strong arms moving north, operating some six hundred miles from one another. MacArthur's strategy was to push one arm of the giant nutcracker up through the Solomons on the right, and the other up the New Guinea coast on the left.... This would be Bear Hug Number One."

For servicemen and women, holidays could also mark the passage of time, as one corporal stationed in Oro Bay put it in a letter to his grandmother. "Soon [it] will be Easter," he noted. "Three years ago in Texas or Louisiana, then last year in Brisbane and then this year in New Guinea."

Christmas, Easter and the Fourth were not the only special occasions that clicked through the calendar like cogs that propelled the year. Birthdays and anniversaries rotated by with soldiers unable to do much more than send greetings through V-mails. Soldiers in support roles, rather than in combat, might be able to get to towns to buy gifts, but they were difficult to come by, afford or ship to the U.S. As for those men and women in New Guinea, they had no towns or stores to get to.

On July 11, 1944, Rella's baby boy turned 29, smelling like a man and giving orders to her from afar about everything from her dentures to her love life. As a declaration of the truth, a reassurance to her, or an attempt at self-deception, he wrote:

Well "Old Man" Bailey is still getting about as spry as ever, even if he is a year older today. I believe I feel younger than I ever had. The Army must be doing things to me. Being as today was my birthday, I didn't work so hard. The only thing that I did was to ride on a bull-dozer, which I enjoyed very much.

As with Christmas and New Year's, his birthday in New Guinea could not be a big day. Nonetheless, at the top of the V-mail, he took time to underline the "11" in the date, as if it were a secret code known only to Rella and him.

That tiny gesture of remembrance—and sitting on a bulldozer—were as festive as he could be in Oro Bay, New Guinea.

CHAPTER FIFTEEN

READ ALL ABOUT IT

Letters from home kept Boisseau well informed about Prince George Courthouse and family events, but he also relied on a daily newspaper in Petersburg, Virginia, the city where he had worked for Coca-Cola before the war.

"I don't remember whether I told you or not about the Progress-Index," he told Rella in July 1944. "Well, I have gotten four of them so far. They didn't lose any time getting here. I read every word in them and enjoyed them so much." Two weeks later, he wrote, "I have gotten about ten of them already. They have been coming in more regularly than my mail. I have enjoyed every one of them."

When he began receiving duplicates of the P-I, in one case six copies of the same issue, he joked that "in every paper that I have gotten I have read about the Munt funeral. How many times has he been buried." He would follow that up with, "Mama, call Curtis Lyons [the editor] and tell him I am tired of reading about Mr. Munts death and I would like to have a few new copies of that famous P Index." He also found humor in the fact that the paper reached him more swiftly than his mother's letters. "Am getting more papers now than letters," he informed her. "Guess you will have to have my letters published. Would get them lots quicker that way."

While he found front-page news to be "history" by the time he got his copies, he nonetheless scoured them to "keep up with the local scoundrels." He also enjoyed the comics, either in the newspaper or in "Funny Books" sent to him. That was nothing new. In 1928, when he was 13, Boisseau "was among the winners in the 'Toots and Casper' contest conducted by Jimmy Murphy, creator of this comic strip," according to the Progress-Index. The comic featured a husband and wife who had a baby named Buttercup. The contest, which ran in June and July, may have been a tie-in with the September release of a movie version of the strip.

In his letters, Boisseau quoted catch-phrases from the Sunday funnies. When bad things happened to him, he would scrawl, "Everything happens

159

to Dick Tracy and I." When he got into a fix, he would moan, "I get into more trouble than 'Ella Cinders.'" That comic strip was a take-off on Cinderella, ran from 1925 to 1961, and was even made into a silent movie in 1926. During the war, comic strips and cartoons in newspapers and magazines didn't ignore what was happening in the real world. Superman fought Nazis and defended America, and boxer Joe Palooka enlisted even before Pearl Harbor. While serving in the Army himself, cartoonist Bill Mauldin created Willie and Joe, two grunts who would eventually appear in Stars and Stripes, the service newspaper.

Another enlisted man, David Breger, created a single-panel cartoon, "Private Breger." In one of them, the small, bespectacled main character is shown by his cot during basic training. Behind him are full-year calendars for 1941, 1942 and 1943, delineating how long he would be in the Army. Hovering over him, an imposing officer demands to know, "Well, young man, and how do you like the Army?" The character of the private was in the Quartermaster Corps, which may have been of particular interest to Boisseau.

One possible reason the Progress-Index's page-one news was stale to Boisseau is that he had an alternative. It was a newspaper published in New Guinea for the troops. As he told his mother in a June V-mail, "We haven't gotten our one and only newspaper in four days. So we have nothing at all to read." Boisseau surely must have read the July 21, 1944, issue because he wrote his mother that "things look really brighter in both theaters of war." That issue's front page contained headlines that read "Tojo's Cabinet Resigns; Drift in Pacific Alarms Leaders" and "Big Nazi Force Cut Off By Own Trap North-East of Caen" and "Americans in Italy Take Leghorn Base."

The newspaper was Guinea Gold, a daily that began printing in November 1942 with the promise "to present the news concisely, accurately, without bias." A member of the editorial staff described it as "a unique four-page Australian army newspaper which day after day....published a record number of world scoops" from 1942 to 1946. The scoops were made possible, he continued, because MacArthur "gave it permission to publish his communiqués 20 hours before the release time for the rest of the world's media." The general maintained that "news and information on current events are the very breath of modern existence. To the combat soldiers they are as necessary as bread and bullets."

While Stars and Stripes, the American military newspaper, was circulated to personnel in Europe, it did not publish a New Guinea edition. Guinea Gold, which printed Australian and, later, American editions, had a peak circulation among service personnel of 64,000 issues and an estimated readership of 800,000 because issues were eagerly passed from soldier to soldier. One of its printing locations was at Oro Bay.

Said the staff member, "The front and back pages concentrated on up-to-the-minute news from around the world, including coverage of major sporting events on the back page. Page 2 was devoted to extracts from Australian and U.S. newspapers published a few days previously, which air transport crews delivered to Guinea Gold." Boisseau, with his interest in both baseball and boxing, probably found the sports news a welcome break from his surroundings. He could have also been intrigued by an unusual competition. At one point, the editorial member recalled, "the newspaper promoted a 'Girl I Left Behind' contest, [and] 1,700 photos of wives, sweethearts and baby daughters swamped the editorial office." Jane's picture might have lain among the snapshots.

In its December 6, 1943, issue, Time magazine's profile of the journal noted that a poll of Guinea Gold's readers discovered preferences for "war news first, political news from home second, educational features third. There are a few standard informational sections (movie schedules, lost & found, etc.). The rest of Guinea Gold is packed, seven days a week, with more than 100 solid news nuggets, many filched from short-wave broadcasts."

The American edition of the island newspaper for July 14, 1943—printed on 8 ½"x 11" paper—includes this banner headline on the front page, "Allied Offensive in Sicily Develops Favorably," and small front-page story, "Rabaul Raid Lasts Three Hours," about a strike in New Guinea. Says the article, "Many high explosives, incendiaries and fragmentation bombs were dropped and the fires were seen 60 miles away.... One U.S. bomber is missing." The back page updates battle news from Italy and the Pacific.

Six months later, Guinea Gold's American edition sported a front-page photo of a woman in a bathing suit. Under a headline of "Glamor," the caption read, "Lass in abbreviated swim-suit might be a 'pin-up' girl from appearance. Actually she is a hard-working AWAS—L/Bdr. N. Longmore—after a swim in Brisbane." (AWAS, the Australian Women's Army Service, had a rank of Lance Bombardier, that is, artillery corporal.) The paper is dated eight days after Boisseau's first surviving letter, the one to his sister Charlotte.

A murder committed in June 1944 in Australia by an American soldier, Private Avelino Fernandez, might have made news in the paper. It certainly made news when the condemned man was transferred, under orders signed by General MacArthur, to Oro Bay to be hanged. In a drunken rage after being asked to pay for the sex he had just had with a woman he met in a bar while on leave, Fernandez had beaten her to death. In November, following his last meal and a failed attempt to commit suicide with his dinner knife, the private was hanged on a scaffold constructed on the Oro Bay beach.

Probert, the officer who briefly led Boisseau's unit, speculated that the execution might have been timed to make an impression on servicemen who had not been around women in a long time but who had recently been joined by WACs. "Every company was required to send a witness to the execution," he recalled. "The purpose was to prevent additional rapes."

The Oro Bay scaffold had been built just a month earlier for six black men—all of them members of the Quartermaster Corps stationed at Milne Bay, New Guinea. They were hanged after being convicted of raping two white WACs the previous spring. In a book about that case, "A Rape of Justice: MacArthur and the New Guinea Hangings," Walter A. Luszki, who was in charge of the New Guinea Detention and Rehabilitation Center at Oro Bay, wrote that Army engineers were brought in to put up the gallows, a task they accomplished in 48 hours. To carry out the executions, Luszki revealed that

> an Australian "professional" hangman, Mr. Wilson, was
> hired. His main task was to cut the rope which sprung the
> trapdoor.... He emphasized that a successful hanging was one
> which resulted in the least amount of suffering
> and strangulation.

162

Wilson fiddled with his ropes and calculated each prisoner's weight, while also finding fault with the Army's capital punishment rules. The author reported that Wilson said, "If you are going to hang a man, hang him and be through with it and don't put on a big show."

But the Army did just that. As if at a wedding, the witnesses—including some WACs—were placed on either side of a central aisle that led to the gallows. Two at a time, the prisoners were marched down the aisle and up 13 steps to their final moments. Wilson decried the number of stairs as an unforgivably ghoulish touch. Boisseau might have been among the spectators on hand for the horrifying moment when one of the men, after being hanged and declared dead, exhaled loudly, his literal last breath rattling through the silence.

In addition to getting information from hometown newspapers and Guinea Gold, some soldiers had access to handmade journals put out by various units. Typed up and mimeographed like high school newspapers, they came crammed with "did you know?" items, trivia questions, sports news, personality profiles and jokes. The pages were open to anyone who had something to contribute.

One scholar estimates that more than 3,200 such publications existed by the end of the war. They were often colorfully titled to indicate what branch of the armed forces published them. Army Air Corps publications ranged alphabetically from Ace-Pursuiter to Wing Tips. Corpsmen tended toward medical terminology when naming their newsletters: Bed Pan, Bandage Roll and Caduceus. Banners also gave clues of a unit's location: Jungle Mudder, Southern Cross, South Sea Reveille and Sand Script. Soldiers also got away with utilizing crude words blatantly (Bull Sheet) and more subtly (Snafnews). A Signal Corps unit stationed at Finschhafen, New Guinea, called its paper "Damfino," an elision of "Damned if I know," which one soldier said when asked what the publication should be titled.

Another example was "Bulldozer," a weekly published by the 757th Squadron, which ran the Engineers Parts Supply Depot in Milne Bay, south of Oro Bay. The first issue included a contest to name the 8½ x 14-inch paper, and the editors complimented the winner because the title "identifies the paper with our business and at the same time notes the 'bull' we fill it with." A typical June 1944 issue included:

- A cartoon of a man being led to the draft board by a cop;

- News about the progress of the war, noting that "the largest daylight raid on Germany" had been carried out, "hitting Oil Plants in Hamburg";

- An expression of sympathy, including a Scripture quotation, toward a soldier whose father had died;

- A profile of "Billy Boy" Ricketts from Texas, who could whistle Verdi, type with precision and play trumpet, and who longed to return to his wife, baby and college studies;

- Announcements of what movies were playing that week, such as "Nine Girls," starring Ann Harding and Evelyn Keyes.

The first issue also contained a lengthy poem about New Guinea that ended with this quatrain:

> *Somewhere in the Pacific, where the ants and lizards play,*
> *And a hundred fresh mosquitoes replace each one you slay,*
> *So, take me back to the U.S.A., let me hear that mission bell,*
> *For this God-forsaken outpost is a substitute for hell.*

In Port Moresby, troops could read "The Jungle Journal," published by the Special Service Section, Base D&22nd Port Headquarters (TC). Its March 26, 1944, issue was heavy with sports news, comics and trivial tidbits from the states, as well as an editorial boosting the right of soldiers to vote for president in the fall:

> *The soldiers are overwhelmingly in favor of participating in the coming US elections this year. That can be readily ascertained from the long-drawn discussions and great concern over problems which they'll have to face in the post-war period. They realize, too, that their vote may be decisive in the forthcoming elections and will vitally effect their very future.... Every citizen who is good enough to fight is certainly good enough to vote. That sacred privilege to vote is the very thing we are fighting for.*

One of the most specialized of the hand-made sheets was "Star of David," directed at Jewish soldiers and printed in Finschhafen, a port town east of Oro Bay. The four-page newspaper identified its date by the Jewish calendar. Thus, July 6, 1945, was designated as 25 Tammuz 5705. A note on the front page announced that Hebrew class would be held Tuesday at 1850 hours, with a Bible lesson to follow.

That issue's cover, headlined "Jewish News of the World," predicted one feature of the post-war world. "Jewish soldiers of the Polish Army, liberated from German PW camps," it reported, "say that they wanted to remain in Germany under Allied supervision until they could emigrate to Palestine. The soldiers felt that they 'had nothing to return to' in their country of origin."

Aboard the U.S.S. Rigel, which saw major service in New Guinea as a repair vessel and sometime transport, The Rigel Morning Star was loaded with news ("Sentiment Grows That Pacific War Nears End"), pin-up photos and drawings, gossip ("Mr. Gerwig is passing out the cigars") and gags ("Boy: 'What's that gurgling noise?' Girl: 'It's me trying to swallow your line.'"). It also declared, in an August 1945 issue, that "it may be a trifle early to start breaking out your blues, but that old 'Home alive in '45' looks better and better every day."

Boisseau could also listen to the radio in New Guinea, although he never mentions doing so. One station was WVTB of the Armed Forces Radio Service. Its schedule was peppered with popular programming like big-band music, the Hit Parade, Bing Crosby, the National Barn Dance, comedians Burns and Allen, and Charlie McCarthy, the ventriloquist's dummy. WVTB was located in Nadzab, which lay northwest of Oro Bay.

Back in Prince George Courthouse, Boisseau's friends and relatives had a reliable source for news about the war in New Guinea—his letters, which must have seemed as if they came from Mars and which they must have read with avid interest. They also heard from other Prince Georgians in the service. However, Boisseau chided his mother on more than one occasion about believing what two particular men were saying in their mail. One of them, Fenner Bishop, apparently spread the word that soldiers were starving. "Don't listen to Fenner Bishop and his wild stories," Boisseau advised Rella on June 17. "He has always been a liar and always will be." A week later, he repeated the admonition:

> As I have said before, don't pay any attention to what Fenner Bishop has told you. We are getting plenty to eat and the best. We have fresh eggs, steak, pork (hold your nose), lamb and almost everything else. That doesn't sound like we are starving, does it?

Both Fenner and Boisseau were carving a slice of the truth because food supplies sometimes came in spurts. In his book, Taaffe describes typical rations for soldiers in the field as "tinned fruit, canned vegetables, dehydrated potatoes…[and] eggs, dried milk and soggy pancakes." However, since he lived on a permanent base, Boisseau had access to food that was a cut well above C-rations. In a letter, Robert Tuttle of Ohio recited the dinner he enjoyed at Oro Bay in January 1944. "There is the chow call," he wrote before breaking off to eat. Returning to his tent, he drew a line to indicate his absence and then revealed that "we had salmon patties, potatoes, peas and carrots, pineapple, coffee and bread and butter."

On the other hand, in a reminiscence about her time at Oro Bay, a WAC named Helen Strzelczyk wrote that

> the food…at Oro Bay was not good. With the exception of Thanksgiving and Christmas, we did not have fresh meat, eggs, fruit or vegetables to eat…. At times [the food] was inedible. Most of the food used for cooking was dehydrated, and the meats conditioned to prevent spoilage…. It was not unusual to miss the noon meal when one learned that the menu wasn't worth standing in line for.

Another factor was the New Guinea climate, which could wreak havoc on food supplies. "A survey of the canned food…in the Oro Bay area…revealed that 40 to 50 percent of the evaporated milk, 20 to 40 percent of canned fruits, and 20 to 25 percent of canned vegetables were unfit to eat," according to Alvin P. Stauffer's book, "The Quartermaster Corps: Operations in the War Against Japan." Another estimate, he continues, was that 40 percent of the rations in the Southwest Pacific were "spoiled or unconsumable."

Factors undercutting the food supplies included spoilage, theft and shipping problems. Stauffer reports that "distribution of food supplies reached a critical phase in the opening months of 1944.....Oro Bay needed 1,300 tons [of flour] but had on hand only 526 tons." The same shortage was recorded there for sugar, salt, lard and butter. In January 1944, Oro Bay needed to feed 232,000 men but had no fresh beef or poultry.

When Boisseau gave his list of foods, he may have been describing the "prince" side of what was called "prince and pauper" supplies. When bases received more food from Australia than they could store, it had to be immediately eaten or it would spoil. Stauffer records that Oro Bay had about 30 1,800-cubic-foot refrigerators for storage of perishable items. When they were packed full, any leftovers had to be consumed or thrown away. In November 1943, as an example, soldiers were given daily rations of 19 eggs and stacks of beef. When those were exhausted, the men went back to canned foods.

As much as he slammed Fenner Bishop, Boisseau was even more decidedly dismissive of William Roach:

> *He is a bigger liar than Fenner Bishop. I don't know what fun they get out of lying like they do. If Bill has killed two Japs I have killed ten thousand. He might make the people back home believe that stuff but, I know where he is and was. There hasn't been any action where he is or was for six months.*

Exaggerating their own fierceness was not unknown among soldiers. Taaffe records that "censors confiscated a bushel basket full of Japanese skulls from GIs trying to impress—or, more accurately, deceive—friends and family as to their military prowess."

A poignant and real reminder of the high cost of war was mailed home from the Philippines in October 1945 by First Lieutenant Zillich of El Paso, Texas. "Enclosed is a postal card found on a dead Jap," he told his wife, Emily. "It evidently is from his folks or sweetheart. You know, honey, it makes me wonderfully happy to think of you and...to realize how blessed I have been to have you as my wife. I love you with all my heart Sweetheart and will to the end of time."

His use of the words "sweetheart" and "wife" in back-to-back sentences indicates how deeply the Japanese postcard had touched him. The "end of time" for Lieutenant Zillich would not come until 1998 when he was 82—and still married to Emily.

CHAPTER SIXTEEN

THE YEAR 'CASABLANCA' WON

Boisseau spent most of 1944 in New Guinea, even enduring an extra February day since it was a leap year. He longed to be home with his mother and Jane. He wanted to be back at work for Coca-Cola. He wished he had his friends around. Such thoughts must never have been far from his mind, although he could be distracted for a time as he labored in the warehouse, read the news and watched boxing matches. But he was severed from the everyday events—even the trivia—of life that could have occupied his thoughts. And 1944 had more than its share of those.

In March, the Oscar for the best movie of the previous year went to "Casablanca," a classic romance-thriller, with its director, Michael Curtiz, getting his own statuette and the three screenwriters being honored as well. Since it told a story of war-weary people finding the courage to keep pressing against Nazism, men in uniform were invited to attend the Academy Awards ceremony at no charge.

In April, the United Negro College Fund was founded, according to its website, "by the presidents of private historically black colleges and universities to make a collective appeal for support to the nation on their behalf." President Franklin D. Roosevelt and philanthropist John D. Rockefeller got on board, and $760,000 was raised in the first year.

That August, the first fire-prevention poster featuring Smokey Bear was released, with the slogan, "Smokey says—Care will prevent 9 out of 10 forest fires!" In Boston, the chairwoman of the city's licensing board banned performances of "The Drunkard; or the Fallen Saved," a play that was more than a century old. It told the story of a man whose alcoholism ruined his life, marriage and family. Mary Driscoll, the censor, said the title itself was offensive enough to keep the play off the stage. If Boisseau had heard about her decision, he might have pointed out that Camp Lee had no trouble staging a play titled "Ten Nights in a Barroom."

Having already served three terms, more than any president in U.S. history, Roosevelt won an unprecedented fourth term in November, burying his opponent, Thomas E. Dewey, in the electoral vote, 432-99. The entire south, including Virginia, went for FDR. Servicemen voted for him, too, but not unanimously. One newspaper speculated that GIs, weary of the war, would cast their ballots for Dewey. A soldier theorized in letters home—and his theories went uncensored—that the president had known about plans for the attack on Pearl Harbor and let it happen in order to justify entering the war. He wrote home before the voting, "Evidently most of the people aren't interested in the obvious and probably would prefer Roosevelt to George Washington or anyone else. Well, we'll all have to pay for it." Another serviceman snidely said that Americans had nothing to worry about after the war because FDR had made sure that they all would be taken care of by the government.

Babies born in 1944 would have a major impact on American culture in the 1960s, '70s and '80s, such as journalist Carl Bernstein, activist Angela Davis, rockers Roger Daltrey and John Sebastian, athletes Joe Frazier and Denny McLain, film director George Lucas and actor Michael Douglas, and politician Rudy Giuliani, who would have to confront an attack on American soil that was instantly compared to Pearl Harbor.

Those infants came into the world as others left it, including failed presidential candidates Al Smith and Wendell Willkie, baseball czar Kennesaw Mountain Landis, fey silent-film actor Harry Langdon and bespectacled band-leader Glenn Miller. He was lost in December, when his airplane disappeared as he flew from England to Paris to set up a musical performance for the advancing troops.

The fall 1944 World Series was an all-St. Louis affair. That city's National League team, the Cardinals, battled its American League club, the Browns, a perennial loser that sneaked into the post-season because so many top-line players from other teams were in the service. All six Series games were played in one stadium, Sportsman Park, with the Cards winning, four games to two.

Throughout 1944, Americans spent hours each day listening to the radio, no longer the new-fangled device that the 1930 census quizzed the Baileys about. It had grown into an essential medium—and not just to access the president's fireside chats about the progress of the war.

Listeners had many more choices than those servicemen and women in New Guinea who could tune in to WVTB. Back home, listeners laughed during comedy shows hosted by Abbott and Costello, Jack Benny, and Red Skelton with his catch-phrase "I dood it," quoted by Boisseau in a letter. They thrilled to dramas such as "The Lone Ranger" and "The Shadow." They stayed up-to-date with news from Lowell Thomas and H.V. Kaltenborn.

Whether by listening to their radios, playing 78-rpm records at home or going out to hear live music, Americans tapped their toes to music from Sammy Kaye, Kay Kyser, Tommy Dorsey and Dinah Shore. When they sang, they crooned new tunes, many of them about distant loved ones or deep-blue nostalgia, like "I'll Walk Alone," "Sentimental Journey," "Dream (When You're Feeling Blue)," "I'll Get By (As Long As I Have You)" and "I'll Be Seeing You." The last song, published in 1938, came into its own in 1944 with lyrics freighted with a sense of loss and longing:

> *I'll be seeing you*
> *In all the old familiar places*
> *That this heart of mine embraces*
> *All day through...*
>
> *I'll find you in the morning sun*
> *And when the night is new.*
> *I'll be looking at the moon,*
> *But I'll be seeing you.*

Pulitzer Prizes went to a stellar collection of creative people for their work in 1944. John Hersey won for his novel, "A Bell for Adano," about soldiers in Italy. James Reston of The New York Times was cited for his reporting on diplomatic meetings that would lead to the creation of the post-war United Nations. Composer Aaron Copland was honored for scoring the ballet, "Appalachian Spring," a celebration in music and dance of American pioneer values. Joe Rosenthal was recognized for his iconographic photo of the flag-raising on Iwo Jima. Sergeant Bill Mauldin was named for his cartoons of life in the trenches.

The prize for "distinguished volume of verse by an American author" went to Karl Shapiro, who had trained at Camp Lee. In 1944, he published "V-Letter and Other Poems," a collection of more than 40 poems, all of which, save one, were written in New Guinea. In a poem named after the island, he wrote:

It fell from Asia, severed from the East;
It was the last Unknown. Only the fringe
Was nervous to the touch of voyagers.
Business and boys looked close and would have come.

In war did come, crashing the gifts of iron
Created on crazy trails where by our blood
The rat-toothed enemy is backward inched,
And forest bulldozed, busted into streets.

CHAPTER SEVENTEEN

THE ELUSIVE JANE

No name is invoked more often in Boisseau's V-mails than Jane's. And his letters are packed tight with names, such as Judges Binford and Temple, Courtenay Figg, the Gays, various Burrowses and Seberas, Ned and Rachel Eppes, Eddie Minor, the Kanaks, Buck Scarborough, and a trio of nicknames—Pinkie, Possum and Flora Dora. Even a one-legged man called Martin B. was mentioned. Most people make one-time appearances, but Jane's name is written approximately 50 times.

Nevertheless, she remains unknown.

The arc of their rocky relationship runs through all of his mail and comes to a conclusion in his final extant letter in the spring of 1945. During the preceding summer, his ardent affection for her grows. Then he aches deeply in his heart when she doesn't write him. He exults joyously when she does but then claims diffidently that he doesn't care for her anymore. He restates his zealous love and happily announces to his mother his plans to marry Jane, father loads of children and settle down in the home he grew up in, adding a third generation to the house across the road from the sheriff's place.

He also reveals what seems to be a little fear of her. When WACs arrive in New Guinea, he tells his mother that he didn't inform Jane lest she suspect he will two-time her, something he vows he would never do. In another letter, he writes that he forgot to inform Jane about a letter he received, "and I know that I will catch hell about it."

It's regrettable that none of Boisseau's letters to Jane survive. Many husbands and boyfriends who had been sent to Europe and the South Pacific penned sensitive and passionate love letters home. In return, wives and girlfriends waiting in Iowa, Florida and Arizona whispered sweet nothings across the oceans. For example, on July 13, 1944, Private Kopplin told his wife in Illinois:

To me...your just every thing cause your such a swell wife
and I will always love and honor you. Being I love you so. You see

"Dear", when I married you, I knew I got the right girl and don't
think I'm not proud as I am, Sweet Heart, ever so proud. Yes my
Love, it was the most wonderful thing I ever did in my whole
life, cause "Sugar" what I mean I love you. There could never be
any one else. Love really is a beautiful thing[;] ours is extra special
and will always last.... Your letters are like gold flowing from
Heaven, and [I] wait patiently for them.

In just a half-dozen letters, he went through a thesaurus of pet names
for her: my loving wife, angel, dearest, blondie, my love, dear, sweet heart,
sugar, precious, sweet blond wife, dearest darling, honey, blond dish, blond
beauty, kid, sweet wife, honey, doll, dearest love one, duchess, beautiful and
sweet bundle of joy.

Not all men maintained such devotion. In battle zones, servicemen
and women, single and not, dated, fell in love and even found somewhere
private to consummate their relationships. One WAC recalled going
to the New Guinea beach to swim and seeing a couple coupling on a
blanket. A Tennessee lieutenant told his wife in a V-mail about a G.I. who
impregnated a woman, brought the baby home on leave and convinced his
wife to forgive him. "I can just see you doing that," he joked, hastily adding,
"I'm not about to get in that situation."

The loss of love announced from the other side of the correspondence
was also a harsh fact of life during World War II. The phrase "Dear John
letter" was born during the 1940s as soldiers, sailors, Marines and pilots
got mail informing them that their wives and girlfriends had found
somebody new. On August 17, 1945, a newspaper in Rochester, New
York, informed readers:

"Dear John," the letter began. "I have found someone else
whom I think the world of. I think the only way out is for us to get
a divorce," it said. They usually began like that, those letters that
told of infidelity on the part of the wives of servicemen.

Kopplin, writing from Maui prior to shipping out for New Guinea,
informed his wife, Vera, "A lot of single guys get letters from their gals

back home saying they are getting married." A military policeman already in New Guinea told his sister why he was feeling low:

> Not having heard from Dot [his girlfriend] since May I have
> been rather discouraged. The last letter from her...was only one
> page.... I am inclined to think she has stopped caring for me and
> has met someone else.... Seems like she was just a dream.

The devastating impact of such a letter is captured by Bergerud in "Touched With Fire," his account of the land war in the South Pacific. "Although a motif in many bad movies," he wrote, a "Dear John" letter "was a very serious matter. It was a generation that took marriage seriously." His book also contains a soldier's account of how another man reacted to being dumped:

> One of our buddies read his letter and slowly rose from his
> bunk sobbing and growling. He picked up his metal bunk and
> threw it halfway through the barracks wall.... All of us hated that
> faraway woman we had never seen nor knew, but we hated her
> then for all the hurt she was causing our buddy.

When love endured, its expressions—from baby-talk affection to erotic wishes—survive in the V-mails and letters sent home from overseas, such as this one:

> Dearly Beloved,
> I could do for some cuddling and snuggling—an' some
> necking too—tonight. We sure have a lot to catch up with. Oh boy!
> Remember my Pet, I love you always and miss you no end.
> Love & Kisses,
> Honey XXXXX

Some letters were more ardent:

> Darling,
> I got the sweetest letter from you to day.
> Yes darling it would be a nice night to lay in bed and make
> love. I can think of nothing nicer.

*You know sweetheart you are very pretty. You are pretty all
over. I think you have the best looking legs in the whole world. I
would like to start in with your feet and work up to your head.*

I would love to...

And that's where propriety draws the curtain.

In December 1942, Hubert R. Enders of Connecticut, a Signal
Corpsman stationed at Camp Kohler in Sacramento, California, wrote to
his girlfriend, Elsa Mildred Brown of Brooklyn:

*I must be with you, Darling. Do you think you might come
out—we'd be married and live in Roseville—off the Post....
Would you think of this, Loveliness?*

Five days later, she typed on a sheet a paper that she used as a
makeshift diary:

*Hube asked me in a letter to come to Calif. and marry...
Yippee! California here I come!*

In a subsequent letter, he responded to her detailed plans for their
upcoming wedding, particulars that didn't interest him:

*I love you. I LOVE you. I love YOU. I LOVE YOU!!...So long
as I can once more hold you in my arms and kiss your lovely mouth,
and sweet lil' nose...and make love to you...no more will I ask.*

In June 1943, Elsa hand-wrote her last entry in the diary:

*We were married Easter Sunday April 25th, Little Church
Around the Corner,...NYC. Arrived Davis Calif July 31st. We
are ideally happy.*

After five years in the Army, rising from private to second lieutenant,
Enders returned to Aetna Insurance. He had begun working there in 1935
as an office boy and would retire as National Marketing Director. A fire
commissioner, Mason and banjo player, he died in 2007, after 64 years of
marriage to Elsa.

Amorous letters also came from the other direction, as wives and girlfriends reminded soldiers of who—and what—was waiting for them at home. Helen Arney of Oregon dispatched a V-mail to her husband, Sergeant Clarence P. Arney, a finance officer with an infantry division in Europe:

> *I just cannot express to you in the way I'd like the love I feel*
> *for you, too—it just goes too deep as I've often said before. And you*
> *may be sure that as each day goes by, I know it is that much closer*
> *to the time we will be back together again.*

No such happy ending happened for Boisseau and Jane, despite the fact that he told his mother he was eager for a wedding. On August 13, in the letter about his rash-covered hands, he writes, "Maybe they will get well before I get married. Hate like hell to be all bandaged up my first night of married life." Such an offhanded remark hints at a previous letter in which he declared he would marry Jane as soon as he got home.

A conflation of his summer/fall letters of 1944 into one imaginary V-mail captures the ebb and flow of their relationship:

> *Its awful not hearing from you and Jane.... The rest of the*
> *mail was from you and My Only Jane.... I still haven't heard*
> *from Jane lately. Is she mad with me about anything or do you*
> *know. She hasn't had any cause to get mad lately.... Was glad to*
> *hear that Jane still loves me.*
>
> *She is not writing as often as before. Her excuse, working*
> *nights.... Didn't hear from Jane today, guess she had to big a time*
> *at the beach to write me.*
>
> *Gosh, it was great to hear from you and Jane again.... Did*
> *you and Jane enjoy the drive in my car? I hope so. Is Jane a good*
> *driver? She used to drive on the wrong side of the road when I*
> *used to let her drive.*
>
> *Why isn't Jane writing me. I hardly ever get a letter from her.*
> *Tell her to get on the ball.*
>
> *I also got two [letters] from Jane, about the sweetest that she*
> *has ever written Me! ...Jane has been doing just a little better*
> *about writing lately. Five letters from her.*

Still haven't heard from Jane and you keep saying how much she loves me. She is too busy thinking about the beach to write me I guess. She will have a dose of her own medicine because I haven't been writing myself for the past week. If I don't hear from her soon, I'm not writing to her anymore. She has written thirty-six letters in the past ninety days. Some record, eh?

What in the world has happened to Jane? I don't hear from her anymore. Is she getting married or something? I have only gotten four letters from her this month. I'm not writing to her until she writes me. Its not worrying me so don't let it worry you. If that's the way she wants it that's the way it shall be.

Well, the ice has finally been broken, again. Got two letters from Jane. They made me feel lots better.... You wont have to worry about Jane and I not taking the entire upstairs. We will need it. Just wait and see.

Still haven't heard from Jane. Is she mad with me?... Thanks for the encouragement about Jane writing me but, I personally don't think she is. I have only gotten three letters from her this month. It must be her as all the other boys from Virginia are getting their mail.

In his first surviving letter, penned in January 1944 to his sister, Boisseau talked about rushing to the judge to get married. In his summer letters to his mother, he refers to "My Only Jane" and promises to stock the upstairs of the Bailey house with grandchildren. In between, he is whipsawed by Jane, who fails to write, writes again, disappears, reappears and tortures the distant sergeant with her coyness. While she has flirted from Virginia, he has saved her letters and can count how many she mailed in the course of three months—three dozen.

So who was this woman who alternately tortured and thrilled the quartermaster in New Guinea? No one in Prince George Courthouse from that time period remembers her among the girls he dated. Edwina, Naomi and Jeannie, yes. Jane, no. A search of thousands of names in the 1930 census of Prince George County for women named Jane who would have been about the right age to date Boisseau turns up five candidates:

- Jane E. Collins, who would have turned 16 in 1944, was the child of Luther and Susie Collins of West Hopewell;

- Jane A. Daniel, who was 17 in 1944, was the daughter of Garry and Virginia Daniel of the Carson area of the county;

- Jane A. Johnson, 16, was the offspring of Harvey and Pearl Johnson from the Woodlawn area;

- Mary Jane Len, 19, was the daughter of Eric and Kathleen Len of Crescent Hills; and

- Betty Jane Owens was 20; her parents were Arthur and Opal Owens of Crescent Hills.

If the Mary and Betty can be eliminated because their first name wasn't Jane, three candidates remain, of whom two are likelier because of their fathers' jobs. Jane Daniel's father was a mail carrier, establishing a possible link to Rella, the postmistress. Jane Johnson's father was commissioner of revenue, the county position held by both of Boisseau's parents.

Boisseau describes his Jane as coming down and coming over to see his mother, expressions that imply Jane did not live in the center of town. The Johnsons lived about five miles away. But, when Jane Johnson's name is mentioned to Boisseau's contemporaries, no one's face lights up. "It's a good possibility" is as far as one of them would go. However, at 16, Jane Johnson could have been too young to work, and Boisseau describes Jane as working at night. The difference in their ages (he turned 29 in 1944) might not have been a factor, however, since it matched that of Boisseau's parents when they married.

It's possible that "My Only Jane" did not live in Prince George County and was not known in the courthouse area.

Late in the research for this book, another candidate surfaced. She was Mary Virginia Fletcher, who roomed with the Buren family, the store-owners who lived only a few doors from the Bailey house. In so many ways, she fits the profile:

- She lived up the street and would have "come down" to the Bailey home;

- She was known to have dated Boisseau before he went to New Guinea;

• She had an income of her own, so she was in a position to pay his car bill;

• She could have worked at night, given her occupation;

• She was the right age, just five years younger than Boisseau.

In short, she was in the right place (the courthouse area) at the right time (the early 1940s) at the right age (she was 24 in 1944) and with the right income to pay someone else's debts.

Fletcher was an accomplished woman for her times. A native of Russell County near the southwestern toe-tip of Virginia, she was a graduate of Virginia Polytechnic Institute with a BS in home economics. She would later earn a master's degree in dietetics from Purdue University in Indiana.

At the time she could have dated Boisseau, she was a home demonstration agent in Prince George County. In that role, she would have taken on a number of assignments that kept her working at night, such as teaching girls to sew, can fruits and bake bread; convincing mothers to serve healthier meals; and teaching families how to be thriftier in their spending. During World War II, agents also helped families plant Victory Gardens in order to raise their own food. Her work could have encompassed organizing 4-H Clubs as well. Any of those duties would have required her working in the evenings, when husbands were home, wives were not occupied with daily chores and children were not in school.

If Boisseau was cowed by her, as indicated in his V-mails, it might have been the result of her superior education and her achievements.

And then there are these three items. Late in the war, she joined the WACs and was sent to the Philippines, where she would have been at the same time as Boisseau. She had reddish hair and freckles like him. And she never married.

Was she Jane? So many clues point to Mary Virginia Fletcher, but the main clue is glaringly absent. Her name was not Jane.

Although the 1850 census of Russell County records a Virginia "Jane" Fletcher, indicating that one branch of the family linked the names, none of her relatives remember her being called Jane—although the list of those relatives includes two named Mary Jane. The family remembers something else that is tantalizing. In the early 1950s, a man came to see Mary Virginia in Russell County. Family lore holds that he was a soldier she had loved and that her father ran the man off the farm because he wasn't good enough for her. A Coke driver with a high school education might have fit that description.

Was the soldier Boisseau? Was "Jane" a nickname he had given her? Had they seen a Tarzan movie together, with him joking afterwards, "Me, Tarzan; you, Jane"? Did she take him up on the joke, with the appellation becoming a secret between them? Or was "Jane" a code word between Boisseau and his mother for Mary Virginia so that prying eyes in Prince George did not discover their secret love?

Boisseau's Jane remains a missing person whose portrait was painted in words by a soldier in New Guinea who loved her.

CHAPTER EIGHTEEN

LETTERS FROM HOME

V-mails from the front lines of Europe and the South Pacific can still be read decades later because families preserved them—sometimes lovingly and sometimes haphazardly—in attics and trunks, dresser drawers and hall closets. Tied with ribbon or tossed in a jumble into shoeboxes, they were kept as memories of a frightening time in all of their lives.

Less common are preserved letters from the U.S. to "over there." The reason is that many servicemen and women did not save them. For one thing, the amount of mail became too bulky for troops to cart around. For another, they were warned not to carry information that would be helpful to the enemy if found on their bodies, alive or dead. One wife even told her husband what to do with her letters, "Tear 'em up in little pieces & throw 'em away. I'll do the same to the ones home here. No sense saving 'em. You'll never reread them."

No letters to Boisseau Bailey are known to exist, but several to Sergeant Lynn Knapp were saved by him. On October 11, 1943, for example, his mother wrote him about the weather, his relatives and hometown events. A week later, she was in a complete panic. Her letter had been returned, so she airmailed it again, this time with the APO address the post office demanded. But it bounced back a second time. "We are wondering where you are," his fretting mother said in a new letter that she added to the original one, "and very anxious to hear from you.... It has been 2 weeks since we have heard from you. Hope you are all right."

The final five words disguise her fear that he was dead. She didn't know that her son had been shipped to England and had no way of telling his family until he arrived there, safe and sound. On May 3, 1944, a relative sent him a birthday card and remarked in an accompanying letter:

A few years ago if you had been told that you would spend
last years birthday in Va [at Camp Lee] and this yr. in London
England you would have thot they were having a fever dream—if

183

it only was a dream.... Why can't this dreadful thing come to an end? A foolish question of course—no one can answer it. Sincerely hope your Birthday has some bright spots. Trust the next one will be spent in the good old U.S.A.

Lieutenant Irvin Michelson's wife wrote him almost every day from West Virginia, and he stored her V-mails in a neat stack in his quarters in New Guinea. Writing in 1943, Jo—who jokingly chided him when he addressed her by her full name, Ida Jo—told him about their baby, Carole Ann, after whom he had nicknamed his jeep, and how a test of an air raid siren had frightened her. She also recounted neighborhood doings, such as how Ernest went "moosing."

In several letters, calling herself "your little red-head," she expressed something more significant, namely, her feelings for him:

Say! What I wouldn't do with a couple of days with you now after these months. I know I'd give you the loving of your life, because I'm still so crazy about you. Goodnight, Darling and with all my love and kisses—forever. And then some more love.... Honey, I've changed my theme song. It used to be "Scatterbrain," Now it is, "Don't Get Around Much Anymore." That's because I'm waiting for you to come back to do my getting around. That's on account of it's no fun "getting around" without you.... Goodnight, Darling, and Sweetest Dreams and I love you more and more and more every day if possible. Just wait 'till you come home. I'll show you.

Writing on June 27, 1943, three weeks shy of their second anniversary and worried that his recent change of address meant that he was going in harm's way, Jo typed a V-mail that charted the depth of her love:

It has been seven months since I've seen you. I certainly hope it won't be seven more before I see you again 'cause I think my li'l heart will surely burst open if I try to store very much more love for you in it but it does seem as though I love you more and miss you more every day and speaking of that old feeling of loving someone—not a day goes by that I don't feel that, too. I thought

*I loved you to the limit on that very happy July 20, 1941 [when
they married] but two years have shown me that that was mild to
what one can feel because, honey, I love you so much more than I
ever thought one person could possible love another. When you come
home, I'll show you what I mean. Gee, when I think of that happy
day, I get all jumpy inside, a shiver goes up and down my spine
and duck bumps pop out all over me and that's putting it mild.*

On Thanksgiving Day 1943, Mary Ellen McDavit dispatched a letter
to her husband, Herbert, at Camp Lee. Given the holiday, his absence
and the hope they would see each other around Christmas, she grew
lyrically nostalgic:

*Remember the sport hop, the flat tire, the kiss in the kitchen at
Orchard Rd after I put iodine on your cut finger; the iodine on my
dress? You don't remember the buzzing in my ears or the tremble
in my knees—but I do. I remember them well —'cause…you still
affect me that way!!*

A few letters from his wife to Sergeant Courtright exist because they
were sent to him in June 1945, when he was already on his way home.
While Liz didn't know that, the Army did. His address was exed out on the
envelopes, and a notation was penciled in that read, "Returning to the U.S."
Back to the correspondent went the airmailed envelopes with their six-cent
stamps. Liz collected her letters alongside his, preserving rare insights into
the other side of wartime mail.

In a June 6 letter carrying the salutation "My dearest darling," for
example, she expresses her hope that no mail from him is good news and
signifies that he is en route to America. "I have a premonition you will"
soon be home, she wrote, a day that would be "the happiest…of my life."
Then she recounts a hunting trip she took with his father. "We got one
squirrel," she said proudly, "and I got it. I shot it right thru the head & am
I proud. First shot, too…. I feel proud of myself!!"

On June 16, 1945, Liz wrote a second letter that ricocheted back to
her. In it, she tells about taking their son to see some Disney cartoons,

including Donald Duck. "It was darling," she enthused, "all in Technicolor. The coloring was simply gorgeous." She, too, sensed the end of a black time and the coming of a bright future. "I'm just living in a stage of expectancy," she stated. "I just hope you are home soon. That's all I think about and dream about."

In her neat, printed hand, she wrote the next day:

> Here it is Father's Day—Jim [their son] & I didn't send you anything to you for fear it would get lost if you are on your way home. Jim dictated a letter to you this morning and I'm enclosing it. Jim has the most ideal & perfect father in the world. Jim will always have a high example set by his daddy and he will always have reason to be proud of you & respect you & admire you. We love you so very much.
>
> We went to Sunday school & church this morning. Jim started in on a new class for tiny tots—ages from 2-4. He'll enjoy it so much.... It seems religion is so neglected in most homes today. Maybe its because the parents are too busy having parties etc....
>
> I just wonder how long it will be before we get word from you. This waiting is terrible, but someday I'll know one way or the other. You can't possibly know how badly I want you to come home. It will be like heaven to be together again.

Others wives also ghostwrote letters from their children to their daddies overseas. For instance, Mrs. Michelson sent a letter to her husband that was supposedly from their baby:

> Dearest Daddy,
>
> I know this is Mother's Day, but I keep thinking, Father's Day isn't far off so I thought I'd get a letter off to you and maybe you'd get it by Father's Day
>
> I wore a red carnation today in honor of mama and when Father's Day comes on the third Sunday in June, you can think of me and know that I'm wearing a red flower for you, too because I love you, Daddy and confidentially, Mama loves you, too.

"Nite"—with lots of love,
Your little Honey

On miniature sheets of paper, decorated with a puppy and two kittens, and sporting handwriting and vocabulary suspiciously like his mother's, Jim Courtright wrote to his father:

Dear Daddy,

Happy Father's Day. I wish you were here with me. We'd have lots of fun. I'm sorry I didn't send you a present but Mommie said maybe you are on your way home & your box would get all lost. Thank you Daddy for my seargent's stwipes and Air Corps badge. I got your letter too and I just love it Daddy.

Daddy I think you are the sweetest Daddy and I love you so much! My Mommie says I can be awfully proud of you 'cause I got the best Daddy in the world. When I grow up to be a big man I'm going to be just like you. I'm going to be big & tall and wear glasses and a uniform just like you. I use to want white hair like Gwandfather Courtright's but now I think I want black hair just like yours.

This morning I started my new Sunday school class. Kenny Kerr & Judy Jones are in it too. Judy was awfully naughty—her layed down on the floor & cried and Mrs. Jorden had to scold her. I was a good boy. We said our prayers & sang 'Jesus Loves Me' and the lady read stories about God to us. I say my gwace at every meal. I put my hands together and bow my head & say 'Father bless the food we take. Bless we all in Jesus sake. Amen.' Mommie got me a new youth bed. Its so pretty. It's soft & nice. I love my new bed. When you come home you can see it.

Goodbye Daddy. Happy Father's Day. I love you so much.

Love & XXXX.

Below the kisses, in a child's scrawl guided by his mother's hand, was an attempt at his signature.

CHAPTER NINETEEN

THE DARK SIDE

The deeply emotional side of Sergeant Bailey can be found in his letters, but it has to be meticulously prospected like a squint-eyed search for the final dust in a played-out gold mine. Seldom is he overly demonstrative, but his happiness, disappointment and other feelings can be teased out. However, on a few occasions, he bursts the confines in which his upbringing or nature or circumstances penned him. There is no more blatant a display of emotion than a V-mail written on August 15, 1944. The cause may have been what he was becoming aware of in July as hypodermic needles were being jabbed into his arm.

Penned a day before the August 15 letter, another V-mail betrays no growling beast about to be unleashed. In that one, he is chatty, telling his mother about souvenirs he is sending for her, Charlotte, Virginia and Jane. "I tried to have them made exactly alike so there wouldn't be any fussing or feuding," he lectured in the parental voice he sometimes assumed. What the four souvenirs were is not clear, but "the ones with the green on them" were for his sisters. Perhaps they were hula skirts or trinkets crafted by natives. In his book about his service in New Guinea, Jules Archer wrote that "almost all of us sent home native gifts—grass skirts, hair combs, shell necklaces, and woven palm baskets." In her diary, Private Walker records trading with natives for tapa cloths, a bamboo pipe and a gourd with a stopper.

Then, on August 15, came Boisseau's roar of rage, opening with the more formal "Dearest Mother" salutation he had not used in weeks:

> Dearest Mother,
>
> Four letters today and not a one of them helped a bit. I have never been as disgusted in all my life as I am now. You people back home must think that I'm a Chaplain or something of the sort. Everybody is telling me all of their troubles as if I didn't have troubles of my own. I hate to say this but, if all of you can't write more interesting letters to me, please stop writing me altogether. All of you should be in our shoes just for a little while, then you would find out

what hell is. I know its tough and all that but, after all you are at home. Here, we have to listen to every body and [that] pleases no one. At home you are at least free to do and go where you please without someone questioning your every move. It seems that its such an effort for any of you to write and God only know[s] I don't want to put any of you to any trouble. I have been away from home long enough not to care whether I hear from anyone anymore. I'm writing to Jane tonight and tell her the same thing that I have written you. Only a little stronger. I'm not mad, just disgusted as all of you seem to be.

    Love,

    Boisseau

He could deny he was mad, but his explosion of red-hot fury surely rattled the windows in the Bailey house in Prince George. He was angry at Army life, over his distance from home, about Jane's fickleness and, perhaps, at not being able to dive into a drink in order to forget where he was.

Two days later, Boisseau tries to unobtrusively clean up the debris in a letter meekly addressed to "Mama" instead of "Mother":

    Dearest Mama,

    I don't know whether I will have time to finish this letter or not but, the first thing that I want to get off my mind is that sassy letter that I wrote you Aug. 15. Mama, I just couldn't help it that night, I was all to pieces. This place is driving me nuts along with the other millions that are over seas. Between your troubles, Jane's troubles and troubles of my own its more than I could [carat inserting can] stand. If it were so I could help it would be a different story but, over here its nothing that I can do about it."

But he is still simmering as he finishes the note:

    Thank God Jennie May has had her baby and that's over with. Glad it's a boy. who's next on the stork list? Anyone in particular? I might as well share their pains with them. I do everyone elses.

    I Love You,

    Boisseau

The allusion to the arrival of Jenny May's baby (the child, who would be named Wayne, is now a funeral director in Hopewell) is perplexing because, the next day, Boisseau writes as if he did not know about the birth. And he scrawls hortatory sentences that suggest a depressed exasperation:

Tell Jenny May to make up her mine. Either have that baby or don't. Its no use in letting it linger. If the poor kid could only realize what kind of a world it's coming into, I know he wouldn't want to be born. I know I wouldn't.

Expressing a belief that the world is a horrible place, followed by the wish never to have been born, has more than a tinge of suicide in it.

That was not the only deeply troubling element about this string of letters. Not only do they contain the strongest and most negative statements in his mail, but they also show a collapse of his writing skills. Words are misspelled ("mine" for "mind" while "Jennie" struggles against "Jenny"); sentences are garbled ("If it were so I could help it would be a different story but, over here its nothing that I can do about it"); words, punctuation and individual letters of the alphabet are missing.

Such raw emotion and communication lapses could have resulted from a combination of factors, not just his feelings about matters at home but also the work stress he was experiencing and maybe the added fuel of alcohol.

On August 18, three days after his blast across the ocean, Boisseau, perhaps having recognized his own emotional state in the meantime, maybe even scared by his own wish not to exist, told his mother, "Wish I could get a furlough. I really need one. Haven't had one in twenty months." But a leave was not in his future. On the contrary, he would soon be riding landing crafts in the Pacific, dining on C-rations and listening to the cacophony of battle.

An anger very similar to Boisseau's was expressed around the same time by Private Kopplin, who was also on the island. In a schizophrenic August 9, 1944, letter to "my Sweet Wife," he swings between praising her for how she is handling their money and his absence ("you are a doll in all ways") and telling her that they're through because she has nagged him about writing her parents to thank them for a gift:

*I'm quite burned up. So if that's the way you feel about me not
writing your folks about the package allrite. Don't bother sending
me nothing cause I just don't feel like writing and get no answer
and don't tell me they can't write as I know different and besides
I did write. I sure as heck can't help if they didn't get it yet. I fully
realize this letter will hurt you Vera as yours sure hurt [me] in
as much as to bring tears to think you wrote me as you did. But I
guess thats the way you feel. I have enough trouble yet you write
me as you did. So I guess to make it plain[:] I'm just no good.
So thats that. . . . If you don't think I'm doing right and not the
husband you want[,] the best thing would be let me know and you
did a very good job of expressing your self.*

That flare of anger burned brightly just after he had penned sentences
like "I can't begin to tell you how grand you are" and "I can't express my self
enough what a wonderful job your really doing, a bang up job believe me[;]
I sure got to hand it to you, which more than proves what a wonderful wife
you are."

Disturbing August letters from two soldiers in New Guinea, both of
whom had been safely working in warehouses for many months, indicates
that something important had changed in their lives, perhaps something
that might place those lives at dire risk. Unable, amid censorship, to state
flatly what was nagging at them, or maybe unwilling to pass their own
primal fears along for relatives to bear, they bottled up their emotions. But
their emotional strain pressed on them so heavily that it burst out despite
their struggles to contain it.

Comedian Joe E. Brown, who toured the island, later wrote a book
about his experiences entertaining troops and what he learned from
spending so much time with them:

*The spirit of our kids, both officers and privates, took the
hardship [of New Guinea] as a challenge and lifted the whole
difficult business into another realm. Not romantic adventure—
don't think that for a moment. It was too grilling and grueling to
be called adventure. But it was an experience and the kids who*

*come back are going to have a special toughness of character that
they learned at Oro Bay, Milne Bay, Gona, Buna, Cape Killerton,
etc. If a kid was going to go on existing he had to kill the weak
stuff in himself and put in its place something strong and durable.*

Their letters betray that Boisseau and Kopplin were in the midst of the
process Brown describes. They were shedding the skin of innocence and
security, and donning the armor of toughness that they would need to survive.

Boisseau had not been in imminent danger during his first months
in the South Pacific. In August 1944, however, that was about to change
because the drive to oust the Japanese from Dutch New Guinea, which lay
to the west, had ended. John R. Kennedy notes in "The Dictionary of the
U.S. Army":

*In just over four months, the Allies advanced 1,200 miles
from the Huon Peninsula to the western tip of Vogelkop Peninsula,
fighting major battles at Hollandia and Biak Island.*

Now a new target was in sight:

*New Guinea became the springboard for MacArthur's
promised invasion of the Philippines in October.*

To achieve that goal, MacArthur needed the docks and warehouses
of Oro Bay as central receiving and distribution points. They had been
that for his moves along New Guinea. They would also be staging areas
for his next step across the Pacific. Boisseau and others knew full well that
the Philippines invasion was coming because they had spent the summer
preparing for it. The exhaustion he wrote about so often was a result of a
build-up.

Writing in Quartermaster Professional Bulletin (Spring 1999), Dr.
Steven E. Anders, historian at the U.S. Army Quartermaster Center and
School at Fort Lee, noted several factors that made the QMs' job in the
Pacific region "uniquely onerous." They included the Army's "Europe first"
policy that emphasized getting Hitler out of the way before Tojo, long
supply lines that had to span the breadth of the Pacific, underdeveloped

countries that couldn't provide much assistance, harsh weather and terrain, and MacArthur's policy of "island hopping," which meant that

quartermasters in the Pacific had to become increasingly adept at joint operations (working under Navy guidelines) while learning to perfect the demanding procedures required to support amphibious, over-the-shore type supply operations. The new tactics called for rapid logistical planning, tailored inventories, and quick development and movement of bases—in short, it meant functioning in a very unsettled environment, where routine supply procedures had to make way for far greater flexibility.

Martin reports in his book that "the Australians had called the New Guinea war a 'Q' war. 'Q' meant quartermaster and the supply problem was critical. Reefs were so rough that you couldn't bring boats in too close. Unloading heavy ammo from a bobbing boat to a pitching canoe on a moonless night had its disadvantages, but not as much as being bombed and strafed during the day by the zooming Zero fighters."

Anders ticked off several peculiar problems QMs had to function under in New Guinea, such as tents that leaked, boots that rotted in the moist weather and a lack of large storage facilities for petroleum. "Quartermaster supply operations in the Pacific faced a challenge of daunting complexity," he wrote. "The task presented them meant, in essence, having to support a new kind of war in a most difficult environment, on an unprecedented scale, against a formidable and tenacious foe. What's more—at a remarkable distance away from the U.S."

To keep up with the breakneck pace of operations in New Guinea, quartermasters were often ordered to work around the clock. Taaffe describes ports like Oro Bay as bustling "with activity as soldiers trained, loaded or unloaded ships, constructed warehouses and buildings, and repaired the implements of war. Huge piles of rations, ammunition and crates dotted the landscape, and rows of jeeps and [other] vehicles filled the motor pools."

In an article, The New York Times delineated the mammoth amount of work involved in "carv[ing] from the jungle elaborate bases that will support the advance on the Philippine Islands and ultimately Japan." At one such base, the newspaper calculated, the Army constructed two 6,000-foot runways, "thirty miles of graveled roads, various docks, a pipeline jetty and a PT patrol boat base." Also erected were "a 250-bed hospital, ten bridges,....operational buildings consisting of a control tower and alert huts at the airdrome, an ordnance dump with five more miles of roads and thirty buildings for quartermasters." Those buildings were the centers of bustling activity in support of forward troops.

That article ran on April 2, 1944. In a report filed for that month for Boisseau's unit, the 343rd Quartermaster Depot Company Supply, First Lieutenant Probert recorded that "the turnover of supplies was exceedingly heavy and called for full cooperation upon the part of all personnel to handle incoming supplies and outgoing shipments. All supply demands were met." As if that exertion were not enough, he also noted that "much time and expenditure of effort have been lavished upon the company area during the past month with consequent improvement in the living conditions and appearance of the area as well."

In May, Probert wrote that "23,500 man-hours of work were performed by the unit...as supply turnover continued to be heavy." In June, the man-hours jumped to 26,880. In July, Probert noted, the "company was inspected by the Inspector General's Office and a few minor discrepancies were found. General overall rating was 'Excellent.'" That same month, man-hours rose again, this time to 27,310.

As the New Guinea winter pressed on, the workload increased. "Quartermaster activities involving labor by men in this organization has in the past month [August] steadily increased, and has hit a new all high in man hours and quantities of items handled," said the unit report issued on September 1. In addition to the routine labor, the unit enlarged the mess hall, built a new recreation room, and erected new tents with flooring to accommodate a returning detachment.

The endless effort left Boisseau worn out. He wrote to Rella on June 26, "Intended answering [your letter] last night but, had to work as usual. Came in last night, went to bed and slept sixteen hours and I can sleep sixteen more now. I am practically exhausted." On July 24, he moaned, "I am still feeling fine except for being so damn tired. I have worked for the past four nights and parts of the days and am so sleepy and tired I can hardly wiggle." On September 3, he concluded his letter with, "My only ailment now is, being so damn tired. We are busier than hell and not any sign of a let up. Well, Ma, its bed time and I am really ready for it."

Given the multiple physical and emotional stressors on him, Boisseau's August 15, 17 and 18 letters become more understandable. Boisseau's next surviving V-mail is dated almost a week later, August 24. It returns to his usual topics, such as his health (his right thumb is broken, probably as a result of the warehouse work, although he does not explain the cause), an accounting of who has written him, his encouragement of Rella's relationship with Joe Burrow and a question about his car.

All the anger of the week before has dissipated, and the unchained beast is back in his cage. Two days later, he sunnily pronounces himself "feeling swell elegant," as if nothing had happened to cause his mother to fret over his state of mind. The expression may have been his way of saying he was back on the wagon.

Dated September 30, Boisseau's final extant email of 1944 is as filled with portents as it is with swell-elegant normality:

Dearest Mama,

I got your letter of Sept. 15th yesterday. The first letter in quite awhile. Thanks for the encouragement about Jane writing me but, I personally don't think she is. I have only gotten three letters from her this month. It must be her as all the other boys from Virginia are getting their mail. The Gov't hasn't notified you that I have been killed in action, have they? Something is radically wrong somewhere. Hope it is in the mail. I am feeling lots better but am awfully week. We are still working our fool heads off. Guess you will read about something big before long. I mean in the war news. Just wish we could move out of this hole and I think we will before long. Wish you hadn't gone to the trouble of fixing me something for Christmas. Its not a thing that I need, except mail. Boy, my morale is way below a thousand tonight. How did "Buck" Scarborough get out of the Army. Tell him to write me and let me

in on the secret. Well, Mama, take care of yourself and give my love
to all. Get Jane on the ball for me.
    Love,
    Boisseau

And then, in terms of surviving communications from Boisseau, there
was silence for 190 days.

CHAPTER TWENTY

NEW GUINEA HEATS UP

Many mysteries, major and minor, envelop James Boisseau Bailey. The official date of his mother's birth is uncertain due to Virginia's not requiring certificates when she was born. Jane's identity will remain hidden unless further evidence is uncovered or Jane herself steps forward. Also unknown is precisely what happened to him between September 30, 1944, and April 8, 1945. No letters have been found from him or his relatives that cover that chasm in time. No witnesses have come forth. More detailed information about his service was lost in a fire.

But there is a tantalizing hint in his separation papers. That hint can be combined with newspapers and books that tell what was happening in the Pacific during that span. Taken together, those resources provide a way to pierce the mysteries.

Early in World War II, U.S. and Australian forces had taken Papua New Guinea on the eastern part of the island, including Oro Bay, but that left the western half to the Japanese. They had to be ousted as part of the Allied plan to leap-frog Pacific islands on their way to the Philippines and Tokyo. The overall plan for New Guinea had been devised in 1943, according to reports by General Marshall:

> *At the Trident Conference of May 1943 in Washington*
> *[attended by FDR and British Prime Minister Churchill] when the*
> *specific strategy of the global war was conceived, it was determined*
> *to step up the pace of the advance on Japan. Then a few months*
> *later, in August 1943, at the Quadrant Conference in Quebec, the*
> *specific routes of the advance on Japan were laid out. Gen. Douglas*
> *MacArthur was directed to continue his operations up the New*
> *Guinea coast to reach the Philippines by the fall of 1944....*

That deadline put pressure on everyone from MacArthur to Boisseau. In a July 31, 1944, letter, Boisseau tells Rella, "We are busier than hell day and night." On August 3, he says, "I had to work again last night.... Am feeling fine, except for being so tired. Working day and night will really get a good man down." On August 4, he complains, "Just think of us poor bastards working like hell.... Ain't no justice do you think?"

The frenetic pattern of work continued all summer. On August 8, he notes, "I have intended writing for the last three nights but, I have had to work." The pace and the pressure exacted their toll on the soldier, both physically and psychologically. In this time span, his hands begin to shed skin. A week later, he issues his emotional diatribe about not wanting to hear everyone else's troubles and labeling his own circumstances "hell." He also dramatically exaggerates his circumstances. When Jane doesn't write, he wonders if she got married. When he doesn't get mail, he inquires if the Army has declared him dead.

The answer to what happened to cause such a shift in work hours, tension, pressure, physical injury (his sloughed skin and broken thumb) and an explosion of emotions lies in what occurred in late July, when, in Taaffe's account, "amphibious landings began [in far western Dutch New Guinea]. Much to the Allies' surprise and delight, the Japanese mounted no opposition.... For the Japanese, New Guinea was now no longer a defensive shield but just another example of the consequences of opposing the mobile American war machine."

To achieve that victory, MacArthur had used massive force carefully and cleverly. Commanding more than 1.3 million troops from the U.S., Australia and Holland, he moved along the northern coast of New Guinea like an experienced and cunning player jumping checkers placed by a novice. Instead of rooting out all opposition with one massive stroke, he isolated it into impotent pockets. Consequently, Japanese forces were broken into unconnected units, cut off from supply lines and communications, and rendered no longer capable of mounting significant campaigns. As Marshall put it,

> We now enjoyed superiority both on the sea and in the air.
> [MacArthur] was therefore able to land his troops where the
> Japanese were weakest and confine their stronger forces in pockets
> from which, because of incredibly difficult terrain and our air and
> sea superiority, they could never break out. As a result there were

*at the time of surrender hundreds of thousands of Japanese troops
isolated in the jungles of the Pacific islands, dying on the vine and
of no further use to their Emperor.*

Maps of MacArthur's east-to-west progress look like the arcs of stones
skipping over a lake's smooth surface. Each successful landing led to the
creation of a new base from which the next successful leap could be made,
using B-25 bombers launched from carriers and what had been enemy
airfields. A veteran of New Guinea in the Army Corps of Engineers
described it this way in an interview for this book:

> *We would bomb an airstrip the Japanese had. Then paratroopers
> would be dropped in to secure the airstrip. Then we would go in to
> fix them so U.S. planes could bring in even more troops.*

In one case, MacArthur sidestepped 50,000-60,000 Japanese troops
in what Frazier Hunt, the war correspondent, called "a 750-mile forward
pass." The job of cleaning out the Japanese installations MacArthur avoided
was given to the Australian army. One commander noted that his men
recognized that their role was "mopping up and that they were not vital to
the winning of the War." Nonetheless, "they got on with the job at hand,
fighting and dying as if it was the battle for final victory."

News coverage of what happened in New Guinea during the closing
months of the summer, the span when Boisseau's tension was ratcheting up,
tells of Japanese mass attacks into withering fire and Allied dynamiting of
caves to bury their enemies alive rather than face endless battles against them
or draining efforts to root them out. By the end of August, tens of thousands
of Japanese and American troops were dead. A sampling of headlines from
The New York Times during those days counts off mounting U.S. successes:

- July 3: NUMFOR RECEIVES A RECORD BOMBING

- July 8: THIRD AIRDROME ON NUMFOR IS WON

- July 10: 213 MORE JAPANESE DIE IN BIAK MOP-UP

- July 13: 45,000 JAPANESE IN WEWAK TRAP LAUNCH
  SUICIDAL BID TO ESCAPE

- July 14: MANY JAPANESE DIE IN NEW GUINEA TRAP

- July 17: JAPANESE CUT OFF IN NEW GUINEA STAB

- July 20: JAPANESE FORCED INTO HILLS IN NEW GUINEA

- July 22: JAPANESE THRASH IN NEW GUINEA TRAP

- July 26: JAPANESE RETREATING IN NORTH NEW GUINEA

- July 31: M'ARTHUR BATTERS ENEMY AIRDROMES

On August 4, the Times wrote, "In an amphibious leap of nearly 200 miles from the previous advanced position on Numfor Island, American troops seized the Sansapor coastal area of Netherland New Guinea and the islands of Amsterdam and Middelburg off the coast, giving the Allies control of virtually the entire New Guinea coastline."

By September 17, the newspaper could inform readers that "M'ARTHUR BUILDS GHQ IN NEW GUINEA JUNGLE." Previously, his headquarters had been in Brisbane, Australia, 1,000 miles to the south. In the same issue came this hopeful headline: "COMING ATTACKS ON JAPAN MUST COVER VAST DISTANCES; But by the Conquest of the Philippines We Can Cut Her Huge Empire in Two— ADMIRAL HALSEY."

The same time-span during which New Guinea was secured also saw the Marine-led invasions of Guam (July 21-August 8), Tinian (July 14-August 1), Mariana and Palau (June-November), islands that would be used as air bases on the way to bomb and then, if necessary, invade the Japanese homeland.

Those headlines are laced with exotic place names. Author James Jones opined, "A year it had taken, from Guadalcanal to Sansapor. And how many invasions? Fifteen? Almost all of them names people in the United States never heard of." But the place names must have become all too familiar to a small-town boy from Virginia accustomed to the simplicity of Newville and Richmond. To Boisseau, the names must have carried with them the smell of death and the noise of war in the air, on the beaches and throughout the jungles, a pervasive odor and din that explain the darkening tones in his letters.

It is certain that Boisseau was directing his men to load and unload ships that were carrying supplies to the distant campaign. As ships docked in Oro Bay, the buzz of fighter planes was heard throughout the area. The activity must have seemed endless. Stauffer writes that "Quartermaster troops...participated in simulated landings and distribution of items to troops on shore." On July 8, Boisseau was cleaning a filthy rifle and practicing on the firing range. He had to suspect, if not know, that those tasks signaled he would soon be pressed into combat.

How tight did his chest feel? How weak were his knees? How sick to the stomach did he become when he thought of what lay ahead of him? The answers can be found in a July 22 letter in which Boisseau wrote a portentous sentence that must have caused his sensitive and frail mother to fret. "All of us can't come back," he noted, "but I hope the Lord spares me." It was a rare mention of God in his letters.

The small prayer might have been sparked not only by his workload but also by the pricks of needles in his arm. In June, he was inoculated against tetanus. In July, he was immunized against typhoid. He could have easily guessed why. He was headed somewhere new, somewhere in the direction of Japan. With the success of his New Guinea operations behind him, MacArthur turned his face toward the Philippines.

The unit reports for the 343rd Quartermaster Depot Company Supply record that the hectic activity of June, July and August began to wind down in September. A detachment that had been separated from the 343rd returned to bring the unit to full strength. According to a unit report, "a company dance was held on 11 September at the W.A.C. Detachment.... Approximately 90 couples were in attendance. Light refreshments of fruit juice and sandwiches were served."

Man-hours dropped from the all-time peak in August to 25,000 in September, and "a regular schedule of time off for all men" was created. Another sign of the lessening of activity was the creation of time for literacy classes, with 14 men being taught to read and write "simple phrases and sentences." Second Lieutenant Dale D. Ingalls, company historian, reported that "excellent food, adequate recreation facilities and promotions [have] made the morale of this organization excellent."

It was a month of relative calm before the storm of war that was literally over the horizon. Boisseau hinted about it in his September 30 letter when he almost whispered, "Guess you will read about something big before long. I mean in the war news. Just wish we could move out of this hole and I think we will before long.... My morale is way below a thousand tonight."

The solution to his clues came two weeks later, when the Philippines were invaded, beginning with the Battle of Leyte Gulf. Boisseau was definitely among the soldiers who participated in it in some manner. According to military records, the 343rd Quartermaster Depot Supply Company was involved in the Leyte and Luzon invasions. Luzon, the northernmost Philippine island, was one embarking point for striking at Japan itself.

What had occupied Boisseau and his depot company throughout the previous three months no doubt involved supplying the final attacks in New Guinea and prepping for the Leyte invasion. Van der Vat notes in his account of the South Pacific campaign:

> The armada that was to return Douglas MacArthur to the Philippines was the strongest in the history of the world, with 157 combat ships and 581 other vessels of the Seventh Fleet protected by the 106 warships of Halsey's Third Fleet. The Seventh Fleet assembled at the sweltering ports of Hollandia, New Guinea (Northern Transport Group), and Manus in the Admiralties (Southern).

In "The War in the Pacific: Leyte, Return to the Philippines," M. Hamlin Cannon states that "the landing of the American forces on Leyte... brought to fruition the long-cherished desire of MacArthur to return to the Philippine Islands and avenge the humiliating reverses suffered in the early days of World War II."

When the first landings were made, Guinea Gold's banner headline roared: "AMERICANS INVADE PHILIPPINE ISLANDS."

The battle was horrific and costly. Eighty percent of the Allied infantry was killed or wounded. "The entire land campaign for the recapture of the Philippines," Van der Vat records, "cost the United States 10,380 killed, 36,631 wounded—and 93,400 sick or accidentally injured." Cannon reports that "the commanding officer of Headquarters Company and the division quartermaster, together with the latter's executive officer, were wounded. Many of the division headquarters personnel were killed or wounded." Forty-one quartermasters were killed, while 67 more were wounded and nine were missing in action.

Boisseau was amid the chaos of battle.

One member of the Quartermaster Corps, a first lieutenant who made the Leyte landing, described it this way:

> The LCI came into the sandy shore, grating against the
> bottom. The ramps smacked down into the water, and men
> struggled up onto the higher beach. They spent that first night on
> the sands, surrounded by rations and dead Japs.... The unit finally
> took over a Jap signal dump, which was on somewhat higher land
> than the paddies. The QMs had quite a bit of luck here, and picked
> up nine partially assembled Jap trucks with the necessary parts to
> put them in running order. Personnel slept that night in nipa huts
> which had housed Japs less than a week before.... Next stop was
> a coconut grove which nestled against a high ridge.... This turned
> out to be a hot spot, as Jap aircraft were continually sneaking over
> the ridge and zooming down the valley in search of juicy targets.

The Quartermaster Corps had a mammoth task to accomplish in bringing supplies to the island from various points, including New Guinea. Said Cannon:

> For an invasion force of 150,000 men, the War Department
> figures showed that, for the landing period alone, 1,500,000 tons
> of general equipment, 235,000 tons of combat vehicles, 200,000
> tons of ammunition, and 200,000 tons of medical supplies were
> required. Thereafter, 332,000 tons of equipment would be required
> every thirty days.

Within two weeks of the invasion, 120,000 troops were on Leyte, requiring (according to Cannon's account) "ammunition, 1,400 tons a day; rations, 1,000 tons a day; bridge timber, no specified amount; landing field mats, 500 tons a day; and aviation gasoline, 1,000 drums a day."

Boisseau's precise role in the massive undertaking is not known. If he followed the route mapped by the 757th Engineers, he left Oro Bay, crossed the ocean to Leyte, moved up the western side of the Philippines and wound up at Luzon. If so, he continued delivering the services provided by the Quartermaster Corps. It is certain that at least one platoon from the 343rd made it all the way to Manila. In an interview for this book, that platoon's commanding officer, Second Lieutenant Jack H. Crouchet, talked about joining them in the Philippines. "There were 20 men or so," he recalled. "They came from New Guinea." He joked that he and the platoon "roasted coffee for the entire Pacific," but they also operated "one of the biggest depots in the Philippines."

Such a depot would have needed an experienced warehouseman like Sergeant Bailey.

Crouchet, who trained at Camp Lee, remembers some of Boisseau's unit, including First Lieutenant William T. Hall Jr., First Lieutenant Earle J. Pettinger, Private First Class Ovis Pratt and Tech5 Paul J. Nieder Jr. A welder in his early twenties from Pennsylvania, Nieder would be busted to a private. He was "a rascal," his former CO said:

> I remember him well. He liked me. I broke up a knife fight he got involved in. I stepped in and told him to hand me the knife. I knew he wouldn't hurt me. He didn't get along with anybody, so I had him drive my jeep. After the war, he wrote me a letter.

While Crouchet does not remember Boisseau, another "rascal," one fact is certain. He served in the Philippines and was awarded a Philippines Liberation Ribbon. Whether he went in with early waves of troops as a rifle-toting soldier or came later as a quartermaster, he would have had some fascinating stories to tell.

The span during which Boisseau did not write home—September 30, 1944, to April 8, 1945—is matched by a break-off in issues of

Bulldozer, the newsletter of the New Guinea Engineers. On October 2, 1944, issue 3 of volume II came out. Issue 4 would not appear until June 10, 1945, eight months later. What had caused the hiatus? A simple answer might be "history." As the editors of Bulldozer put it when they resumed printing:

> We've seen a lot of history made—the fall of Germany—the election of a 4th term President and his death in office—the start of heavy bombing of Japan itself. At the end of Sept. 1944, when last we went to press, big events were in the offing. Down in New Guinea, we were scheduled to move. Where—we didn't know. Everyone guessed it would be Mindanao. But we all guessed wrong. (Which is usually what happens in figuring out Army moves). The Marines were still engaged in the now famous battle of Bloody Nose Ridge on [Peleliu] Island. The Philippines were being subjected to heavy air attack by carrier borne planes. Even Tokio was bombed occasionally by the Superfortresses.... Japan, the unpredictable, put most of her cards in an all out attempt at Leyte. She played—and lost the Philippines. Now,...she is reduced to a war of retreat and attrition.

Like the engineers, Boisseau had been on the move and perhaps was too busy to write. He might even have been forbidden from writing.

On October 20, 1944, one of the iconic moments of World War II—indeed, of military history—occurred when MacArthur strode through the Pacific surf, marched onto the beach of Leyte with wet trousers and declared, "People of the Philippines, I have returned."

Without the supply operations in New Guinea and the quartermasters' roles in the Philippines, MacArthur might not have been able to make that ringing statement.

In some small, definitely less boastful, way, Sergeant James Boisseau Bailey of Prince George County played a role in advancing the U.S. toward Japan and victory.

CHAPTER TWENTY-ONE

WHEN WILL THE WAR END?

From the Pacific to Europe, one question was on the minds of weary servicemen and women: When could they go home? The answer depended on how another question was resolved: When would the war be over? In letter after letter, Corporal Fox, the Massachusetts quartermaster, speculated on that date. He was ever hopeful—and always wrong. Boisseau was more reserved, almost as if he didn't dare become optimistic.

They certainly were not alone in speculating. A V-mail, sent on November 21, 1942, less than a year after Pearl Harbor, by an Ohio branch of the American Women's Voluntary Services, showed a cartoon Santa Claus in a turban, hovering over a crystal ball. The image was surrounded with these words, "Kno all the Yank predicts Allied Victory for '43." In September 1944, shortly after ending his years as commander of the British Eastern Fleet, Admiral Sir James Somerville projected, "There has been a grand D-Day in Europe, and it is only a matter of time before we shall see an equally grand D-Day in the East." Such an invasion of Japan, in fact, would never occur.

In that same fall, legendary Mayor Fiorella La Guardia of New York City spoke on radio about how Victory in Europe Day—VE Day—should be marked, criticizing those who planned to "get plastered, tight, or lit up." He followed up with a shaming question, "What would the wives and mothers of dead servicemen, or those still fighting in the Pacific, think of a disorderly and destructive demonstration?"

VE Day would not come until May 8, 1945, but the colorful mayor had already begun working with the police to plan for whatever mass celebrations would occur when an armistice was announced. British Prime Minister Winston Churchill had a better grasp of how long the war would continue. In a message to the House of Commons, delivered around the same time as La Guardia's message, Churchill was grimly realistic, warning that "many experts have good hopes that the war in Europe will be over by the end of 1944, but on the other hand no one, certainly not I, can guarantee that several months of 1945 will not be required."

"NO END OF WAR IN 1944 SEEN BY CHURCHILL," ran the headline, in all capital letters, on the front page of Guinea Gold's September 30, 1944 issue. Read by Boisseau in his Oro Bay tent on the same day he wrote his last extant letter of that year, those nine words could have compounded his dark and nervous mood as the final hours ticked away before invasion of the Philippines. In light of the article, parts of his letter take on a deeper meaning:

> *My morale is way below a thousand tonight. How did "Buck"*
> *Scarborough get out of the Army. Tell him to write me and let me*
> *in on the secret. Well, Mama, take care of yourself and give my love*
> *to all.*

Then came his long silence. His realism, if not pessimism, toward the length of the war was stated succinctly in a V-mail he had written four months earlier. "The news certainly sounds encouraging now," he said, "but I'm afraid the end is a long way off."

Writing in August 1944, Sergeant Tuttle, the Ohioan who was also at Oro Bay, was more optimistic. "The war news is looking better every day," he noted. "I don't see how it can last any too long." Similarly wishful thoughts were salted throughout Fox's mail. As early as March 26, 1943—about six months before Italy was invaded, more than a year before D-Day and two years before the war in Europe would end—the quartermaster, who was then in North Africa, told his family, "Our boys are doing a wonderful job over here… I don't think it will be too long before we will be headed for Europe." More than six months later, still optimistic, he wrote, "I am only predicting; but, I think that the Germans will crack up in about four months. Boy, won't that be the day."

"The day" was actually more than 19 months in the future.

On Leap Year Day 1944, Fox shared an article he had read in a Philadelphia newspaper. "Most of the war correspondents predict this war will be over this year," he wrote. "I have stood it this long and I guess I can take it until then, but I hope it is over before then."

Two days after D-Day on June 6, 1944, which General Dwight D. Eisenhower termed "the Great Crusade toward which we have striven these many months," and "this great and noble undertaking," the ever-optimistic Fox jotted a note to his mother and father, enthusing about the landing in Normandy:

> It makes me feel good that an invasion has started, and that things are going good. The majority of the boys look to see the war in Europe over with by the end of the year. Let's hope that their guesses are right.

From Fort Belvoir in Virginia, a quartermaster named Lester W. Short wrote his wife at 7:45 a.m. on D-Day:

> Hey "Sweetpea," I suppose the good news is being discussed there by all, as it is here. That was the first thing we heard this morn, and hasn't stopped yet. Hope the boys keep rolling over there and have it over with soon. It makes all us fellows on this side wish we were over there with them.

On the same day, Courtright, the airplane technician then stationed in England and soon to move to France, wrote to his wife, Liz, saying, "Well, honey, this is a day to remember. A lot has happened as you know. I guess this date will go down in history. From now on I suppose we will be quite busy." In a later letter in June, he noted, "There is a lot in the papers about the war ending soon, but I don't think so. I hope I am wrong."

Around that same time, Courtright bet a fellow soldier that the war would not be over by January 1, 1945. He collected 800 francs from the loser, an amount equal to about $15.

In the wake of the Normandy landings, signs of the war's end were imagined everywhere. In New Guinea, Private First Class Seth Hillsberg received several letters from his hometown of Syracuse, New York. The missives were filled with predictions. On July 3, 1944, for example, his father typed, "It commences to look to me that we are getting in the finish of the War. I don't see how either Japan or Germany will be able to stand it very much longer. They will be knocked out."

Two months later, a friend in the Army shot a V-mail overseas to assure Hillsberg that "I do think the war is about finished. Now we are set for an offensive and invasion of Japan." At the same time, Hillsberg's brother, Carl, a Coast Guardsman aboard a ship in the Pacific, prophesied they would soon be seeing each other after two years apart. "It won't be long, kid," he said. "Germany is on the verge of utter collapse, and you know the Japanese situation well. Supplies will lick them."

Barrington, the New York combat soldier in training, wrote in October 1944 that "there was a commentator on the radio the other night who predicted the fall of Japan before that of Germany. That would be really something wouldn't it."

The war, more horrific than ever, continued in Europe and the Pacific. The passing of more months, however, failed to deflate the optimism of the father of the Hillsberg brothers. At the end of March 1945, he told his son in New Guinea that "it looks that Germany will crack soon this time sure. It don't seem possible that they can endure it longer. And that will make a great big difference in the Pacific. Japs will be finished soon too. Things usually go together that way."

That same month, Fox told his sister, "Today's news said that Finland had ordered Germany to withdraw her troops, or they would be made prisoners of war. It sure looks bad for Germany now with all the countries turning against her. It would not surprise me to see her give in any day now, although one cannot tell."

Having pushed into Germany with an armored division, Captain John Ross wrote to his parents in Albany, New York, on Holy Thursday, March 29, 1945. But Christians were not on his mind:

> Today I was riding through a German city and on one corner was a large sign: "Passover Services—One Block." It is certainly a wonderful day for the Chosen People. They had one service in Goebbels' castle and if I had known in time I would have gone myself.

Three days later, Courtright replied to a question his wife, Liz, had posed. If the war ended in May, she asked, when would he be home? "I don't want to throw cold water on your hopes," he said, "but I am afraid it will be some time yet even if the war with Germany was over with today." The sergeant predicted that an air force would be left in Europe after a peace treaty or that he would be forwarded to the China-Burma-India theatre. "I don't look to be seeing the States this year," he continued. "Perhaps Germany will fold this summer....There is a lot of tough days ahead of us."

In the Signal Corps in New Guinea, Private Hull, starved for information, sent a V-mail to his father on May 6. "All the war news sounds in my opinion to be very good," he declared, "that is for the Allies, bad for Hitler and Tojo. Did you ever hear what happened to Mussolini for certain? If so would you pass the news along to me." The Italian dictator had been captured by partisans and executed on April 29.

On May 8, Germany, bruised, battered and bombed into submission, proffered its unconditional surrender. On that day, Sergeant Courtright penned one of his longest letters to his wife:

> Well darling today is the official V.E. day. Victory is ours after so many long months & years of fighting the Germans....
>
> At last there is peace in this part of the world. What a wonderful feeling it is.... I am glad it is over. It will be a wonderful day when it is over in the Pacific too. And with the air strength going there from here will help turn the time up when the Japs will give up....
>
> Lord how I want to be home with you now.... My job is done here. I have done my small part as best I could. As a crew chief I have more combat missions that any other in this Sq. No pilot or gunner has ever been hurt in any of the ships I have crewed. Of course it is all luck, but luck seems to set in my lap....
>
> It's all over, over here. What wonderful words they are. I can't tell you in words how happy I am.... I hope the men who have laid down their lives for this war...haven't done so in vain.... I am glad God saw it fit to let me return to my loved ones.

In New Guinea, the news of VE Day was greeted with mixed feelings because the horrifying war in the Pacific continued. On May 9, Private

Walker, the WAC stenographer, jotted in her journal:

We heard the news yesterday early in morning.... Some kids yelled an uncertain Hurrah—but most of [us] I guess were sort of mum about it. One expected to feel exhilarated.... We are the victors, yes, and it was a terrible struggle; and we are glad it's over. But I can't really be jubilant about it when I think of what the victory cost.

In his monthly report for June 1945, as the ouster of the last Japanese from the Philippines was being finalized, First Lieutenant Ingalls, unit historian, noted that the 343rd Quartermaster Depot Company Supply was packing up in New Guinea and "preparing to close the base." Stocks had been sent forward. "Warehouses in the Depots have been torn down when they become empty," he wrote. "Company buildings such as the recreation hall, bakery shop and a few tents have been torn down to facilitate a hasty departure."

Boisseau, no doubt wondering about his role in the coming invasion of Japan, was sending letters again.

CHAPTER TWENTY-TWO

FINAL LETTERS OF MOTHER AND SON

Although Germany had surrendered, the fighting in the Pacific still had months to go before planes that took off from Tinian in August 1945 dropped two atomic bombs on Japan that effectively ended World War II.

Where Boisseau had spent the months between October 1944 and April 1945 is unknown. Perhaps he moved with MacArthur through the Philippines, marching from Leyte to Luzon or elsewhere. Fighting continued through those months as troops converged on Manila and seized Corregidor. Certainly, his services were needed. MacArthur said the achievements of quartermasters in the Pacific were "without parallel in the history of warfare."

Brigadier General William F. Campbell, chief quartermaster in the Southwest Pacific, offered this praise:

Not once did our attack falter because of a lack of Quartermaster supplies! Never before in any war have supply lines been so long. Never before has so much been supplied over such distances. I am confident that logistics experts a few years ago would have said that the execution of the supply operations you have accomplished in the last four years [was] impossible. I am equally confident that historians in the years to come will write of your supply achievements as one of the miracles of this war.

Whatever his role might have been in the Philippines, Boisseau was back in Oro Bay on April 8, 1945. On that date, he wrote to Charlotte, putting "New Guinea" so boldly at the top of his first page that it almost declares, "I'm home, and I'm safe."

How safe he had been in the Philippines and New Guinea before that is debatable. Even if not in the line of enemy fire at Oro Bay, he had heard about other ways to die there. There were malaria and other diseases, as well as accidents, like the Utah teenager who had been killed when a mortar shell exploded on the firing range, or the Iowa PFC who drowned.

Boisseau's message to Charlotte was not a V-mail but a regular letter on two sheets of Army stationery that were 6 ¼ x 10 ½ inches. While the letter was intended for her, he addressed the envelope to his mother, drawing an arrow from "Dearest Charlotte" to a notation at the very top edge of the first sheet. There, he wrote, "Mama, please mail this to Charlotte. I have forgotten her address, again."

Did Rella have enough self-control not to read the contents of the letter before passing it along to her daughter? If she didn't, she would have discovered that one of the paragraphs referred to her, a paragraph that may have caused her to gasp. The letter also contained, in effect, a blunt farewell to Jane:

> *Dearest Charlotte,*
>
> *Got a letter from you yesterday. Say, you are really on the ball now. Keep it up as I sure do appreciate it. Your letters mean a lot to me. So don't let the Old Sarge down please.*
>
> *Every thing around this here joint is just about the same. No hits, no runs and a plenty of errors. Am still tired of this place.*
>
> *Thanks for telling me about the Midway. We heard about it the day it was launched. You should have gone to the unveiling of such a ship. Oh, heck, I should have said launching, shouldn't I? Guess I'll be seeing it one of these days I hope.*
>
> *Sis, I want you to do me a favor as soon as you get this letter. I want you to call Mama and cheer her up some. You and she won't be hearing from me for several days. I have just written her about it and I know she is going to worry. So please help me out. Please!*
>
> *Am feeling fine for an old man. Aint that "wunnerful." Hope you are in good health. Haven't heard anymore about being drafted, have you? Stay out of this damned mess if that is possible.…*
>
> *Did I tell you I heard from Jane about two weeks ago. She is trying to warm up old soup but, it's no use.…*
>
> *Love,*
>
> *Boisseau*

The letter, partly because it is the last extant one from him and partly because of its significant content, merits line-by-line explication:

> • *Got a letter from you yesterday. Say, you are really on the*
> *ball now. Keep it up as I sure do appreciate it. Your letters*
> *mean a lot to me. So don't let the Old Sarge down please.*

A year from his first V-mails, Boisseau is still eager to hear from home and from his family. Emotionally and psychologically, he has not separated himself from them. The use of the self-applied nickname, "Old Sarge," indicates further maturing on his part. He sees himself as a man, not as a youth.

> • *Every thing around this here joint is just about the same. No*
> *hits, no runs and a plenty of errors. Am still tired of this place.*

Those lines imply that he has re-assessed New Guinea upon returning and found it to be as awful as ever. The use of the baseball metaphor underlines his interest in the game.

> • *Thanks for telling me about the Midway. We heard about it*
> *the day it was launched. You should have gone to the unveiling*
> *of such a ship. Oh, heck, I should have said launching, shouldn't*
> *I? Guess I'll be seeing it one of these days I hope.*

Charlotte lived in Newport News, where the Navy built and launched ships. The USS Midway, an aircraft carrier, slid down the ways there on March 20. Nearly 1,000 feet long, it held a crew of 4,000-plus sailors. Boisseau would not see the Midway. While it made a shakedown cruise in the Atlantic, it was not involved in any action during World War II. In fact, it was not commissioned until September, after the war had ended. The Midway did participate in action during the Vietnam War and Operation Desert Storm. The carrier, decommissioned in 1992, is now the San Diego Aircraft Carrier Museum.

> • *Sis, I want you to do me a favor as soon as you get this letter.*
> *I want you to call Mama and cheer her up some. You and*

*she won't be hearing from me for several days. I have just
written her about it and I know she is going to worry. So
please help me out. Please!*

Asking one part of a family to protect or support parents, especially
mothers, was not unusual. Writing from Okinawa around the same time
as this letter, a soldier told family members about snipers and then added,
"Don't say anything…to Mom about that[;] she worrys enough. I hope I
don't ever see anymore now but you never can tell."

Boisseau's paragraph, if it was read by Rella, would have been chilling.
Even if she had already received her own version of the news, this
reinforcement would have underscored her concern. Where was Boisseau
disappearing to this time? What would silence him for several days? Was
he returning to the Philippines or going off with a detachment on special
assignment? Another possibility is that his malaria had flared up again,
sending him to the hospital.

• *Am feeling fine for an old man. Aint that "wunnerful."
Hope you are in good health. Haven't heard anymore about
being drafted, have you? Stay out of this damned mess if that
is possible.*

Again referring to himself as an old man, Boisseau may have been
thinking ahead to July, when he would turn 30. The expression "Aint that
'wunnerful'" was one he used in other letters. It could have been a family
catch-phrase.

As for Charlotte being drafted, she was an RN and therefore much in
demand by the military. Tens of thousands of women served in the Army
Nurse Corps. It wasn't just battle wounds that they treated. Nurses also dealt
with diseases. A general rule was that four men were admitted to medical
units for illnesses for every one admitted for battle wounds.

On January 6, 1945, in his State of the Union Address, President
Roosevelt said, "Since volunteering has not produced the number of nurses
required, I urge that the Selective Service Act be amended to provide for the
induction of nurses." A 1945 bill to draft nurses was narrowly defeated and
then rendered moot when Germany surrendered.

Boisseau's description of World War II as "this damned mess" and his encouragement of Charlotte to avoid the draft if she could are indications that he was weary of the war, beaten down by his own experiences and protective of her. Throughout his letters, he shows a preference for Charlotte over Virginia, who is seldom spoken of. No mail to or from her survives.

> • *Did I tell you I heard from Jane about two weeks ago. She is*
> *trying to warm up old soup but, it's no use.*

Those two sentences mark the end of the up-and-down relationship between Boisseau and "My Only Jane." He now dismisses her with a wave of his hand, a gesture that provides a melancholy ending to their romance.

The final Bailey letter that remains was neither written by Boisseau nor to him. The author is Rella herself, showing some of the qualities that inspired Boisseau's steadfast devotion. Undated, the letter may have been written on April 17, 1945, about a week after her son wrote his sister. Rella's letter is also to Charlotte. Penned with blue ink in a delicate hands, the letter is written on 8 ½"x 11" stationery that is headed:

RELLA B. BAILEY

POSTMASTER

PRINCE GEORGE, VA.

My darling,

We had such a wonderful day with you all. You both are charming people to your guests and the food was <u>superb</u>. We got home all right, little crowded but <u>we</u> didn't mind. I'm sending cards also a few AM Stamps, be sure to write to Boisseau. Please come home the <u>first</u> chance you all have. Write to me. I love you all so dearly and thank you from the bottom of my heart for being so sweet to me. Mr. Burrow sends his thanks too for a nice day even if <u>we did</u> get <u>beat</u>. Your apartment is lovely. What <u>would</u> I give to have such a grand place to go to after a <u>hard</u> day out <u>here</u>. I am worked to death. Love to the couple downstairs. I liked them a lot.

All my love.

Devotedly

Mother

The thank-you letter is so pregnant with meaning, especially given the cataclysmic event that would follow, that it, too, deserves in-depth study:

> • *We had such a wonderful day with you all. You both are charming people to your guests and the food was <u>superb</u>. We got home all right, little crowded but <u>we</u> didn't mind.*

The vocabulary Rella uses in the short note nearly exhausts the list of positive adjectives: wonderful, charming, superb, sweet, nice, lovely, grand. They all are chosen to boost Charlotte and her husband, Phil. Many a mother could not have resisted a "but" sentence that said, "The food was superb, but you could do better with the biscuits," or "Your apartment is lovely, but it could probably use brighter rugs on the floor." The underscoring of "superb" is the first of several emphases that demonstrated Rella's deep feelings.

> • *I'm sending cards also a few AM Stamps, be sure to write to Boisseau.*

The encouragement of Charlotte to write her brother was probably not necessary, but Rella did not want to take any chance that her son would be neglected. AM Stamps—Air Mail stamps—assured that the mail got to New Guinea more swiftly.

> • *Please come home the <u>first</u> chance you all have. Write to me. I love you all so dearly and thank you from the bottom of my heart for being so sweet to me.*

According to Boisseau's V-mails and the testimony of a contemporary, Charlotte frequently came home to Prince George to visit her mother. She also was there to help with Aunt Macy. "Glad to hear that Charlotte and Phil got away for a weekend. I know she was a great help to Sis Macy," Boisseau had written on June 29, 1944.

> • *Mr. Burrow sends his thanks too for a nice day even if <u>we</u> <u>did</u> get <u>beat</u>.*

This line confirms that the long courting of Rella by Papa Joe had borne some fruit. They were still together nearly a year later, cozy enough to make the trip as a couple to Newport News, where they played some game—cards? Monopoly? tennis?—with Charlotte and Phil. But Rella and Joe did not marry, perhaps because he was skittish after his two marriages had ended in death and divorce, or perhaps because she was still not ready to move on. Then again, did she really want to become the stepmother of 11?

> • *Your apartment is lovely. What <u>would</u> I give to have such a*
> *grand place to go to after a <u>hard</u> day out <u>here</u>.*

This compliment is interesting in that Rella's house was far larger than her child's apartment. Yet, Charlotte's apartment was a lovely, grand place.

> • *I am worked to death.*

Her son's mail often referred to his mother's working too hard, and he urged her to cut back. From her own testimony, she did not listen to him.

> • *Love to the couple downstairs. I liked them a lot.*

Rella even extended her graciousness to the neighbors, a comment she did not have to make, but the sort of compliment that must have made Charlotte glow.

> • *All my love. Devotedly Mother*

Rella uses "love" (in one case as "lovely") four times in the short note. That she closed with "devotedly" is almost to be expected in light of the remainder of the message. She was thoroughly devoted to her children, whom she had raised alone for 14 years. They had turned out well. Her daughters were married. Charlotte was a nurse. Boisseau was a sergeant in the U.S. Army, risking his life for them. It is no wonder, then, that he was so solicitous in return and that he always signed off with "love" himself.

Another aspect of her letter is its perfect spelling and grammar. If she stopped her schooling at 16, when she got married, Rella had less education than her son, who went through the 12th grade. Yet her letter is impeccable, while his contains many spelling and punctuation errors.

Rella's letter is all the more touching because of what happened several weeks later, something that The Washington Post took notice of. Early on

June 16, she died, never having seen her son again. Only 46, she passed away at Charlotte's apartment, the "grand" place she had visited so often. Decades later, her friends said that her heart failed her. Perhaps she had, indeed, been "worked to death."

In a letter the previous summer, Boisseau had told his mother,

> *I did get the telegram that you and Jane sent.... Naturally I was a little frightened at first. I thought something had happened to you. That telegram certainly made record time.*

This time, a telegram contained the news he had feared then. What his reactions were is not known, but perhaps they imitated those of another soldier. In April 1945, Private First Class Anthony Battaglia from Illinois, in ordinance supply at Oro Bay, said in a V-mail to relatives:

> *Yesterday [April 1, 1945] was Easter Sunday and I made my Easter duties just for my mother and in the after noon I recieved 2 letters.... [One was] from my wife saying that my mother passed away March 17. OK, you really don't know how hard it really hit me. Why, I couldn't finish the letter. I started to cry like a baby. I had to leave the office and went to my tent and it was time for chow but who could eat after that news—of all the days to receive news like that it had to be Easter Sunday. Really, I cain't believe it that my mother is gone for good. I just can't put it in my head that she is gone and I will never see her again.*

Irella Olivia Boisseau Bailey is buried in Blandford Cemetery, near Petersburg, with her husband, James Benjamin. They share a headstone. Beneath her name are carved just two words: "At rest."

At last.

CHAPTER TWENTY-THREE

BOISSEAU BAILEY ON THE COUCH

Who was James Boisseau Bailey? ¶ That appears to be a question he rarely, if ever, pondered. His writing, full of so much information about his skin problems or his mother's teeth, are empty of self-reflection. Conscious self-reflection, that is.

When they are examined for what hides between the lines, his V-mails actually disclose a great deal about their author. Playwrights can advance their stories by having characters say what they want or how they see themselves. Boisseau shared his desires for home-cooked fried chicken, for something to be done about his mother's blues, for an end to her worry, for his childhood bedroom, for marriage. From that, his simplicity, ties to Prince George, wishes for normal life and love can be detected. He also provided a list of who he was: a Prince Georgian longing for home, family and Jane…a soldier totally exhausted and ready for sleep…a son sorry for neglecting his mother.…a soldier afraid the war's end was a long way off…a human being "never…as disgusted in all my life as I am now." That list moves ever more intimately into his life, divulging what he kept from the world.

In not openly sharing his emotions or unveiling his soul in letters home, Boisseau was like millions of servicemen in the 1940s. Rather than plumbing deep feelings, their mail skims lightly over surface events. Far from allowing the release of classified information about their fundamental beliefs, they pack their letters so full of everyday trivia that nothing of their secret inner code can escape. That was how they were brought up, and that was what society expected. But, occasionally, firefly flashes of something deeper flickered in the correspondence. A connection to the divine was one of those glimmering signals. On D-Day 1944, for example, Private Joe Barrington was at Camp Croft, South Carolina, well aware that he was in training to go overseas. He told his parents:

> *All the Catholics in the camp marched to the Catholic chapel,*
> *and the same with the other religions and the chaplains conducted*
> *a service for the safety of the boys over there.*

Religion appears often in V-mails written by Sergeant Alexander, the Mississippian in New Guinea. He told his parents that "often times when the world is going our way we forget God until we need him to help us and then we get humble again. May Jesus help me a sinner for I am not worthy of the kingdom of God.... Pray for me these days and I shall always remember you in my prayers."

Vern Haugland, an Associated Press journalist who was lost for days in the New Guinea jungles when he had to bail out of a bomber, revealed that the experience made him

> surer and surer about profundities I long had questioned. I
> knew at last for certain that somewhere there was God and that I
> was in His hands, and that he was merciful.

Did Boisseau ever have such spiritual feelings? Only his small prayer for survival hints that he did. Nor does he dream big or imagine a new profession or think about going to college. He wants only to travel back— certainly toward the small confines of Prince George Courthouse, but also through time to become once again what he was before he was drafted. That was the notion in most men's minds when the war ended, but all of them had encountered people, events and changes in the service that affected them. Boisseau doesn't seem to understand that he could not pick up where he left off because time had altered everything, including two of the most central parts of his world. Jane was out of his life, and his mother was dead. Nonetheless, picking up was precisely what he would try to do when he returned to civilian life.

There is something else missing in the mail. Boisseau doesn't talk much about his fellow soldiers. There is no appearance of closeness to the men not just on the other side of the barracks but also across the ocean from him. It's as if he were in the war by himself, hunkered down and hoping it would pass overhead without damaging him. Although he mentions a few Prince George residents he has run into, he never refers to another soldier, sailor, Marine, airman, WAC or nurse in New Guinea by name.

Even though he was surrounded by thousands of men and women, and despite supervising dozens of soldiers for hours a day, whom he refers to collectively as "the boys," Boisseau never writes about specific individuals, like the ones who were in his unit at Camp Lee: Thomas Driver, the actor from North Carolina; Seymour Barris, the single sales clerk from Newark, N.J., or Harry Jennings, the married sales clerk from Arkansas; John Chopack, the Pennsylvanian nearing 40; Ovis Pratt, the teenaged Missouri mechanic; or Ralph Rosenbluth from Cleveland, Ohio, who had enlisted in the Army nine months before Pearl Harbor.

In contrast, Private Clarkson, the Army baker from Michigan, jotted this note to his parents in the summer of 1944 about his bunkmates, Ward and Tennessee:

> *Ward wanted me to tell you about the washing machine he made for us, it's really nice, works by hand, but does a swell job on the clothes. Old Ward is sure proud of it, he says he's going to patent it and sell them to G.I.'s. You know, it's Tennessee & Ward who sort of look out for me. Tennessee is 28, and Ward is 32, both of them are from the South, of course. Tennessee is from where he got his name, Ward is from N. Carolina. Since I'm the youngest they always look out for me.... Another cook just came in from town, and he's telling the boy's all about his date. Another one is hitting me on the arm, trying to make me stop [writing] while he tell's me about his girl.*

Corporal Gerald Fox, the Massachusetts quartermaster, wrote from Corsica that "I have a lot of good friends here at Camp.... One couldn't meet a better bunch of fellows than there is here at Camp; that is, as far as getting along with each other. We all seem to realize that we have our troubles and try to make the best of it."

In just one letter, penned on March 13, 1945, Fox paints a portrait of camaraderie in three ways. They watch movies together, organize "a ball game between two of the platoons" that would be "comical to watch" because "none of them are any too good" and, of all things, dance solo to a record player that was being passed around:

> *There is a new victrola in Camp, and we have it in our room tonight. The boys are sitting around listening to the victrola and dancing by themselves. Well, it is something to pass away the time.*

In more than three dozen letters, however, Boisseau never looks up from the paper he's writing on to describe what's going on around him. For all the goodness people saw in him and despite his eager willingness to do favors when asked, he seems very self-absorbed.

Or so an amateur psychologist might conjecture. After reading Boisseau's letters as if they had spent two or three hours with him, two experts arrived at some conclusions about him—or, as one of them put it more cautiously, to "a series of tentative hypotheses subject to revision in the face of additional data."

A therapist who runs a counseling center believes that Boisseau "would probably be treated for compulsive disorder and separation anxiety" if he presented himself to a psychologist with the information contained in his letters. As evidence of his compulsiveness, she cited his frequent tendency to list the people who wrote him and to count Jane's letters. "There's also lots of repetition about the money he is always sending to his mother to pay for the car or her teeth," the therapist said. "There were the same themes over and over."

She pointed out that "he sometimes wrote every other day to his mother. It seemed to me that most of his communication was to his mother, even when he was writing others."

Another view was offered by an analytical psychologist who said:

Boisseau had a strong sense of responsibility. This assertion is based on research studies of birth order. To have this strong sense of responsibility brings pluses and minuses, strengths and weaknesses. The letters reveal evidence of a pattern of "over-responsibility" for and toward his work and the welfare of his mother. This becomes entangled with his emotional dependency on his mother. To use a metaphor, "he has not cut the umbilical cord." He has not developed a healthy balance in relationship to his mother. On the basis of limited data, I would not dare to speculate the matter of degree of his emotional dependency upon his mother, but the problem is there throughout the letters.

Boisseau's relationship with his mother—from constant expressions of love to paying for her teeth and even the threat to spank her—"places him,

226

at times, in a neurotic conflict," the psychologist said, "where his sense of over-responsibility will lead him to overwork and then feel like a martyr. My guess is that his other neurotic bind is felt as he feels the urge to marry. It conflicts with his perceived sense of responsibility toward his mother and some degree of emotional 'un-freedom' from his mother."

Pointing out that Boisseau was 29 in 1944 and unmarried, the psychologist observed that he lived at a time when "men were expected to marry at a younger age. The letters suggest that he experiences considerable discomfort in making the actual step of marriage to Jane. It seems that he is waiting for her to 'stumble' so that he can justify to society the break-up of the relationship."

The psychologist has a second hypothesis about Boisseau:

> *His French Huguenot background plays an influence on who he is as a person. The French Huguenots were Calvinists with Calvin's strong emphasis on predestination, [being] the chosen ones, that they were "special." In small, subtle ways, [Boisseau] makes known that his work is important. His father had a special place in the community; the mother has a special role as postmistress. As such, she is the center of community information and communication. She is "special," probably as "special" as the local newspaper.*

Picking up on the anger that exploded in Boisseau's August 15, 1944, letter, the psychologist sees what is missing amid the rage. "His refusal to feel empathy for the troubles of people back home suggests a self-centered narcissism," he said. "It might well be that he perceived himself to be the center of the world. This type of narcissist does not have friends and lacks the ability to see the feelings of others."

The analyst also spotted the absence of spirituality, noting, "I am puzzled that the letters do not have references to prayer and seeking the protection of Divine Providence."

Together, the two analysts detected in Boisseau compulsive disorder, separation anxiety, over-responsibility, emotional dependency, neurotic conflict, lack of empathy and narcissism. Those characteristics do not add up to a healthy person, and they are factors often present in someone with alcohol dependency.

After he presented his assessment of Boisseau, the psychologist was told that Boisseau was probably an alcoholic. "That corresponds to his pattern of grandiosity," his sense of being special, the expert commented. "One of the characteristics of an alcoholic is yielding constantly to grandiosity. The alcoholic suffers from a neurotic bind: He sees himself as a demigod, but he has low self-esteem. I am not judging him as being sinful; a neurotic bind is an objective disorder" and, therefore, not something Boisseau chose.

The risk factors for alcoholism, as listed in the 21st century by the Mayo Clinic and the U.S. National Institute of Alcohol Abuse and Alcoholism, read like a short biography of Boisseau. He was a male who drank at an early age and who consumed too much liquor over a long period of time, he had a family history of alcohol abuse, and he experienced anxiety or depression.

But, in the 1940s, subjective moral weakness, not objective disorder, was often seen as the cause of alcohol abuse. Alcohol abuse was judged to be a character flaw or condemned as a sin. The drinker was a weakling, a loser, a bum, a failure, a disgrace. Those assessments weren't made only by observers. They were also the inner sense of the drinker of himself. Boisseau the child had watched his father drink too much and grow maudlin or angry or weepy. When Boisseau the adult brought drink after drink to his own mouth, his memories of revulsion were likely directed at himself.

Those feelings and his overall psychological state may have led to unconscious efforts to keep Jane from marrying him so that she did not experience what Rella had with Ben. Told that Boisseau never married, the psychologist responded, "I would have predicted that" because marriage would have meant the recognition of someone else as special, someone else having feelings and the importance of someone other than himself. The therapist said, "I didn't really sense that he loved Jane. If she wanted to call it off, it was okay by him. I wonder if he was ever treated for depression."

"At the same time," the psychologist emphasized, "allow me to say that the letters portray him as a patriotic American, risking his life to serve in the military in a time of war."

If the therapists are correct in their assessments, it must have been exceedingly difficult for Boisseau to surrender himself to the Army, leave home and go halfway around the world, and be separated from his mother. What got him through must remain as one of the puzzles of his life.

Boisseau never earned a Purple Heart, but he could have pointed a finger at himself as he resonated to something aphorist Jose Narosky said, "In war, there are no unwounded soldiers."

CHAPTER TWENTY-FOUR

"'TIL HE'S HOME ONCE MORE'

Atomic bombs were dropped on Hiroshima and Nagasaki, Japan, on August 6 and 9, 1945, scarring the sky with fiery exclamation points to the multiple horrors of World War II.

From Luzon in the Philippines on August 9, Corporal Morris Finkelstein of Troy, New York, wrote to his mother:

The news of the last two days has really put an optimistic view on the finish of the struggle over here. No doubt you have heard of the new "atomic" bomb that was so deadly and devastating when dropped. With a country facing total destruction there is but one alternative.... Looking at the overall picture at this last stage of the struggle, one cannot but feel a little lifted and a bit more optimistic.

But the war did not instantly end. While Japanese leaders weighed their catastrophic losses and dwindling options, Allied assaults on the island-nation continued with conventional bombs. Guinea Gold reported that "a record B29 strike was launched on Honshu" after the atomic attacks, and that "800 B29's and 200 fighters took part. Six thousand tons of demolition and fire bombs were dropped during this air onslaught."

As the bombs fell, half a world away at Fort Bragg, North Carolina, Private Harold McKee of West Virginia was in training to be sent overseas with an artillery unit. Beginning on August 11, his emotions swung wildly as he wrote his mother a succession of letters about the news on the radio, including premature reports on surrender:

About 8 o'clock this morning our switch board rang and the operator answered it. What you think? The war was over. Boy we really had a time for a while. Then they said it wasn't official, but almost. Tonight the radio sounds pretty good.... About 9 o'clock a news flash came over the radio [and] said Japan had give up then in about a minute they said it was a mistake. Boy you could [have] knocked all of us over with a fether. But I don't look for them to hold out mutch longer.

Finally, on August 15, Hirohito, the 124th emperor of Japan whose reign was known as the time of enlightened peace, announced, through a radio address, that his government had accepted Allied terms for ending the war. It was the first time his subjects had heard his voice.

The front page of Bulldozer, the Engineer Battalion's newsletter, declared in huge lettering: "EXTRA! NIPS AGREE to SURRENDER!" The page was decorated with a crude drawing of a stereotypical Japanese soldier, waving a white flag and meekly saying, "So solly." The lead article credited what already was being called "the A-bomb":

For Japan it meant a blood bath, chaos and destruction—for the Allied nations it held the hope of early peace—for the future of the world it [posed] a threat and a promise.... It is a weapon of destruction, the magnitude of which staggers even the most agile of man's faculties, the IMAGINATION.

Guinea Gold shouted, "IT'S OVER," in capital letters that were two inches high and added:

Even as the dramatic news...was being flashed simultaneously from Allied capitals, hundreds of Allied carrier-borne planes were over [Tokyo]. They were only a few seconds from their targets when word of Japan's unconditional surrender came in over the aircraft's radios. It was the voice of the commander of the US 3rd Fleet, Admiral William ("Bull") Halsey, saying: "It looks like the war is over".... So the Anglo-American pilots held their fire and dropped their bombs into the sea on their way back to the carriers.

When the war ended, Boisseau Bailey was somewhere in transit toward home. He had left his last duty station (probably Oro Bay) as the nuclear explosion erupted over Nagasaki. If he was at sea on August 15, he might have witnessed a celebration like the one Private First Class Robert W. Shackleton reported to his girlfriend in Connecticut:

V-J day was officially announced to us at 5:30 last nite just
as we were eating supper. It set off celebrations aboard ship which
was fun for all. The band played, everyone cheered & sang. Then,
everyone started throwing their hats overboard & started tearing
each others shirts off & throwing them into the sea also. If anyone
in the crowd had a hat on—over it went. Even the ship's officers
threw theirs. A Marine guard very reluctantly gave his shirt &
hat for the cause.... The nurses & officers threw their bars over as
their donation.... Most of the fellows were bare chested when they
finished with dozens of shirts over the side—and some pants.

Then came the real fun. Our C.O., Capt. Harris came down
to our end of the ship...& his shirt was torn off his back & used
in a tug of war & then ceremoniously thrown overboard. The other
officers suffered the same, one by one. Temporarily stripped of their
rank, they were given brooms & swept the deck....

Shackleton and his shipmates had an extra reason for joy. They had
been headed from Europe to the Pacific for the anticipated invasion of
Japan. By the following day, this Battle of the Bulge veteran was thinking
about the fighting he would not have to do:

This morning, the ship was decorated with flags & their were
flag-raising exercises and also a prayer by the ships Chaplain. There
are religious services on board today, also. Since today is a Holyday
[the Roman Catholic Feast of the Assumption] for us our Mass had
a double meaning. I expect to go to Communion this afternoon. I've
been to Mass every day & I expect to keep it up until we reach port.

The exultation was felt in the U.S. as well. In an August 16 letter to her
husband in the Pacific, an Ohio woman shared how she learned about and
celebrated the news of the war's end:

What a wonderful evening it was yesterday.... [We] took
a picnic dinner and went to Turkey Creek for dinner and some
swimming. We just got things started...when another car pulled in
next to us.... This man had the car radio on, and...he called over

233

to us that it was all over with.... It was not long before we could hear the horns blowing at the docks, factories, and round house. It really was a wonderful sound, so gay, with the air of relief that has not been for such a long time, that it is almost hard to remember.

She did not get to bed until 3 a.m.

From Fort Bragg, McKee reported:

Happy day, the war is over and we have the day off. We had a big prade this morning and the General give us a big speech, and the band played all sorts of music. Marches, Polkas, swing and every thing. Sure was a great morning. Boy last night they announced the war was over and they liked to have took the place, turned all the beds over, hollered and stomped for about 1 hour. I don't think any one went to bed till about 2 o'clock.... What we are doing now will never be needed.... I won't have to do any fighting.... I thought of you as soon as I heard the news. I could just see you laffing and crying at the same time. Right?

In Leghorn, Italy, Corporal Fox, the quartermaster, wrote to his parents:

I don't know how to start this letter as I am so nervous and excited. You can probably tell that by my writing. Honest, this is the happiest day I have had since coming into the Army and there are happier days to come. Now take it easy Mom, take it easy Dad. Oh the hell, I might just as well come out with it. Dam it, I can hardly write as my hand is shaking so much. Don't pass out now for God's sake. Your long lost son will be home on a furlough in a very few weeks. It may be a month or may be six weeks, but I am coming home.

Don't know just when I will leave, but it will not be too long. I have sweated it out for almost 33 months and I can surely sweat out a few more weeks. I'll bet those weeks will drag by....

We have been going through a training period for the past five weeks; infantry drill etc. We had orders to go direct to the Pacific from here. Today our orders were changed to go to the States. Imagine that; the United States of America. Oh! Good old States. What the hell is it like there anyhow? I'll dam soon find out....

*I'll be seeing you all soon.... Whoopee, Wow, Oo lah lah, Mama
Mia, I am going to the States.*

Still at sea, 22-year-old Shackleton, who signed his letter "Butch,"
told his girlfriend:

*Now we can look forward to the happy reunions that are to
follow in the near future.... My thoughts were of you last nite
[when he learned the war was over] darling knowing you'd be
thinking of me. I seemed closer to you than I've ever been and the
months to come will bring our dreams to reality.... Hope you're a
bride very soon, honey. AND HOW!!!*

On September 2, the war in the Pacific and World War II formally
ended aboard the battleship Missouri. Japanese representatives signed a
document that read, in part:

*We hereby proclaim the unconditional surrender to the Allied
Powers of the Japanese Imperial General Headquarters and of
all Japanese Armed Forces and all Armed Forces under Japanese
control wherever situated.*

From Okinawa, Corporal Thompson wrote to his parents in Missouri.
"I guess you were as glad to hear that they now have all the papers signed,"
he said, "and knowing that now for sure we can begin to work for some
thing besides war."

Zillich, the Texan who belonged to an anti-aircraft artillery battalion
that had been poised in the Philippines to attack Japan, turned reflective. He
wrote his wife to say, "I've been reading a considerable amount about [atomic
bombs]. Frankly, I don't like it—thinking about it (atomic energy) from a
standpoint of its future use in war. If we could be certain that it would be
used for peaceful use only I think the uses it can be put to are many."

On September 3, the U.S.S. Rigel's daily newspaper, "The Rigel Morning
Star," printed a message from the commanding officer, congratulating the
crew on its efforts "from Pearl Harbor right down to our victory over

Japan." But, amid the joy and celebration, an editorial admonished sailors:

> *Jubilation and pride should be but passing. Technological developments made during this war, particularly the development of the atomic bomb, with its as yet scarcely hinted at potentialities for destruction on a scale hitherto undreamed of, should give all mankind pause to think of the future.... It will be up to the veterans of this war to give sum and substance to the desire of mankind that war may be abolished from an earth that reeks of blood and despair.*

As the reality of peace, rather than a dream of it, began to settle in people's minds, thoughts of coming home filled V-mails. One wife wrote her husband:

> *I have not been able to get the thought of when you will get home, out of my mind. Seems like you certainly will get home by Xmas, oh Darlin, if only you do.... You know there is one wonderful thing about it, now we don't have to think about you getting a furlough and then having to let you go back again. Now you can come home for good.*

The official Quartermaster Song includes this lyric: "From the day he joins the Army 'til the time he's home once more...." Boisseau might have had those words running through his mind as he made his transpacific voyage as a member of one of the first large groups of men and women returning from overseas duty. To get home, they would experience something new. It was called demobilization. The process has been under discussion since well before VE Day, and servicemen and women scoured the news for details about it, quizzed their relatives back home about what they had learned and pored over government handouts.

The Midpacifican, a military daily that billed itself as "the Armed Forces' Newspaper of the Pacific Ocean Areas," provided some details as early as February 3, 1945. Its front-page headline promised "What Every GI Should Know About Becoming A Civilian." The article attempted to answer 12 questions, such as "How long does the discharge process take?" and "How does the 'point system' of demobilization work?" One cartoon accompanying the article showed some of the elements that would constitute discharge points, including decorations, time served and children. Four pages provided the details about moving millions of soldiers, sailors, airmen and Marines back to their normal lives.

In a new monograph written for this book about what each man—including Boisseau—went through to get home, Dr. Mason R. Schaefer, archivist at the U.S. Army Center of Military History, explained the point system and outlined the "multiple steps and layers" that service personnel would have to get through in order to re-don their civvies:

> *Each soldier would receive an Adjusted Service Rating*
> *(ASR) card, on which he would be assigned a numerical score*
> *based on several different criteria. All theater units filled out*
> *ASR score cards and turned them over to records units for*
> *consolidation and transmittal to theater headquarters and, in turn,*
> *to the War Department.... After Japan surrendered and the rush*
> *to redeploy gained speed, the Army quickly winnowed down*
> *the list of essential (and retainable) specialties to three:*
> *orthopedic mechanic; transmitter attendant, fixed station; and*
> *electrocenphalographic specialist.*

In May 1945, Major General William F. Tompkins, director of the special planning division of the War Department General Staff, said the point system reflected the views of soldiers themselves. In a survey, they recommended that men who had served overseas, who had been in the military the longest and who had children should be demobilized first. Tompkins released details that reflected that view, with points awarded for combat credit, medals won and parenting responsibilities. The general gave an example:

> *Let us suppose that a soldier has been in the Army thirty-*
> *six months, has served overseas for eighteen months, has won*
> *the Silver Star and Purple Heart and participated in three*
> *major campaigns and is the father of a child under 18. He*
> *would receive thirty-six points in service credit, eighteen points*
> *in overseas credit, twenty-five points in combat credit and*

twelve points in parenthood credit. His total score would be
ninety-one points.

That fictional man was free to go because 84 points equaled dismissal
from the military. Those with the highest scores would be released first,
unless "military necessity" required their continuing in uniform.

Writing home from her barracks in New Guinea in May 1945, Leatha
Walker, the Ohio WAC said:

In the last week or so since Germany collapsed, everybody's
been counting their points like mad.... The demobilization plan
is terrifically complicated, but it is so because it is being done
individually and not collectively and under the fairest means possible.

Observing that men with dependents got extra points for each child,
she wisecracked, "That's been causing fresh material for new Army jokes."

Schaefer noted that military personnel cleared for demobilization
"received a movement order, which stated the shipping number and table
of organization, the port of embarkation, the amount of equipment to be
carried, and other pertinent information. The order also set two dates—
the availability date (by which the unit had to be ready for movement to
the assembly area command) and a readiness date (when the unit would
leave the assembly area for the staging area). The unit dropped most of its
equipment at its home station, retaining only essential gear; there, soldiers
received cursory physical exams and the unit met all financial obligations.
It would then be ready to move."

In May 1945, even with the war in the Pacific ongoing, 2,500 men had
attainted high enough scores to be released. Fox, however, voiced doubts
about whether they would actually be sent home from Italy. In a May 19
letter, he told his parents:

We are the oldest outfit of its kind in this Base. According
to the point system, we haven't many [points] because we have
no decorations.... I don't think the points mean a hell of a lot
anyway. When they get ready to send us home they will. If they
need us here, well here we will stay.

Fox's cynicism may have been inspired by another feature of the point system. Because "units often contained a complex mix of high- and low-scoring soldiers," Schaefer explained, "a theater commander would often transfer low-scoring men from a unit scheduled for demobilization. Simultaneously, the Army might transfer in high-scoring men from units not slated for demobilization." Thus, units of men about to leave were created, while low-point soldiers sustained units at full strength.

In France, Courtright, the airplane mechanic, added up his points for service time, time overseas, a dependent son and medals—and fell just shy. "I only have 82 points," he moaned to his wife in a May 16 letter. "I guess I am headed to the Pacific bigger than life.... If I did have a lot a points it wouldn't matter anyway, because I am essential (anyway they say so)."

In Ohio, Erma Sunderland typed a letter to her husband, Hugh, a sailor in the South Pacific, about her efforts to figure out the point system:

> In the paper there was an article of questions and answers
> regarding servicemen. And one of the questions was whether a
> wife is a dependent.... Nuts I just called the Navy dept. to see
> what they had to say on the subject, and it does not matter how
> many dependents you have you are still only allowed 10 points
> for dependents. Whether it is five or one...oh heck, that means
> only 39-1/2 or 35-1/2 points for you.... Cuss the luck if that isn't
> disappointing.... I'm so very anxious for you to come home.

Alger, stationed in England, was grumpy about his chances of heading back to Oregon. He described to his girlfriend the signs around him that troops would be going home. For example, the PX and Red Cross were closing, deadlines were announced for sending money orders and packages to the U.S., the troops were packing up equipment and putting it on railroad cars, and make-work assignments were handed out, leading him to find secluded spots where he could loaf away the day, well out of sight of his superiors.

"I am not in a receptive mood," he wrote. "Frankly I think that [the point system] stinks and is full of discrimination."

In that frame of mind, Alger would have been livid had he read an article in Time magazine, revealing that all 54 members of a football team had been sent home when only 13 of them qualified for discharge.

After Japan's surrender, the total points needed for demobilization were lowered from 84 to 80. On September 19, President Harry Truman promised that troops would be "coming back home....as fast as the services can get them out." Less than a week later, 139,000 were returned to civilian life. A month after Truman had made his vow, the Army lowered the point total to 60, and 1.1 million men were headed home.

But not fast enough to suit many of them. In France in September, Sergeant Knapp, like Alger in England, was being driven crazy by what he considered make-work assignments, like moving all of the desks in the offices across the hall. Noting reports that soldiers 35 and older, like him, might be discharged earlier than others, the 40-year-old wrote to his wife, Bobby,

> *I'm trying every angle I can think of.... Probably I should be
> all excited and thrilled and looking forward to getting a boat home
> next week or the week after that but knowing the army as well
> as I do I just see a fight to get out even after that good news in the
> paper today, "Age limit dropped to 35."*

As Alger sneaked off to avoid work and Knapp shifted furniture, Jacob Zillich was drumming his fingers on Leyte. He swam in the ocean and tanned in the sun. He played ping-pong and volleyball, he fiddled with a radio and took photos of Filipinos fishing and doing laundry, and he experimented with ways to keep his woolen clothing from turning moldy in the moist tropical heat.

"Today a little piece of paper came around and I had three choices," he teased his wife, Emily, on October 23. "1. Stay in the Army until June 1947. 2. Stay for any number of months up to six. 3. Go home when I become eligible and its my turn. Which do you think I chose?"

Still stuck on Okinawa in November, Corporal Milton Thompson asked his wife, Sara, for help:

> *Would you get our Senators name. I don't know it. And find
> out just how I would address a letter to him, if any thing goes*

wrong with this [outfit] and I don't get to come home with it. I want to find out just what is going on.

He would not get back to Missouri until early 1946.

In "X-Ray, X-Ray: A Citizen Soldier Remembers WWII," an unpublished memoir, Lieutenant Liven A. Peterson, a Minnesotan stationed in Japan, shared a letter he wrote on Thanksgiving Day 1945. In it, he vowed to his aunt, "If I am still in the Army next Thanksgiving I think I'll blow my brains out."

But, with agonizing slowness, orders were arriving. Finkelstein, working in a dispensary in Luzon, had been marking time by playing pinochle and volleyball, laboring to replace the termite-infested bamboo floor of his tent, touring the area, taking pictures and seeing movies. Then, on October 18, he wrote his mother:

At long last it has happened. My orders finally came thru and fifteen of us are leaving this camp tomorrow morning for Manila to join another outfit that is waiting transportation home. This doesn't mean that I will be on the boat the end of the week because we may have to wait two or three weeks, maybe less; maybe more. In any event, it is the 1st step back and even if we don't leave the Philippines before the 1st of Nov., at least we know we will be home for Christmas. That's if everything works out smoothly.

It did. That was his final letter from overseas.

When he got his orders to go home, Staff Sergeant Amico, who had been snatched out of a Connecticut high school by the Army and ended up with the occupation forces in Japan, was assigned the duty of making sure the men in his unit were all present and accounted for when it came time to board the U.S.S. Kenton to go home. "Like someone wasn't going to show up," he scoffed as he recalled the moment of the roll call.

On December 7, four years to the day after Pearl Harbor was attacked, Zillich got his chance to pen a final letter from overseas:

Its here—this is it!!! We load on board ship at 8 tomorrow morning! Boy! Am I happy—happy as can be.... Just found out a

*few minutes ago.... This is my last letter darling—no more mail
after tonite.*

But getting notice that you were going home and actually leaving were
not the same thing. There was a tedious process of medical examinations
and red tape to unravel before embarkation. Then, the voyages themselves
could take weeks, if not months. Boisseau's own transit over the Pacific
took seven weeks from start to finish.

Those delays gave servicemen and women time to sit and ponder. In
a 1945, issue of TopoGraphic, a newspaper put out by an Engineer unit
stationed in New Guinea, Jack Olivier offered his thoughts:

> *There are many things...we've all forgotten. Not really
> forgotten, but slipped into the far deep recesses of our mind.... Can
> you imagine the thrill you're going to get from your first look at
> a pair of high heeled shoes supporting some lovely gams?... We're
> all tired of girls in slacks. Not that we see many of them, but give
> every long-lonesome one of us in New Guinea or anywhere, an
> armful of silk and perfume. Yeah, that's all brother!*

There were also thoughts of the country they were returning to:

> *Perhaps the statue of Liberty, standing high and proud or the
> towering spires of the Golden Gate bridge will thrill us. For many
> it may be just a river ambling along that will be "it." A sleepy
> town, or a hurrying city—a well-kept farm. But my guess is that
> you and I are really looking forward to the simple things....a good,
> hot bath...a soft bed...clean sheets...or good home brewed java.
> Set down and talk to your favorite person...mom, Dad, or the girl.
> Then you're home, pal!*

Although some troops returned to America in airplanes, it is most
likely that Boisseau headed toward the U.S. by sea, stopping along the way
to refuel and maybe pick up other passengers. He began his journey on
August 9 but would not step on U.S. soil until September 26. Allowing
for a three-week ocean cruise, that still leaves a month to account for. It

is probable that he spent part of that that span getting from Oro Bay to Australia, waiting there for other transportation to arrive and be loaded, and perhaps pausing at way-stations along the trip home. It might have been the Philippines, for example, or even Hawaii.

Private Albert A. Griggs, a Californian, told his hometown newspaper about his 1945 return:

We left Oro Bay, New Guinea, aboard the Liberty ship Joseph Porter on September 9 and arrived in Manila September 22. There were 900 of us on board and it was rather crowded, but we said we'd ride any kind of a ship if they would get us out of there, so we couldn't gripe.

From his account, it took him two weeks to get just to Manila. Private Griggs added that his group then moved into a camp to wait for another transport ship, adding to the length of the journey.

Whatever his itinerary along the watery way, Boisseau must have thought about his Army life and how very different it was from Prince George Courthouse. There, he had been bathed in stability. He had lived in the same county since birth. He had worked for the same company from 1936 until he was drafted five years later. He had lived in the same house from the time his parents bought it when he was a toddler until he marched away. Even his time in the service began with two years in the same camp, located in the same county.

Then he had been torn away from what he knew.

During his two years in Oro Bay, he had lived in a tent, worn a uniform that rotted in the extreme humidity, contracted malaria and a skin disease, worked ceaselessly, worried about his family, wrote and read letters, stared at different stars, boiled under the equatorial sun, and lost a mother. So, whatever his route home, it is unlikely he missed any aspect of New Guinea as it faded behind him. The island had been bluntly summed up by Thomas R. St. George in "Proceed Without Delay" as "the leading and original bunghole of creation," a place of "rain, heat, mud, dirt, bully beef, blood, brutality, boredom, bombs, and sudden death."

If he was like most men coming home from the war, Boisseau did not—perhaps could not—drop those memories into the sea. Instead, he sank them within the deep ocean of his identity. From that bottom, they would occasionally arise, often unbidden.

And, like most men who made it home, Boisseau probably thought about those who didn't, like Robert Kopplin, the Illinois soldier who had so many pet names for his wife. In July 1944, responding to a letter in which she outlined plans for their future after the war, Kopplin replied, "I'm all for your plans my Dear but as I said before I make no plans for the future as I have been disappointed to[o] many times. But its nice to think about."

A member of the 136th Infantry (33rd Division), Kopplin was stationed in New Guinea and participated in the invasion of the Philippines. On March 19, 1945, as an assistant squad leader, his men were pinned down by Japanese soldiers along a road on Luzon. He would earn a Distinguished Service Cross for what he did there, as told in his unit's history:

> He immediately took command of the situation. Designating one squad to clear the road and form a base of fire, he led the others to a partially covered position off the highway. Corporal Kopplin reappeared on the pavement a moment later armed with an automatic rifle. Firing from the hip, he started toward the bluff. Unable to resist such an inviting target, the Japanese brought all of their fire to bear on the corporal. Miraculously weathering the hail of lead tearing up the concrete at his feet, Kopplin shouted to his comrades to leave their cover and follow him. Still spraying the bluff as he moved forward, the corporal led a bold counterattack which spilled over the hill, causing the enemy to fall back. A parting shot from a retreating sniper killed him as he stood on the edge of a Nip emplacement and fired down into it.

The previous July, he had lovingly calmed his wife's worries about him:

> Now then "angel" I assure you I'm in no danger, really safe, so please don't worry about me "Dearest," and besides you know Kopplin will take care of him self so he can come home to his waiting wife who he is deeply in love with.

In November, he had reiterated his caution while simultaneously boasting:

> *I have heard that w[h]ere we came from the Japs more or less*
> *made a counter attack. I sure wish I had been there. Sure would*
> *like to sack a couple. No don't worry Darling they wouldn't get me.*
> *No ma'am, cause Kopplin watches out for him self.*

On the day before his death, his wife, Vera, unaware of what would happen, wrote him a letter with the salutation, "my Doll." She continued:

> *I miss you more every second.... Knowing your well & safe*
> *means so much to me.... I'm proud to be your wife.... Take care of*
> *your precious body. I want that body home here this yr. you know,*
> *ok? Don't let me down now!*

When the letter was returned to her, it was stamped "Deceased."

Around 400,000 U.S. servicemen would never return to their loved ones. In a letter to a newspaper, Staff Sergeant George A. Ross of Iowa, who was in graves registration in New Guinea, described how the Army treated one of its fallen, in this case, someone from Ross's hometown:

> *He is buried in an established U.S. cemetery, where his*
> *grave will have all the care it is possible to give it. As there is a*
> *permanent party stationed there, it will have such care until such*
> *a time as it is possible to return his body home for reburial, if that*
> *is the wish of his family.... [His] folks may feel sure that he has*
> *been given every possible attention, with a full military funeral in*
> *accordance with his religion.... I was sorry to hear of [his] death*
> *as war strikes just a little closer, even over here, when it is someone*
> *from the home town.*

Soldiers were buried where they fell or nearby—or sometimes very far away and after several moves, as a grim letter to the editor of Time magazine revealed after the war:

> *Sirs: Last February [1945] I was Chief Motor Machinist*
> *Mate of a Coast Guard-manned small Army F boat which carried*
> *116 corpses from Oro Bay, New Guinea to Finschhafen, New*

Guinea, where a cemetery was being established for the Southwest
Pacific Area.

Many of these bodies had already been moved two or three
times, namely from the Solomons and New Britain to the
beautiful little cemetery at Oro Bay, in which also the dead from
the Buna–Gona campaign had been buried.

After all this moving even the all-steel coffins were showing
the effects of wear and handling and many had been damaged
and broken. Due to the damaged coffins and the advanced
decomposition of the bodies, the nauseating job of disinterment for
transfer to Finschhafen was given to native labor, but American
G.I.s had to load them on the ship....

Why can't the Army let its dead rest in peace where they
fell? We, the crew, saw nothing but desecration in the above
performance. If the relatives think otherwise, why not let them do
the moving?

An article in the Quartermaster Review in 1946, revealed other
difficulties faced in New Guinea:

Isolated graves are sometimes located far in the mountainous
interior, and overland transportation, confined to native trails,
is slow and difficult. Some New Guinea natives refuse to disinter
bodies, and this means that at times the actual digging must be
done by limited graves registration personnel. The task of locating
isolated graves is sometimes complicated by the rapid growth of
vegetation, the tall kunai grass in some areas, and the dense jungle
undergrowth in others.

As a quartermaster, Boisseau might have brooded on such tasks, now
behind him physically as he sailed east, but remaining among his memories.

He probably reached the west coast of the U.S. at San Francisco
and Camp Stoneman, from which he had departed two years earlier. On
September 26, the date given in his Army records, eight ships docked in
San Francisco Bay with 7,000 returning Americans on board. The Oakland

Tribune listed the vessels as:

- U.S.S. Roi (small carrier), due at Alameda Naval Air Station, with 252 Navy and 490 Marine passengers;

- Kadashan Bay (small carrier), due at Naval Air Station with 634 Navy and Marine passengers;

- Charles E. Smith, four Army passengers, no dock listed;

- Sea Corporal, due at Pier 15, San Francisco, with 23 Navy men, 45 Army officers, 2,074 enlisted Army men and 20 civilians;

- Wilfred Grenfell, no dock listed, 15 Navy passengers and three Army passengers;

- Wake Forest Victory, no dock listed, two Navy passengers;

- Brazil, Pier 15 in San Francisco, five Navy passengers, 335 Army officers, 3,651 enlisted Army men, 439 Army hospital cases and 149 civilians;

- Utahan, no dock listed, 10 Navy passengers.

Based on that accounting, it is most likely the soldier from Prince George came ashore from the Brazil or the Sea Corporal. If it was the former, its captain was also a Virginian, and the ship had previously been named Virginia. Those would have been good omens for a returning serviceman from Prince George.

In its September 22, 1945, issue, The Tribune, reporting on "the first time a contingent of Pacific veterans [was] returning to the States," chronicled the hoopla that greeted the troops, such as blaring bands, thousands of civilians crowding the docks and lining the streets to Camp Stoneman, cheers and laughter as the veterans paraded by, and promises of steak dinners.

Said Schaefer, "Once a soldier reached the U.S., a new series of procedures began. Returning troops underwent a flurry of physical exams, disease preventive measures, customs inspections and records checking."

The Tribune outlined the process that men arriving at Camp Stoneman had to make their way through before heading to separation centers around the country:

The San Francisco Point of Embarkation…has a "flow chart"
which neatly catalogues 10 specific steps a man must go through
from the moment he debarks until he heads for his separation
center. The chart makes the separation processing look like a simple
matter, an accomplishment of a few hours. But the returning men
find out…the actual job is a tremendous one. There are too many
men and too few hours in a day. Sweating out this last phase of
their Army life is a tedious time for the men, but there's plenty of
anticipation, hilarity and fun tangled in with the necessary red
tape to make the 24 to 48 hours pass quickly at this disposition
center.… The fellows dash, at the first opportunity, for a bottle of
beer at the nearest post exchange. There is a rush to telephones and
the telegraph center.

To assist soldiers eager to place a call home, the California State
Military Museum notes that

The largest telephone center in the world was operated at
Camp Stoneman in 1945, consisting of 75 phone booths capable
of handling 2,000 operator-assisted long distance telephone calls
each day.… Telephone service was operated on a 24-hour basis. A
telegraph office was also located on base, with the most frequent
message being, "Arrived safely, be home soon."

Once through the gauntlet at Camp Stoneman, Boisseau entrained for
his East Coast destination, which was Fort Meade in Maryland. There, still
more hoops to jump through awaited him. At a separation center, soldiers
"reported to the Arrival Station, specifically the Incoming Records Section
of the Enlisted Men's Record Branch," Schaefer noted, adding:

At many centers, this station worked around the clock.…
First, soldiers attended briefings on the demobilization process.
Then they filled out several War Department forms and reported
to the Initial Clothing Shakedown Station, where they turned
in all unauthorized government clothing and equipment.…
Separatees then went to their assigned processing company,

[where they were housed]. Demobilizing soldiers then underwent physical exams.... A board of four medical officers, including a psychiatrist, ruled on a man's fitness for discharge. During this stage, soldiers could file for disability claims. [They also] underwent counseling [and] received instruction on the transition to civilian life, information on their rights and benefits as veterans, and vocational and educational guidance.

What each soldier wanted as a reward for their service and patience was War Department Form No. 53-55, the Discharge Certificate. At one processing center, clerks typed a thousand every day. Schaefer explained:

Separation centers created an assembly line procedure. Soldiers first filled out a Separation Qualification Record, which was a resume of a GI's education and training. The Suspense Section handled all incomplete or irregular case records, plus men who had lost their records or were being retained for physical reasons [such as recovery from illness or injury]. The Outgoing Records section provided the final coordination point for a separatee's documentation. There, he assembled all his papers for the much-anticipated final discharge ceremony. A soldier then underwent the final clothing shakedown. Attendants checked his uniform for neatness and fit. The Financial Branch effected "prompt and accurate payments" to all officers and men about to leave the service.

At last, a departing soldier underwent his Departure Ceremony, the last step of all. A field grade officer and a chaplain presided over this event.... With the speeches concluded and the decorations issued, the soldiers walked past the officer in charge to collect their discharge certificates. The Army next pointed them to a railroad or bus station, where they would buy a ticket for their desired destination.

The process wasn't always perfect. When Courtright arrived at Seymour Johnson Field in North Carolina in September 1945, he wrote his wife in Kansas enthusiastically:

I went through processing today and I did get my ten extra points. That makes the total 92 as of right now. And I hear they lowered the points to 80 for discharge. I have turned in all my extra clothes. I go from here to a seperation center which will be back to Ft Levenworth I believe.... I will be a civilian again in just a short while.

Or so he thought. Instead, he began sitting on his cot, playing bridge, going into town (which he described as ten times filthier than his hometown) to see a western movie, swimming in Woodland Lake, sending home the 45-pound toolbox that went through the war with him, declining a bonus to re-up in the Army and worrying about getting the job he wanted in airplane maintenance so he didn't have to return to selling insurance.

After three weeks during which "I wait & wait & wait," Courtright told his wife:

Everything is so screwed up here they don't know their A— from a hole in the ground.... They gave me a recount up to V-J day. And that gives me a total of 98 points. So I don't know what the hell. Why don't they turn me loose? I am so disgusted with the whole set up here I don't know what to do.

After more than a month in North Carolina, he signed papers and waited for separation orders. "I think I will be a civilian in about a week," he told his wife. "I signed up for private transportation out of here. The government will pay 5 [cents] a mile and I can ride a bus or train cheaper than that."

At last, on October 6, 1945, Courtright wrote the last of the hundreds of letters he had sent home from California, Oklahoma, Georgia, Utah, New York, England, France and North Carolina:

Well darling I am in course of processing for discharge. I look to be out of here Wed [October 10]. I don't know how I will travel yet. Wheather I will take the train or bus. But I will take the one that gets me home the fastest.

As they hurried home, soldiers also had jobs on their minds. As early as September 1944, The Rotarian magazine published a column by Lewis B. Hershey, the head of the Selective Service System, titled, "The Ex-G.I. Joe and You." In it, he said:

> These returning men have given something to the nation. They have carried some of the load that belonged to us. We have retained privileges, rights, and comforts because they went.... A job is their right—one on which they can give honest service in return for the opportunity to earn a living.... Work is the best restorative of confidence.

The same month, Life magazine printed a lengthy article under the heading, "When You Come Back: Here Are the Answers to Your Questions about the Future." It promised servicemen that "the federal government, state governments and private groups of all kinds have built up for you a comprehensive program of benefits which is by far the best and most thorough ever planned." The story went into fine details about jobs, education and care for disabled men. It also outlined what individual states were offering and noted that Virginia had plans for educating war orphans, rehabilitating veterans and assisting men in tapping into federal programs.

But, in a letter home, Lieutenant Commander Coppersmith cautioned:

> It will take no little time to make these men realize that the world does not owe them a living simply because of their participation. Even the loans they will make must be repaid. A completed college education takes effort and sacrifice in the way of study and deprivation of an otherwise possible married normal family life.... Jobs may be promised and guaranteed upon their return, but they are available only where there is a continued demand for labor, and it is up to the man to hold and retain the job he returns to. How I wish the serviceman was made "aware"— there are so many limitations to assistance that is doled.

An article in the Journal of Higher Education asked, "How are our universities and colleges going to receive the veterans of this war as they return to civilian life and seek further enlightenment in our institutions of higher learning?...Are we going to receive them intelligently and sympathetically or ineptly and ruthlessly?" The author listed, among his suggestions for providing servicemen with credit for their war experiences, such as "for work in the finance or quartermaster departments, and the like."

While thoughts of higher education and jobs were on the minds of returning servicemen, their main focus was on getting home. For Boisseau, that meant Prince George Courthouse, and he was tantalizingly close as he was processed about 150 miles away at Fort Meade in Maryland.

In the four years since he had lived across the street from the courthouse and next door to the Seberas, he had earned several decorations and citations: a Good Conduct Medal with clasp, a Meritorious Unit Award, an American Defense Service Medal, an American Theater Service Ribbon, an Asiatic Pacific Service Ribbon, a Philippine Liberation Ribbon and a World War II Victory ribbon. They were nothing extraordinary, but they were honors he could be proud of and emblematic of his devotion to what he had been summoned to do.

As for "wounds received in action," his discharge papers recorded "none." Malaria and skin diseases did not qualify, no matter how long they lingered.

Because of his length of service, the number of months he spent overseas and other factors, including his ribbons, Boisseau received an Adjusted Service Rating (ASR) score of 81, one point over the magic number he needed to be discharged ahead of other men who had been in uniform for shorter periods of time or who had not been in combat zones. His papers also noted that he had "no days lost under AW 107," the Article of War covering desertion and other absences, including time in the pokey.

That meant, despite any heavy hangovers he may have experienced while at Oro Bay (if he drank at all) or deep longings for his nearby home while at Camp Lee, Sergeant Bailey had been perfect in his steadfastness during his time in the military.

After duty split almost precisely between "continental service" and "foreign service," he was leaving the Army, in the words of his formal separation papers, for the "convenience of the government" due to "demobilization."

Half a globe away, the place he had lived and worked and written letters for two years was about to be consigned to history. In mid-September, Guinea Gold printed its final edition for Americans. There weren't enough Yanks left to read it. Roger Sykes, the member of the 491st Port Battalion who lived on a hill above the 343rd Quartermasters, recalled:

> *I was at Oro Bay until the end of the war. After the war was ended, most buildings built by Americans were burned down. Ammo dumps were burned. Our camp on Chinaman's Ridge was completely destroyed the day we left for Manila. Oro Bay was pretty well deserted in October 1945.*

Letters sent to APO 503, Boisseau's home address for two years, would now be delivered to a new location: Tokyo.

At Fort Meade, Boisseau was due $300 in "mustering out pay." He signed up for insurance and promised to pay the next premium by New Year's Eve. He was issued a lapel button nicknamed "the ruptured duck" because of the uncomfortably posed eagle on it. The pin identified him, once he climbed back into civvies, as a veteran who had been honorably discharged.

He gave his home address as "c/o the postmaster, Prince George County, Va.," where mail was now being received by someone new and not by his mother. Boisseau was handed $8.40 in travel pay to get back to Prince George Courthouse.

On November 29, 1945, he was finally free to go—1,513 days after he had been inducted. More than 800 of those days had fallen off the calendar since he had seen any member of his family. As he traveled, perhaps he felt in his heart what a Signal Corpsman who served in New Guinea had said in a letter:

> *Our work weeks [were] of the seven day variety, however one doesn't mind too much if the work day is long...for we're paid off in self satisfaction in the knowing that our job is well done and is having a direct effect on the outcome of the war.*

Like Odysseus home from war, Boisseau arrived in Prince George Courthouse after an adventure filled with peril and separation. The Greek hero proved his identity after the long passage of time by pointing to a scar and naming trees around his house. The returning soldier could have shown his right thumb, busted in New Guinea, and pointed to the inconspicuous shed beside his home, saying, "This was my mother's post office."

But, as he approached the house he had known since he was five years old and climbed the 16 steps to his high-ceilinged bedroom, there was no one to call out to him to challenge, "Who goes there?" Charlotte and Virginia lived elsewhere, and Rella rested in Blandford Cemetery.

In all the ways he understood, the house was no longer home.

Ten months after his mother had passed away, the Bailey property—so storied for its rollicking good times—began a slow move out of the family's control:

- On April 11, 1946, Charlotte and Virginia, along with their husbands, conveyed their interest in the house and surrounding 38.23 acres to Boisseau "in consideration of assuming, paying off and discharging the indebtedness of" their mother. Boisseau—identified in the legal documents as being "sometimes known as Boisseau B. Bailey"— sealed the deal with a symbolic $10. In the legalese of the contract, the two sisters granted their brother "quiet and peaceful possession of said land." He now owned the site, but he also owned its debts to the Bank of Virginia.

- Eleven months later, on March 28, 1947, Boisseau, identified as "unmarried," passed three acres to his childhood friend, Joe Sebera Jr. (on which his family still lived at the time of this writing). The bank agreed to the transfer. Boisseau was given "valuable consideration," which may have included payments to the lien-holders.

- On March 4, 1949, Boisseau sold the remaining land (35.13 acres) to W.R. and Alva B. Horne for $3,500, only about $400 more than his parents had paid for it in 1920. Mr. Horne had been the justice of the peace who witnessed the exchange of the property from Charlotte and Virginia to their sibling. The Bailey property thus passed out of the family's hands. On August 23, 1963, the entire plot was sold by the Horne children to Joe Sebera Jr. for $11,500.

Rella's little post office beside the family's home—where her three children had played, above which her husband had flown in an airplane and waved to her, and into which flowed scores of V-mails from exotic New Guinea—was turned first into a workshop and later moved behind the home to become a tool shed.

It remains there to this day.

CHAPTER TWENTY-FIVE

'WHAT IS TO BECOME OF ME?'

In 1944, with a sense that the war was nearing its conclusion, William Alexander, the Mississippi sergeant in New Guinea, turned reflective about his future. He wrote his parents to say, "My greatest question is what is to become of me and what have I to look forward to when all this is over."

Those same questions must have occurred to Boisseau, and he began to answer them by going home. Not every soldier from Prince George County did. Killed in the war were 40 residents, including two teenagers. They were a Temple, who was white, and an Epps, who was black.

The Prince George Courthouse that Boisseau returned to had been as sleepy as ever during the war. One resident, when asked what the town was like in those years, replied, "It's not a town. It never has been. It's always been rural and unsophisticated. There was the courthouse, store, post office and bank. That was it." Until the early forties, she continued, "I lived in a house with outdoor plumbing, and the kitchen sink had a hand-pump to get water."

Dennis Sebera, who grew up in the courthouse neighborhood, retains sense memories of how quiet the place was. "There was not a lot of traffic," he said. "You could hear the whistles blowing from the steam engines at the two crossings about four miles away. You could even tell which way they were going. I remember laying in the front yard with my father, gazing at the stars. A car would come down the road, and he knew without looking who it was from the sound of the motor."

Regardless of how much it was cut off from the world, Prince George was nonetheless touched by the four-year war that scarred the earth, reduced countless cities to rubble and claimed millions of lives from Pearl Harbor to Poland, from New Guinea to Norway. Willie Horne, who grew up in the courthouse area, recalls that "there were a lot of small farmers in the area. When [the war] started, a lot of them went to work at Camp Lee as carpenters, firemen, mechanics. There were several bivouac areas in the county, and soldiers in full gear would march through" the town.

As those workers headed toward the camp, recruits walking away from it hiked along the main road, headed for those bivouacs. They would sometimes stop in yards to ask for water to replenish their canteens. Kids would parade gallantly alongside the men, aping their pace while toting makeshift rifles fashioned from broomsticks and branches.

Horne remembers that everyone was patriotic and went to church. The secretaries who worked in the courthouse took part in another sort of ritual. They would process outside during lunchtime, sit on the lawn, bring out a Ouija board and ask the mystic powers to reveal the fates of the men in their lives who had gone away. Given his reputation as a ladies' man, Boisseau must have been among those whose names were incanted.

With reminders of the war all about (a tank rested on the courthouse lawn when bond drives were held), Prince George still went through its routines. A white woman who was a grade-schooler during the 1940s remembers walking an oak-lined lane to get to school, where the first three grades were all in one room. She attended sixth grade with only two other pupils. The black children trudged to their segregated schoolhouse. Afternoons and summers were spent playing in front yards and even on the courthouse grounds, fussing with the decorative cannonballs and not always successfully avoiding having a finger crunched by one.

Horne thinks of Prince George Courthouse as a typical hamlet of the times. There was even a village blacksmith named Opocensky, who worked up the road a piece from the Bailey house. "He could fix anything mechanical, especially farm equipment, and also shoe horses and mules," Horne noted. "Between him and Joe Sebera's father, they kept things running during the war."

Like any small locale, oddball characters from Boisseau's time added dashes of eccentricity to the courthouse area. "There was an older black man who everybody called Uncle Bud. He drove a mule team and wagon everywhere he went, and he came to Buren's store a lot," Horne said. Next to the Buren Store lived Beauregard Temple, "a small man who always dressed in a black suit and hat, except when it was real hot. Then he would wear a vest but no coat. About every other day, he would wander around the courthouse complex, picking up cigarette butts, putting them in his pocket and taking them home. I was told he stripped the tobacco out and smoked it in his pipe."

As the war impacted the community, residents were still in the process of getting over the shock of the Depression. Stores and service stations, such as Buren's and Sebera's, allowed customers to charge items until they could pay. People used blocks of ice to cool their food and raised backyard chickens for eggs and meat. Farmers who had pigs and hogs "had smokehouses to cure the meat after 'killing time,' which was usually in the fall," Horne said.

And there were the aromas that no doubt greeted Boisseau as he came down the street, convincing him as much as anything that he was home: the rotten egg stench from Hopewell's paper plant, the scent of smoke from wood and coal fires that curled from the chimneys, the earthy smell of tilled soil, the strong odor from the dairy farm down the road from his house. Back to those familiar scenes and smells and sounds came Sergeant Bailey.

The place had few diversions to offer. What action there was in the area—and there wasn't much—could be found in Hopewell with its one movie theater or in Petersburg, which had three times that many as well as a Woolworth's, cafés, a clothing shop, a jeweler, a billiard parlor or two, drug stores, a bookseller and the Nifty Jiffy grocery. In the summer, a veteran who had recently swum in the Pacific could drive over to the James River shoreline site run by the Costenbader clan or to Moore's Lake up old Route 1. It had a restaurant, tourist cabins, a pavilion, a fun slide into the water and a slogan, "Make Moore's Lake Your Lake."

From such familiar things, Boisseau might have expected to come home to the same place he left, but nothing stays the same. Neither places nor persons, no matter how much seemed familiar on the outside, were left untouched by an event as cataclysmic as World War II. Historians Beth Bailey and David Farber have observed:

> World War II initiated a series of changes that had crucial
> consequences for American society. The demands of war upset
> existing patterns.... The war fostered nationalism and encouraged
> the emergence of a national culture. It laid bare social problems.

Those problems included racism, sexism and classism, which had been witnessed—even practiced—when millions of men from throughout the nation mingled in foxholes, warehouses, ships, planes and barracks. A telling example of lingering racism occurred in Petersburg. During the war, a white soldier stationed at Camp Lee wrote home about the fun he had swimming in Wilcox Lake. He didn't note that use of the lake was limited to white people. In 1954, when a black YMCA official spoke out in favor of integrating the beach, he was fired. A year later, when other blacks pressed a federal judge to issue an injunction that would end segregation at the public facility, city officials took swift action. They obviated the problem by closing the beach to everyone.

In other significant ways, Prince George was no longer the place the ex-soldier remembered. Jane was gone from his life plans. His mother was in the cemetery, next to his father. His sisters had moved away. As if to cling to at least one part of the past, Boisseau resumed what he had been doing before Pearl Harbor—selling Coca-Cola. He guided his delivery truck back and forth from Petersburg to Prince George, stopping at 20 to 40 stores along the way—including Buren's across from the courthouse, and Parker's and Starke's groceries up the road—to pitch the soft drink. Horne also recalls lawn parties held on church or school grounds "in the late summer or early fall. [People] would bring homemade goodies—cakes, cookies, pies—which they sold to raise money. Boisseau [would be there] with his Coca-Cola truck and dressed in his Coke uniform. He'd set up one of the Coke [coolers] with the bottle opener on the front."

The same charms that had won over so many friends through the years could be applied to shopkeepers and crowds at lawn parties. "Red" Bailey, with his winning smile, stack of one-liners and veteran status, had a leg up on other salesmen.

A woman who was a pre-teen when Boisseau came marching home again recalls more "the idea of him" than the reality, but the idea was an accurate précis of his life. "He was a glamorous, devil-may-care guy who showed up once in a while," she said. "He used familiar terms when talking to women—a lot of 'honey' and 'sweetie.' It was his personality—and so typical of men in those days—to use affectionate nicknames."

Ben Kanak, seven years younger, thought of him as an older boy he "palled around with" and who grew to be "a good man who was well-known in the county." Horne, who would be pressed into helping the Coke driver and regret it, described Boisseau as "a real spiffy dresser" who leaned toward sports clothes. "I never saw him in a suit." Said another man, "You never expected to see him in a coat and tie. He was just one of the boys—cotton slacks and everyday shirt, and not always shaved."

Another young man from Prince George Courthouse who returned was Joe Sebera Jr., who had grown up next door to the Baileys and whose father had fixed Boisseau's car. Joe came back to Frances, the Dinwiddie County girl he had left behind when he entered the Navy. He didn't know it when he departed, but he had met her when she was only 14, a fact she concealed from the 20-year-old.

Several dance halls, some sponsored by churches, could be found throughout the county. When he returned, Sebera made his way to one of the dances to reunite with the girl he left behind and had written to during the war. He then invited her to go on a quest to find his pal, Boisseau. "Red" would wander in and out of their lives for years, one time declaring her steaks so perfect—"the best I've ever eaten"—that he felt compelled to wipe his dish with his bread. He even threatened to go after the pan.

Another returning Navy veteran, Herbert Scott Jr., remembers Boisseau as "an attractive guy and a character who got into a lot of escapades." One of them involved the ex-sailor, who lived in Newville, about 10 miles from the courthouse and the place of Boisseau's father's birth.

"I was dating a girl in Prince George," Scott recalled during an interview for this book, "and Boisseau told me to keep my butt in Newville and not get near the girls in Prince George. She was about 18 at the time, and he was 30-something." Scott, then about 21, dared Boisseau to do something about it, a challenge the quartermaster backed down from. (Scott went on to marry the girl, who worked as a clerk in what had been Rella's post office and who was still his wife 60-plus years later.) The pugnacious threat from the veteran may have been a faint echo of the toughness he had assumed just before the invasion of Leyte.

261

More typical of his personality was a natural bonhomie. Horne, who lived in the Bailey house after his parents bought it in 1949, said, "Nobody was a stranger to Boisseau. He was a well-liked employee and a good salesman." Nicknamed "Sonny" by "Red," Horne also remembers that the sergeant's favorite breakfast was a famously horrid Army meal—chipped beef on toast with cream sauce.

Henry Parker Jr., who owns Parker's General Store and has been a long-time chairman of the County Board of Supervisors, can still picture Boisseau arriving in his truck. Dressed in a snappy Coke uniform, he would swap out empties for new bottles of soft drinks, recommend new products and cajole bigger orders. Parker recalled:

> *Everybody in the tri-city area [Prince George Courthouse, Petersburg and Hopewell] knew him or of him. If a kid was in the store, he'd hand him a Coke and rub his head. He was a very good representative for the company. He could have been one of the best ambassadors for Coca-Cola with his gift of gab.*

Raymond Starke, who owned another grocery, labeled Boisseau "a good fella. There was no harm in him. He'd do a favor quicker than anything in the world." One of those favors was joining with Joe Sebera Jr. and Horne to lay out a baseball field in nearby Burrowsville so that it was ready for a game the next day. The soldier had not lost his affection for the game (nor, according to Horne, his slight resemblance to Mickey Mantle of the Yankees because of their common light hair and fair skin).

In June 1955, Boisseau performed another act of kindness by being a pallbearer for the late A. Warren Adams Jr. at the Methodist church in Newville. Other pallbearers, honorary and active, included men with familiar names from his V-mails and town history: Binford, Temple, Buren and Burrow. One of those processing up the aisle alongside Boisseau was Thurman Cox, a Newville farmer who had known the Bailey family before the war and spent hours with Boisseau after it.

"I must have been with him 200 or 300 times," he said. "He was a very good person. Reliable. What he told you, you could believe. We went to ball games together in Burrowsville and Prince George. He played for the Prince George team." When they talked, Cox continued, "it was more foolishness than business. It was always something to get a laugh. He was really comical."

Dorothy Stansell, Boisseau's cousin, recalled his outgoing character but also that "he never settled down." Far from pining for Jane, she said, Boisseau was a ladies' man who seemed to be adept at finding an endless number of female companions. Christine Moncol Belsches, who had dated Boisseau when they were young, remembers seeing him at many socials after the war.

And so life unspooled for the ex-sergeant. He visited old friends, dated new women, cruised his truck along the highway and said "sure" when people asked for a hand, the résumé of a man on the rise.

But, underneath the jolly surface, alcohol abuse began to erode his life. The diverging stories about him were the first signs. On one hand, Boisseau challenges a man to stay out of town. On the other, he is a jolly joker with no harm in him. Occasionally, Parker conceded, Boisseau drove his truck with a hangover. Horne remembers riding with him and being promised money if he would lug the cases of soft drinks in and out of the stores. "He reneged on the pay," Horne said. "I never got a dime and never rode with him again."

Dennis Sebera recalls Boisseau as being as lean as dancer Fred Astaire, but with "a dappled complexion and kind of pointed features. His pants always seemed a little baggy. He had the look of a man who drank his lunch." Where one man puzzled over why the vet didn't rise in his Coke job, another who knew him said, "I heard he could have had his daddy's job if he hadn't been a drinker."

It is peculiar indeed that the returning soldier did not end up with a county job of some sort but went back to hustling sodas. It is easy to imagine his assuming, in his tent in sweaty New Guinea, that he would succeed either his mother or father in their positions. Another Commissioner of Revenue or postmaster named Bailey must have seemed like a birthright in a town with a courthouse oligarchy. But he didn't even rise at Coca-Cola, where he could have certainly applied his considerable warehouse skills to meet their needs.

Something else emerged that was fundamental to Boisseau's post-war personality. It was a restlessness that kept him from rooting. It was patently true that he was a son of the county. Other than his two New Guinea years, he seems always to have been in or next door to Prince George. However, he never stood still long enough to settle down. His interest in any one woman was fleeting. He would show up to visit people and then mosey on. Even his job allowed him to wander.

In many ways, he was there but not there. People had, to use the woman's phrase, "the idea of him," rather than his essence. In some ways, he was disappearing—literally. Described before the war as hazel-eyed and red-headed, a post-war observer said that his eyes were "gray" and his hair "brown." His weight was falling, and he became stooped. It was as if the island sun and long separation from home had blurred and contorted him.

With his mother gone, with the house sold, with his sisters living elsewhere, Boisseau had no fixed points to anchor himself to. He was adrift. So much of what he had packed into his letters as hidden and even overt wishes for the future were no longer within his grasp. The one thing he still had was the one thing that should have been left behind: alcohol.

But he held on to the bottle and lost his job. More than one person believes he was fired by Coke due to his drinking, a notion confirmed by Horne:

The alcohol got to him and destroyed his career. He was such a
good salesman; they gave him many opportunities to get straight before
they fired him. Everyone thought he could have gone far with them.

Twenty years after the war ended, when he was around 50, Boisseau was a rootless, out-of-work drinker with few, if any, prospects. He began picking up odd jobs. He worked briefly at a store he used to service, according to one memory, and briefly at a sawmill, where he was allowed to sleep in a trailer. "He didn't take care of himself," an acquaintance said. "There was no one to cook for him. He would pick up a sandwich wherever he was" when he got hungry.

A man who lived across the street from Charlotte remembers Boisseau occasionally visiting her. "He was mysterious," he said. "No doubt, he was a drinker. He was an odd individual. A drifter."

Hearing praise of Boisseau for his solicitous devotion toward Rella, one of the women who knew him well shot back, "Then he should have behaved himself better. He loved to drink. He caused her a lot of grief."

"Drink was his downfall," declared someone who knew the Baileys. "He was never a mean drunk. He just got funnier. Maybe he needed the attention. It could be he lacked a father figure, but his father wasn't a good example because he drank, too."

The last place Boisseau worked—the place where he finally stood still—was a used car lot up the road in Chester. He had finally left his native county, but not by much. Chester, in Chesterfield County, lies about ten miles north of Prince George Courthouse.

There, he worked for Ira "Big Jim" Smiley, who owned Tri-City Motors. One of the employees, Fred Bilter, believes he was taken in by Smiley as soon as the business opened in the mid-'60s. During the day, Boisseau became a go-fer, picking up parts and other items, a tiny, sad charade of his warehousing days in New Guinea. When the dealership closed in the evening, he transformed into a night watchman. Having no car of his own, he drove the owner's when he needed to fetch tires and carburetors. "He was an all-round Guy Friday," said Nancy Bilter, Smiley's daughter. "He was always there."

The owner looked after the former sergeant, giving him spending money, later insisting that he apply for the Social Security benefits due him from his time with Coca-Cola and providing a place for him to settle down. Smiley "treated him like an older uncle," the salesman said. "'Red' lived on the premises, using two rooms in the back. He was a nice old guy—wiry, freckled face, with a tint of red in his hair, although it was mostly gray."

Added Mrs. Bilter, "He stayed to himself. He had a hot-plate and a cot." The salesman remembers only occasional outings that Boisseau took to a nearby 7-Eleven to eat.

If his roaming days were over, the veteran still seemed able to find another way to disappear. He withdrew into himself. The former car salesman said:

He was trustworthy and a decent old man, but he was a tough guy, hardened, a hard-core veteran. He didn't like people and

*became a recluse in many ways. He was an old Southern, country-
type man—almost like an old tobacco farmer—who believed in
the separation of the races. We used to discuss daily things, like
his health. I know he had his carotid artery cleaned out. He kept
personal stuff to himself. He was not tight with anyone. He knew
a lot about county politics and could get hostile about young people,
like all old men, saying they didn't work and their music was lousy.
He liked country music—Loretta Lynn and Johnny Cash. I'd
bring him coffee and the paper every morning, and he would read
the sports section. He drank, but he was never drunk.*

Mrs. Bilter said, "He was very private and didn't share a whole lot.
I don't know if people who came in even knew that was his home. The
business was everything to him. Any friends he had he met there, but
I don't think he had friends. He had no social life that I know of." She
described him as "a small-built man who always looked old and weathered.
He was not robust; he didn't look healthy."

Occasionally, and often on the Fourth of July, the holiday he had
off even in New Guinea, Boisseau returned to Prince George County.
One resident tells the tale of a little old man, gray-headed, wizened and
"humped over," showing up at the Sebera filling station. "Where's Joe?" he
called out in his gravelly voice. It was a declining Boisseau, back for one
last swapping of stories about the old times with his boyhood buddy and
remembering those delicious steaks, those piano-filled nights at the Bailey
house, perhaps that night camping out in the hurricane.

And maybe those nights in the Pacific, when he would close his eyes
and picture Prince George Courthouse…the fields he played baseball in…
the little post office…an upstairs big enough for a brand new family.

At some point when he visited Prince George, he passed along precious
keepsakes to a friend who still has them: his Army papers and the pistol
W.E. Boisseau never drew in 40 years.

The sergeant was letting go.

He might have been surprised that he had lived so long, and not just
because he had gone in harm's way. When he looked back over his family

history, he could number a series of early deaths. There were his mother and father, both dead at 46, and Sheriff Boisseau's son Richard, killed at 31 in a rail accident. Even his great-grandmother had been slain in her early 40s by lightning, the jagged arm of Jehovah, which seemed so often aimed at anyone named Boisseau. The veteran of a war in the South Pacific had outlived them all by two decades and counting.

Given to reading the comics and sports pages, it is unlikely he ever cracked open William Faulkner's novel, "As I Lay Dying," in which the author wrote, "How often have I lain beneath rain on a strange roof, thinking of home." But Boisseau surely knew that feeling. As he lay supine on his bed in the back of the dealership, a cigarette glowing in a nearby ashtray and a glass of something dark beside it, what thoughts and memories passed through his mind?

Maybe he had heard of a Signal Corps member named Charles Summers, who had met his future wife in New Guinea. They married at Oro Bay on April 2, 1945, less than a week before Boisseau wrote his last surviving letter to his sister. By August 1948, the Summer family included three sets of twins. It was the sort of settled family life that had eluded Boisseau—or that he had deliberately kept at bay—or that alcohol had stolen from him.

As he lay beneath a rain-pelted roof, Rella and how she died without him must have churned his memories as sleep crept in.

Pondering his losses, did he consider them all his fault? Did he believe God had justly punished him for drinking by taking away the wife, children, job and future he longed for when South Pacific monsoons drummed on his tent in Oro Bay? Did Boisseau curse himself for being a failure?

He might have thought, Why shouldn't I drink now? I behaved myself in New Guinea, and what did get me? No mother and girlfriend to come home to. As he had written in one of his V-mails, "Its no sense in it."

Did Jane's face come to him? Did he thank God for the small favors of Social Security and the kindness of strangers?

Perhaps one reason he drank was to keep those thoughts and questions away.

In his most lucid and proud moments, maybe he reckoned how he had served his country from before Pearl Harbor until Hiroshima, wearing a uniform for the entirety of World War II and was proud of that service.

If pressed for his thoughts, as he lay dying, might he have echoed another Virginian, who said, as he served in New Guinea, "I ain't got but one of me. If I lose my body, that's the end of everything as far as I'm concerned. If the world goes on, I won't know it."

James Boisseau Bailey of Prince George Courthouse, Virginia, died around 3 a.m. on January 17, 1985. He sighed his final breath at the veterans' hospital in Richmond, six months shy of turning 70. Cancer got him, according to some. Maybe throat cancer.

One person swears, "He got off the bottle toward the end." Another confirms that "he quit drinking a year or so before he died. I saw him at Parker's one Sunday morning, and he was telling people he stopped."

"The Old Sarge," as he had once called himself in a letter home from New Guinea, had won the final battle of his life.

His two obituaries—one in the Petersburg paper and one in the Richmond daily—consisted of bland boilerplate:

> James B. Bailey, 69, of Chester, died Thursday in McGuire
> Veterans Administration Medical Center.... He was...a veteran
> of World War II.... The graveside service will be Saturday at 1
> p.m. in Blandford Cemetery, Petersburg.... Instead of flowers
> contributions may be made to the American Cancer Society.

Christine Belsches attended the viewing of Boisseau's body. "There was a couple there who were real good to him" as his life waned, she said. "Big Jim" Smiley, the owner of the car lot, and his wife, Lorraine, had come to say their goodbyes.

"When he died," Horne related, "his sisters wanted the J.T. Morris Funeral Home in Petersburg to handle the arrangements. But [Smiley] told them that he had been looking after Boisseau all those years and had already prearranged the funeral and paid the [E. Alvin] Small Funeral Home in Colonial Heights to take care of the arrangements."

The car dealer offered to bow out and let the sisters proceed with their own wishes, but they acquiesced to his care for their brother, which, at that point, had lasted about 20 years.

The Small Funeral Home still has the records of those arrangements, which included finding a Presbyterian or Methodist minister to officiate. Rev. Charles Leedy of Matoaca United Methodist Church was selected. The records also divulge the address of the car lot Smiley owned: 11649 Jefferson Davis Highway. The funeral files show that the same address was given as the home of the deceased and the place to which his Social Security checks had been sent.

A devoted son who gave his mother heartaches and belly laughs, a sergeant who served his nation flawlessly while griping about heat and ringworm, an employee who sold his company's product well but fell too often into a different sort of bottle, a lover who could not claim the woman he loved the most: That was Boisseau. But only a part of him.

A person's entire life cannot be encompassed in three dozen letters with about 9,500 words that were written over 18 months, nor in the fond and fading memories of those who knew—and liked and even loved—him. Such items can be collected and sorted through, but they provide only one angle, tantalizing and true, but neither all-encompassing nor conclusive. Mark Twain said, "What a wee little part of a person's life are his acts and his words! His real life is led in his head, and is known to none but himself."

It is tempting for historians to take what exists as the entire truth simply because it exists. It is a temptation to be resisted. How many more letters, lost or tossed, would tell a different story—definitely a more complete one—if they could be found?

This question must also be asked, Why did those letters survive and not others? One possible answer is intriguing. They were saved by Jane. The collection centers on her more than anyone or anything else. When Rella died, what happened to her boy's V-mails? Were they divided up? Did Charlotte and Virginia sort through them, laughing, crying and shaking their heads at the memories? Did one of the sisters hand the ones about Jane to her? Or had Boisseau done so himself when he got home from the war and began rummaging through the desk and dresser drawers in his house before it was sold?

From the relics of his life—the stack of letters, the remaining memories and the official documents—this much is true: As with all of us, Boisseau was simply—and complexly—a human being. He never charged up a rock-strewn hill to plant a snapping flag atop a Pacific atoll, nor did he single-handedly capture an enemy stronghold, wielding only a rusty handgun and shining bravado. What he did was survive—and more than just World War II. He survived the early death of his father. He survived his mother's demise and the knowledge that he would never see her again. He survived without Jane. He survived being fired. He survived poverty. He survived descending into drink and the loneliness that pours endlessly from the bottle.

There are heroes who win—and deserve—singular medals for instant acts of courage. But there are also heroes who slog through each rough day—day after burdensome day. They are no less valiant for pushing their shoulders against the immovable objects placed in their way by everything from genes and experience to time and fate, and trying to budge them just a bit. Even in failure, they achieve something by pressing on through life, bent over perhaps, but not broken.

Private First Class Kendall Johnson, a military policeman from Wisconsin, wrote from New Guinea in 1944:

All I can say is that [I am] doing [my] work to the best of [my]
ability.... I am only doing my little bit in the effort at securing
Peace and Happiness.

In the introduction to "V-Letter and Other Poems," his Pulitzer Prize-winning volume of verse, Karl Shapiro, who was at both Camp Lee and served in New Guinea, wrote:

In the totality of striving and suffering [of war] we come to
see the great configuration abstractly, with oneself at the center
reduced in size but not in meaning, like a V-letter.

In the preface to "My War," a collection of his own World War II letters, Tracy Sugarman declared: "It is my conviction that every sailor and soldier...fought his own war. It was a struggle that only sometimes permitted him to see the enemy. But as he stared out into the darkness from his ship or beachhead, he very soon began to see himself.... He watched himself grow through fear and loneliness, boredom and exaltation. It was an inescapable odyssey for each of us who served."

Any odyssey—whether actual, metaphorical or a combination of the two—is an attempt to get back home. In his V-mails, Boisseau used the word "home" about 20 times. Even when he didn't say so specifically, "back home" was the great underlying theme of his letters. He craved messages from Prince George and ached so deeply when they didn't arrive. He longed for stories about what was happening back there and felt cheated when writers didn't provide enough details. He dreamed of marrying Jane, moving into the rooms above his mother's and raising a troop of kids. But he had to live with having all of that denied to him.

In his first surviving letter, Boisseau wrote, "Will do anything to get this damn war over and to get back home."

On June 26, 1944, he wrote to his mother from New Guinea in order to assure her that he was not scheduled to be transferred anywhere dangerous. Then he added what could have been the theme sentence of his war experience:

The next move will put us closer home and I can't wait for that day.

Boisseau now lies for eternity close to home, at rest in Blandford Cemetery in Petersburg, near his parents. His marker, flush to the ground, tells anyone who passes:

JAMES BOISSEAU BAILEY

TEC 4 US ARMY

JUL 11 1915 + JAN 17 1985

He was that. But he was so much more. If this book pays him the attention he deserves, maybe he will rest more peacefully with his family in the soil of the county they so dearly loved.

AFTERWORD

Nearly 20 years would go by before another Bailey child died. On October 3, 2003, Charlotte Bailey Branch passed away at age 86. She had lived in Newport News for 60 years. Charlotte earned her RN degree at the Medical College of Virginia, was a supervisor at Riverside Hospital and worked for a doctor. She was also an occupational nurse. Her husband, Phillip, had predeceased her. In the tradition of the Bailey family, who took in Tommy Munt, she and her husband became surrogate grandparents to a neighbor child who had lost his.

Less than a year later, Virginia Bailey Thompson passed away. She was 84. Her husband, Lawrence, had gone ahead of her.

Because none of the three children of Irella Olivia and James Benjamin had any offspring, the direct Boisseau-Bailey bloodline ended.

In her wartime diary, written in New Guinea, Walker, the Ohio stenographer, composed the following:

> I write [this journal] because I want to keep these experiences
> alive somehow, and yet ... The trouble is the deeper things one cannot
> put into words. But perhaps I keep those experiences alive for myself
> by remembering those other experiences through an account of what
> happens. ... Last night something started me remembering thing
> about home. How terribly far away it seems—almost unreal.

This book is an attempt to keep alive the experiences of James Boisseau Bailey and others like him, and to bring closer to mind things that seem so far away and unreal, including World War II, Prince George Courthouse, New Guinea and the 1940s. Tech Sergeant William H. Biesel of Pennsylvania, in a 1944 letter to friends, summed up his experience of the war in New Guinea this way:

> Trucks run here and there, and boats and jeeps and planes, and
> men. Some good, some bad. Efficiency and inefficiency run side by
> side. Good judgment and poor, tolerance and intolerance, decency and
> indecency, faith and lack of it. So it is now, and probably ever will
> be. Amen.

Boisseau could probably have written the same thing.

In his letters home, Boisseau used the expression, "Aint that 'wunnerful,'" which was likely something his family members often said to one another as an inside joke. Perhaps more of his V-mails sit in the corner of some antique shop somewhere, waiting to bring him even more vividly back to life.

Wouldn't that be wunnerful?

NOTES OF APPRECIATION

I am deeply and everlastingly grateful to those residents of Prince George Courthouse who generously shared with me their memories of their town and Boisseau Bailey. They universally demonstrated southern hospitality, and this book would not exist without their endless cooperation.

Appreciation must also go to the experts in World War II, the Quartermaster Corps and other topics who explained elements of military life as well as other aspects of life during the early and mid-20th century, in Virginia, the Army and New Guinea.

Most of all, a very special and italicized note of heart-felt appreciation is offered to Nancy Crowell, who literally took in a stranger, guided his research, introduced him to those with memories to share and drove him around Prince George Courthouse, pointing out such key sites as the Bailey home and Rella's post office. Her repeated and patient assistance through many phone calls, emails and in-person conversations was invaluable.

Others who opened their memories, shared their experiences and memorabilia, pointed me in the right directions, and helped in other ways to make this book come true include:

Martha Shipman Andrews	Jack Crouchet
Lennie Barnes	Conley L. Edwards
Joseph Barrington	Betsy Evans
Christine Belsches	Kenneth Figg
Fred Bilter	Ruth Figg
Nancy Bilter	Shirley Owens Fletcher
Betty Bishop	Frank Forcinella
Richard Boisseau III	Luther Hanson
Carol Bowman	W. Jon Harrington
Barry Burton	Jan Hathcock
Chris Calkins	Wayne Hedgpath
Russ Carter	David Hester
Margaret Colabella	Willie Horne
Dewey G. Cornell	Ben Kanak
Thurman Cox	John R. Kennedy

Jack Long

John Malecki

Kelly McBride

Scott Reynolds Nelson

Patrick Olienyk

Joseph Pape

Henry Parker Jr.

Delia M. Parrish

Mary Jane Pattersoll

Isabel Fletcher Perry

John R. Probert

James B. Richard

Mason R. Schaefer

Herbert Scott Jr.

Dennis Sebera

Frances Sebera

Robert Skowron

Bryan Small

Elizabeth Smith

Anne Bryan Smollin

Dorothy Stansell

Raymond Starke

Anny Stockman

Roger Sykes

Jay Taylor

Steve Taylor

Katherine Munt Tompkins

Victoria Tucker

Gerald Twaddell

Wally Wachter

Gladys Wiseman

Leatha Walker Wood

Mary Wood

Lewis Wyche

Among the many organizations and institutions that aided me are:

The Chesterfield, Va., County Library

Fort Meade, Maryland

The Herndon (Virginia) Fortnightly Library

The Library of Virginia, Richmond, Virginia

The National Archives and Records Administration

New Mexico State University

The Prince George County Historical Society

The Quartermaster Museum, Fort Lee, Virginia

The Surry County Historical Society

U.S. Army Headquarters, Washington, D.C.

The Virginia Historical Society

I am also immensely grateful to the other soldiers whose wartime letters and personal reminiscences provided greater depth and context to Boisseau's story, and to their families for preserving those memories:

Sergeant William H. Alexander of Mississippi
Sergeant Hollis M. Alger of Oregon
Private Alphonso J. Amico of Connecticut
Sergeant Clarence P. Arney of Oregon
Lieutenant J.L. Avery of Washington, D.C.
T/Sergeant James Barrington of New York
Corporal Joseph Barrington of New York
Private First Class Anthony Battaglia of Illinois
Private Bertram C. Behrmann of Indiana
Tech Sergeant William H. Biesel of Pennsylvania
TEC5 John G. Burk of Missouri
TEC3 Ernest R. Carlson of Washington State
Private Jennie Clark of Oregon
Private James Clarkson of Michigan
Private First Class Russell Cobb of New York
Private John C. Coleman [home unknown]
Lieutenant Commander Morris D. Coppersmith of Illinois
T/Sergeant Ben Courtright of Kansas
Private Hubert Enders of Connecticut
Sergeant Morris Finkelstein of New York
Corporal Gerald K. Fox of Massachusetts
Private John G. Gilday of New York
Private First Class Seth Hillsberg of New York
Private Berrien J. Hull of Missouri
Corporal Wallace Hunt of New Mexico

Private Arthur Hurwit of Connecticut

Private First Class Kendall W. Johnson of Wisconsin

Sergeant Lynn Knapp of New York

Private First Class Robert Kopplin of Illinois

Major Grant Levin of New York

Private Herbert McDavit of New Jersey

Corporal Thomas McGee of New Jersey

Private Harold McKee of West Virginia

Corporal Vincent H. McLaughlin of the District of Columbia

Lieutenant Irvin Michelson of West Virginia

Private Martin Norberg of Idaho

Lieutenant Liven A. Peterson of Minnesota

Private Raymond L. Porter of New Jersey

Captain John Ross of New York

Private First Class Robert W. Shackleton of Connecticut

Sergeant Lester W. Short of North Carolina

Private Charles Smith of California

Hugh A. Sunderland of Ohio [rank unknown]

Private First Class Clinton Thomas of Pennsylvania

Sergeant Howard Thomas of Ohio

Corporal Elbert Thompson of Illinois

Corporal Milton Thompson of Missouri

Sergeant Robert D. Tuttle of Ohio

Private J. Volkman of New York

Private Leatha Walker of Ohio

PFC Keith Winston of Pennsylvania

Lieutenant Charles L. Wooster of Ohio

First Lieutenant Jacob J. Zillich of Texas

BOISSEAU'S UNIT

From the unit histories of the 343rd Quartermaster Depot Company (Supply), this alphabetical roster of some of Sergeant Bailey's comrades has been assembled. Where known, their year of birth, state of residence and occupation at time of enlistment are given:

Alexander, Franklin R., TEC5

Anderson, Philip C., Lt.

Baier, Harry F., Pvt., later PFC

Barris, Seymour, Sgt.... 1920...New Jersey...sales clerk

Buchanan, Gene W., 1st Lt.

Buckley, Lt.

Chezar, Abraham, PFC, later TEC5....1911....New York....
mechanic

Chopack, John A., PFC, later TEC5....1908....Pennsylvania....
janitor

Christopherson, Pvt.

Crouchet, Jack H., 2nd Lt.

Curry, Ray H., Lt.

Dexter, Edward M., Lt.

Driver, Thomas F., TEC5, later Pvt.... 1921...North Carolina...actor

Guidry, Armand, Pvt.

Hall Jr., William T, 1st Lt.

Halverson, John R., pfc., later TEC5

Herrington, Robert B., 2nd Lt.

Hollowell, Stanton I., captain....1906....

Huber, Lt.

Ingalls, Dale D., 2nd Lt.

Jackson, Barnie, T/Sgt.... 1916...Tennessee...miner

Jennings, Harry F., PFC, later TEC5....1916...Arkansas...sales clerk

Johnson, Edgar T., Pvt., later PFC

Kulawczik, John, Sgt.... 1918...Ohio...bookkeeper/cashier

Levin, Norman L., 2nd Lt., later 1st Lt.

Marx, Vernon W., Pvt., later PFC

Morton, Marcellas C., PFC, later TEC5....1905...Oregon...laborer

Murphy, Ronald T., Captain, later Major

Nieder Jr., Paul J., TEC5, later pvt.... 1921...Pennsylvania...welder

Olson, Oliver, PFC

Pettinger, Earle J, 1st Lt.... 1914...Illinois...accountant

Powell, Tony P.... 1910...California...mechanic

Pratt, Ovis B., Pvt., later PFC.... 1926...Missouri...mechanic

Probert, John R., 1st Lt., later Captain.... 1919...Ohio...salesman

Reynolds, Lawrence, Pvt., later PFC.... Kansas

Riebel, Arthur S., TEC4

Rosenbluth, Ralph L., TEC3

Smith, Lawrence F., Cpl., later Sgt.... 1915...Oregon...mechanic

Stern, Robert W., Lt.

Thompson, Harry E., 2nd Lt.

Valleroy, George G., 1st Lt.... 1920...Missouri...shipping clerk

Waldman, Captain

Winterbottom, James E., Captain.... 1910...Rhode Island...foreman

Also, found on-line:

Gates, Travis W.... 38082849...Tec4...first platoon...receiving and shipping checker...Asiatic-Pacific Campaign Medal with Bronze Star, Good Conduct Medal...5/24/1914-10/4/1970...middle name: Wayne

Ward, Stephen H.....4/29/1913-3/5/1965...buried in Manitowoc County, Wisconsin

If these men are still alive or if their families have material related to their time in New Guinea, the author would be very interested in knowing about it.

BIBLIOGRAPHY

— "1975 Hopewell (Prince George County, Va.) City Directory" (Richmond, Va.: Hill Directory Company)

— Aerial Age Weekly, Vol. 8, No. 1, September 23, 1918

— "Annual Reports of Officers, Boards and Institutions of the Commonwealth of Virginia" (Richmond: J.H. O'Bannon, Superintendent of Public Printing, 1899)

— "Another Language," The New Yorker, May 8, 1943, p. 12

— "Army Laureate," The New Yorker, December 9, 1944, page 26

—"Birmingham soldier saves 12 from a bomb-wrecked ship at Oro Bay; dies a hero," The Negro Star, Wichita, Kansas, April 23, 1943 (Vol. 35, Issue 51)

— "Books in Wartime," Yank: The Army Magazine, June 9, 1944

— "Businesses, Manufacturers, Merchants, and Tradesmen: Financial Condition for Prince George County, Virginia, 1928" (R.G. Dun Mercantile Agency Reference Book, July 1928)

— "Camp Lee: Home of the Fighting Quartermaster" (undated booklet; issued during WWII to recruits)

—"Camp Lee Models: Mock theater of operations simplifies logistics," Life magazine, October 11, 1943, pages 56-59

—"Camp Lee, Virginia" (prepared by Camp Lee Public Relations Office, ca. 1945)

— "Displaying Australia and New Guinea: Memorabilia for U.S. Forces in Australia" (The Australia Story Trust, 1945)

— "Editor's note," Life magazine, October 18, 1943, page 11

— "First Annual Report of the State Board of Charities and Corrections" (Richmond: Davis Bottom, Superintendent of Public Printing, 1909)

— "Gazetteer of Virginia," 1904

— "Gazetteer of the World" (London, 1887)

— "Getting About in New Guinea" (Allied Geographical Section, Southwest Pacific Area, 4th April, 1943)

— "Graves Registration search and recovery operations after World War II," Quartermaster Review, May/June 1946

— "A Handbook of Information" (QMRTC, Camp Lee, Virginia, undated)

— "A Handbook of Virginia" (Richmond: Everett Waddey Co., Printers, 1909)

— "He Finds Uses for 'Useless' Things," The Literary Digest, Vol. LXX, July-September 1921

— "Historical and Pictorial Review, Tenth Training Regiment of the Quartermaster Replacement Training Center, United States Army, Camp Lee, Virginia (Baton Rouge, Louisiana: The Army and Navy Publishing Company, Inc., 1941)

— "Hopewell and Prince George County Women: 1600-1985" (Hopewell Tourism Bureau, undated)

— "Jungle Warfare" (War Department Field Manual, FM 72-20, 27 October, 1944)

—"M'Cullough's Universal Gazetteer, Volume II" (New-York: Harper & Brothers, 1844)

— "Military History of the United States Army Services of Supply in Southwest Pacific" (typed manuscript, unpublished; located at U.S. Army War College, Carlisle, PA)

— "National Cyclopaedia of American Biography" (New York: James T. White & Company, 1909)

— "Norfolk and Western Railway Company: Industrial and Shippers Guide" (Roanoke: 1916)

— "Numerical Listing of APO's: January 1942-November 1947 (Prepared by Army Postal Service and Strength Accounting Branches, AGO)

— "Official Register of the United States," 1881

— "Official Register of the United States, 1907: Volume II, The Postal Service" (Washington, D.C.: Government Printing Office, 1907)

— "Out There," by George Johnston, Life magazine, Vol. 14, No. 1, January 4, 1943

— "A Pocket Guide to New Guinea" (War and Navy Departments, Washington, D.C.)

— "Prince George County, Virginia: Where History Was Made" (Compiled by the Prince George Tricentennial Committee, Richmond: The Dietz Press, 2003)

— "Prince George County Records" (The Virginia Magazine of History and Biography, Vol. IV, 1897)

— "Quartermaster Base Depot Supply and Sales Company" (War Department Field Manual, FM 10-38, 5 July 1945)

— "Quartermaster Depot Company Supply" (War Department Field Manual, FM 10-22, 22 October 1945)

— "Quartermaster Operations" (War Department Field Manual, FM 10-5, March 10, 1941)

—"Quartermaster Professional Bulletin," Autumn/Winter 1994 (ISSN 08969795)

—"Quartermaster Replacement Center," undated mimeographed document (Camp Lee, Virginia: Office of S-2, Quartermaster Replacement Center)

—"The Quartermaster Review," November-December 1943 (Washington, D.C.: The Quartermaster Association, Vol. XXIII, No. 3)

—"The Quartermaster School: Camp Lee, Virginia" (Richmond: Whittet & Shepperson, Printers, May 10, 1943)

— "Quartermaster Service in Theater of Operations" (Washington, D.C.: United States Government Printing Office, 1942)
— "Report of the Secretary of the Commonwealth to the Governor and General Assembly of Virginia for the Year Ending September 30, 1920" (Richmond: Davis Bottom, 1921)

— "A Search for Gold: An Episode of the War of Rebellion" (The Day, New London, Conn., No. 1358, November 23, 1885)

— "Second Annual Report of the State Board of Charities and Corrections to the Governor of Virginia for the Year Ending September 30, 1910" (Richmond: Davis Bottom, 1910)

— "Speaking of Pictures....Guess What Goes On Here," Life Magazine, December 21, 1942, pp. 14-16

— "Spirited and Moving," The New Yorker, August 7, 1943, page 12

— "Statistical Review [of] World War II: A Summary of ASF Activities" (Washington, D.C.: War Department, 1946)

— "United States Official Postal Guide," July 1911

— "Virginia: A Guide to the Old Dominion" (New York: Oxford University Press, 1940)

— "The War Illustrated" (London: Vol. 9, No. 209)

— "When You Come Back: Here Are the Answers to Your Questions about the Future" (Life magazine, Vol. 17, No. 13, September 25, 1944)

—"World War II Honor List of Dead and Missing: State of Virginia" (War Dept., 1946)

— "World War II Military Field Manuals: Quartermaster Declassified FBI Files" (DVD) (FamousFiles.com)

— "WWII Topographic Maps: New Guinea Series" (DVD) (Australian Bunker & Military Museum Pty. Ltd., 2009)

— Yank Down Under, Vol. 1, No. 38, April 21, 1944

—"Yanks at Home and Abroad: When an Outfit Moves Up in New Guinea, They Always Tell the Quartermaster First" (Yank, The Army Weekly, Vol. 1, No. 44, Apr. 18, 1943)

★ ★ ★

Alcedo, Colonel Don Antonio de, "The Geographical and Historical Dictionary of America and the West Indies" (London: 1814)

Anders, Dr. Steven E., "Quartermaster Supply in the Pacific During World War II" (Quartermaster Professional Bulletin, Spring 1999)

Anderson, Alan, "The Songwriter Goes to War: The Story of Irving Berlin's World War II All-Army Production of 'This is the Army'" (Pompton Plains, NJ: Amadeus Press/Limelight Editions, 2004)

Anderson, Malcolm, "Our Far-Flung Correspondents: Jungle Juice" (The New Yorker, Oct. 20, 1945, pp. 81-87)

Archer, Jules, "Jungle Fighters: A G.I. War Correspondent's Experiences in the New Guinea Campaign" (New York: Julian Messner, 1985)

Bailey, Beth, and Farber, David, "The First Strange Place: The Alchemy of Race and Sex in World War II Hawaii" (New York: The Free Press, 1992)

Bergeron Jr., Arthur W., "Tudor Hall: The Boisseau Family Farm" (Richmond: The Dietz Press, 1998)

Bergerud, Eric M., "Fire in the Sky: The Air War in the South Pacific" (Boulder, Colorado: Westview Press, 2000)

Bergerud, Eric M., "Touched With Fire: The Land War in the South Pacific" (New York: Viking, 1996)

Bergreen, Laurence, "As Thousands Cheer: The Life of Irving Berlin" (New York: Viking, 1990)

Berry, Galia, editor, "When Victory Is Ours: Letters Home from the South Pacific: 1943-1945" (published online at www.topshot.com/dh/Victory.html, copyright 1996)

Berube, Allan, "Coming Out Under Fire: The History of Gay Men and Women in World War Two" (New York, The Free Press, 1990)

Blackmon, Douglas A., "Slavery by Another Name: The Re-Enslavement of Black Americans from the Civil War to World War II" (New York: Anchor Books, 2009)

Boring, Edwin G., editor, "Psychology for the Armed Services" (Washington, D.C.: The Infantry Journal, 1945)

Bradley, James, "Flyboys: A True Story of Courage" (New York: Little, Brown and Company, 2003)

Brown, Joe E., "Your Kids and Mine" (Garden City, N.Y.: Doubleday, Doran and Co., Inc., 1944)

Buell, Augustus C., "The Cannoneer: Recollections of Service in the Army of the Potomac" (Washington, D.C.: The National Tribune, 1890)

Bunkin, Irving A., MD, "Under the Knife in New Guinea," excerpts from his World War II diary (World War II magazine, March-April 2011; also www.historynet.com, February 1, 2011)

Burrell, W.P., and Johnson Sr., D.E., "Twenty-Five Years History of the Grand Fountain of the United Order of True Reformers, 1881-1905" (Richmond, 1909)

Caldwell, A.B., editor, "History of the American Negro: Virginia Edition" (Atlanta: A.B. Caldwell Publishing Company, 1921)

Campbell, James, "The Ghost Mountain Boys" (New York: Three Rivers Press, 2007)

Cannon, M. Hamlin, "The War in the Pacific: Leyte, The Return to the Philippines" (Washington, D.C.: Office of the Chief of Military History, Department of the Army, 1993)

Carter, Rear Admiral Worrall Reed, "Beans, Bullets, and Black Oil: The Story of Fleet Logistics in the Pacific During World War II" (Washington, D.C.: Department of the Navy, 1953)

Catton, Bruce, "A Stillness at Appomattox" (Garden City, New York: Doubleday & Company, Inc., 1953)

Catton, Ellis, "The Other Side of War" (Bloomington, Indiana: AuthorHouse, 2007)

Christian, W. Asbury, "Richmond: Her Past and Present" (Richmond: L.H. Jenkins, 1912)

Clar, William Bullock; Miller, Benjamin LeRoy; Berry, Edward W.; and Watson, Thomas Leonard, "The Physiography and Geology of the Coastal Plain Province of Virginia" (Charlottesville, Va.: University of Virginia, 1912)

Clark, Dr. Walter, "The Story of V....-Mail" (Popular Photography, Volume 12, Number 4, April 1943)

Cooke, John Esten, "Virginia: A History of the People" (Boston: Houghton Mifflin Company, 1883)

Costello, John, "The Pacific War, 1941-1945" (New York: Perennial, 2002)

Coutts, Mike, compiled by, "Invasion of Papua and New Guinea" (Port Moresby, New Guinea: South Pacific Magazine, 1992)

Craven, Wesley Frank, and Cate, James Lea, "The Army Air Forces in World War II, Volume IV" (Washington, D.C.: Office of Air Force History, 1983)

Darnton, Byron, "Natives help American airmen forced down in New Guinea area" (The New York Times, April 23, 1942, page 11)

Darnton, John, "Almost A Family: A Memoir" (New York: Alfred A. Knopf, 2011)

Dixon Jr., Thomas, "The Clansman: An Historical Romance of the Ku Klux Klan" (New York: Grosset & Dunlap, 1905)

Dixon Jr., Thomas, "The Leopard's Spots" (New York: A. Wessels Company, 1906)

Doriot, Colonel Georges F., "Research in the Military Planning Division, Quartermaster Corps" (Journal of Applied Physics, Vol. 16, April 1945)

Dorr, Lisa Lindquist, "White Women, Rape, and the Power of Race in Virginia, 1900-1960" (University of North Carolina Press, 2004)

Doubleday, Abner, "Reminiscences of Forts Sumter and Moultrie in 1860-'61" (New York: Harper & Brothers, 1876)

Dow, Lorenzo, and Dow, Peggy, "The Life, Travels, Labors and Writings of Lorenzo Dow" (New York: C.M. Saxton, 1859)

Drea, Dr. Edward J., "Defending the Driniumor: Covering Force Operations in New Guinea, 1944" (Fort Leavenworth, Kansas: Combat Studies Institute, February 1984)

Drea, Dr. Edward J., "New Guinea: The U.S. Army Campaigns of World War II" (Washington, D.C.: U.S. Army Center of Military History, date unknown)

Edwards, Richard, editor, "Statistical Gazetteer of the State of Virginia" (Richmond: Published for the Proprietor, 1855)

Eichelberger, Lieutenant General Robert L., "History of the Buna Campaign" (report to Army, 1943)

Encel, Vivian, and Sharpe, Alan, "Murder: 25 True Australian Crimes" (Crows Nest, New South Wales: Kingsclear Books, 1997)

Esposito, Brigadier General Vincent J., chief editor, "The West Point Atlas of War: World War II: The Pacific" (New York: Tess Press, undated; original copyright, 1959)

Fairley, Brigadier N. Hamilton, "Medicine in Jungle Warfare" (Proceedings of the Royal Society of Medicine, Vol. XXXVIII, No. 195, March 1945)

Flynn, William J., "The Eagle's Eye" (New York: The McCann Company, 1919)

Ford, Ernest C., "My New Guinea Diary" (Roseville, California: White Stag Press, 2010)

Gale, First Lieutenant Miles W., "Crossing the Pacific Ocean, May 1944" (College Park, Georgia: Static Line, Vol. II, No. 1, April 1, 1999, and Vol. II, No. 2, April 3, 1999)

Gilday, John G., "Our Freedom Was At Stake: My World War II Experiences in the Infantry" (privately published)

Giles, Albert W., "The Country About Camp Lee, Virginia" (Charlotte: University of Virginia, 1918)

Gladwell, Malcolm, "The Courthouse Ring: Atticus Finch and the Limits of Southern Liberalism" (The New Yorker, August 10, 2009)

George, Bob, "Aviation Engineers Avenging Pearl Harbor" (self-published, 1996)

Greenburg, Judith E., and McKeever, Helen Carey, "Letters from a World War II GI" (New York: Franklin Watts, 1995)

Gregory, Robert P., "Letters from the South Pacific: A World War II Chronicle" (Santa Barbara: Fithian Press, 1996)

Hall, Gwendolyn Midlo, editor, "Love, War, and the 96th Engineers (Colored): The World War II New Guinea Diaries of Captain Hyman Samuelson" (Urbana and Chicago: University of Illinois Press, 1995)

Haugland, Vern, "Letter from New Guinea" (New York: Farrar & Rinehart, Incorporated, 1943)

Hepworth, John, "The Long Green Shore" (Sydney: Picador, 1995)

Hershey, Lewis B., "The Ex-G.I. Joe and You" (The Rotarian, Vol. LXV, No. 3, September 1944)

Hines, Walter, "Aggies of the Pacific War: New Mexico A&M and the War with Japan" (Las Cruces, New Mexico: Yucca Tree Press, 1999)

Hodges, LeRoy, "Efficiency in County Government" (letter in "The American City," Volume XIII, July-December 1915; (New York: The Civic Press)

Hodges, LeRoy, "Petersburg, Virginia: Economic and Municipal" (Petersburg: Chamber of Commerce, 1917)

Hunt, Frazier, "MacArthur and the War Against Japan" (New York: Charles Scribner's Sons, 1944)

Hutnick, First Lt. Joseph J., and Kobrick, TEC4 Leonard, editors, "We Ripened Fast: The Unofficial History of the Seventy-Sixth Infantry Division" (Frankfurt Main, Germany: Otto Lembeck, undated)

Jenkins, H. Harrison, "Army Newspaper Names" (American Speech, Vol. 26, No. 3, October 1951, pp. 185-189)

Jimerson, Randall C., "The Private Civil War: Popular Thought During the Sectional Conflict" (Louisiana State University Press, 1988)

Jones, James, "From Here to Eternity" (New York: A Delta Book, 1951)

Jones, James, "WWII" (New York: Grosset & Dunlap, 1975)

Kahn Jr., E.J., "The Army Life: XXIII—Somewhere in New Guinea" (The New Yorker, December 5, 1942)

Kahn Jr., E.J., "The Army Life: XXIV—Somewhere Else in New Guinea" (The New Yorker, December 12, 1942)

Kahn Jr., E.J., "The Army Life: XXIX—The Natives" (The New Yorker, April 10, 1943)

Kahn Jr., E.J., "The Army Life: XXVII—Housekeeping" (The New Yorker, Feb. 20, 1943)

Kahn Jr., E.J., "The Army Life: XXXII—Homeward" (The New Yorker, May 22, 1943)

Kahn Jr., E.J., "G.I. Jungle: An American Soldier in Australia and New Guinea" (New York: Simon and Schuster, 1943)

Kahn, Sy, "Between Tedium and Terror: A Soldier's WWII Diary, 1943-1945" (Urbana and Chicago: University of Illinois Press, 1993)

Kennedy, John R., "New Guinea," entry in "Historical Dictionary of the U.S. Army" (Westport, Conn.: Greenwood Press, 2001)

King, Edward, "The Great South: A Record of Journeys" (Hartford, Conn.: American Publishing Company, 1875)

Krueger, Walter, "From Down Under to Nippon: The Story of the Sixth Army in World War II" (Washington, D.C.: Zenger Publishing Co., Inc., 1979)

Langston, John Mercer, "From the Virginia Plantation to the National Capital" (Hartford, Conn.: American Publishing Company, 1894)

Lardner, John, "Southwest Passage: The Yanks in the Pacific" (Philadelphia: J.P. Lippincott Company, 1943)

Lee, Harper, "To Kill A Mockingbird" (New York: HarperPerennial, 2006)

Lee, Ulysses, "The Employment of Negro Troops" (Washington, D.C.: Center of Military History, 1966)

Leonard, SJ, Rev. William J., "The Letter Carrier: The Autobiography of William J. Leonard, SJ" (New York: Sheed & Ward, 1993)

Luszki, Walter A., "A Rape of Justice: MacArthur and the New Guinea Hangings" (Lanham, Maryland: Madison Books, 1991)

Lutz, Francis Earle, "The Prince George-Hopewell Story" (Richmond, Virginia: The William Byrd Press, Inc., 1957)

MacDonald, Charles B., "Company Commander" (New York: History Book Club, 2006)

Mallett, Ross, "Logistics in the South-West Pacific," chapter in "The Foundations of Victory: The Pacific War, 1943-1944," (Canberra: Army History Unit, Department of Defence, 2004)

Martin, Joseph, and Brockenbrough, W.H., "A Comprehensive Description of Virginia and the District of Columbia" etc. (Richmond: J.W. Randolph, undated)

Martin, Ralph G., "The GI War: 1941-1945" (Boston: Little, Brown and Company, 1967)

Mathias, Frank F., "GI Jive: An Army Bandsman in World War II" (Lexington, Kentucky: University Press of Kentucky, 1982)

Matloff, Maurice, editor, "American Military History, Volume 2: 1902-1996" (Conshohocken, PA: Combined Books, 1996)

Matloff, Maurice, "Strategic Planning for Coalition Warfare, 1943-1944," part of "United States Army in World War II" (Washington, D.C.: Office of the Chief of Military History, Department of the Army, 1958)

Mayer, Sydney L., "MacArthur" (New York: Ballantine Books, 1971)

Mayo, Lida, "The Ordnance Department: On Beachhead and Battlefront" (Washington, D.C.: Center of Military History, 1991)

Mencken, H.L., "The American Language: Supplement Two" (New York: Alfred A. Knopf, 1948)

Middlebrook, Martin, "Arnhem 1944: The Airborne Battle, 17-26 September," (Boulder, Colorado: Westview Press, 1994)

Miles, S/Sgt Charles T., "New Guinea Diary: A History of the 27th Air Depot Group" (Sydney, Australia: S.T. Leigh & Co. Pty. Ltd.)

Milner, Samuel, "Victory in Papua" (Washington, D.C.: Center of Military History, United States Army, 1957)

Mordecai, Samuel, "Richmond in By-Gone Days" (Richmond: George M. West, 1856)

Morison, Samuel Eliot, "History of United States Naval Operations in World War II; Volume 8: New Guinea and the Marianas, March 1944-August 1944" (Urbana and Chicago: University of Illinois Press, 2002)

Nelson, Scott Reynolds, "Steel Drivin' Man: John Henry, The Untold Story of an American Legend" (New York: Oxford University Press, 2006)

Olmstead, Frederick Law, "Journeys and Explorations in the Cotton Kingdom of America" (New York: Mason Brothers, 1861)

Overy, Richard, "War in the Pacific" (Long Island City, NY: Osprey Publishing, 2010)

Pamplin, Jr., Dr. Robert B., "Another Virginian: A Study of the Life and Beliefs of Robert Boisseau Pamplin" (Portland, Oregon: R.B. Pamplin Corporation, 1986)

Peters, John O., and Margaret T., "Virginia's Historic Courthouses" (University Press of Virginia, 1995)

Peterson, Liven A., "X-Ray, X-Ray: A Citizen Soldier Remembers WWII" (unpublished monograph, 2000)

Reynolds, Grant, "What the Negro Soldier Thinks About This War," The Crisis magazine, Vol. 51, No., 9, September 1944, pages 289ff.

Richmond, Keith, "The Counter Intelligence Corps and Its Activities in Australia and New Guinea, 1942-1945" (Sabretache, Vol. XLVII, No. 2, June 2008)

Rigge, Simon, "War in the Outposts" (Alexandria, Va.: Time-Life Books, 1980)

Risch, Erna, "The Quartermaster Corps: Organization, Supply, and Services," Volume I (Washington, D.C.: Government Printing Office, 1953)

Risch, Erna, and Kieffer, Chester L., "The Quartermaster Corps: Organization, Supply, and Services," Volume II (Washington, D.C.: Government Printing Office, 1954)

Rosenthal, Major Julius, "Atypical Lichen Planus" (American Journal of Pathology, Vol. 22, No. 3, May 1946)

Russell, John H., "The Free Negro In Virginia, 1619-1885" (Baltimore: The Johns Hopkins Press, 1913)

Salmaggi, Cesare, and Pallavisini, Alfredo, "2194 Days of War: An Illustrated Chronology of the Second World War" (New York: Gallery Books, 1979)

Scott, Emmett Jay, "Scott's Official History of the American Negro in the World War" (1919)

Shapiro, Karl, "Poet: An Autobiography in Three Parts" (Chapel Hill, North Carolina: Algonquin Books of Chapel Hill, 1988).

Shapiro, Karl, "V-Letter and Other Poems" (New York: Reynal & Hitchcock, 1944)

Simpich, Frederick, "QM, the Fighting Storekeeper" (Washington, D.C.: The National Geographic Magazine, Vol. LXXXII, No. 5, November 1942)

Smith, J. Douglas, and Jensen, Richard, "World War II on the Web: A Guide to the Very Best Sites" (Wilmington, Delaware: Scholarly Resources Inc., 2003)

Smith, Robert Ross, "Triumph in the Philippines," part of "The United States Army in World War II: The War in the Pacific" (Washington, D.C.: Office of the Chief of Military History, Department of the Army, 1993)

Stauffer, Alvin P., "The Quartermaster Corps: Operations in the War Against Japan" (Washington, D.C.: Center of Military History, 2004) (first printed 1956)

Steinbeck, John, "Bob Hope," The New York Herald Tribune, July 26, 1943

Steinberg, Rafael, "Island Fighting" (Alexandria, Virginia: Time-Life Books, 1978).

St. George, Thomas R., "c/o Postmaster" (New York: Thomas Y. Crowell Co., 1943)

St. George, Thomas R., "Proceed Without Delay" (New York: Thomas Y. Crowell Co., 1945)

Stirling, M.W., "The Native Peoples of New Guinea: Smithsonian Institution War Background Studies, Number Nine" (City of Washington: Smithsonian Institution, February 16, 1943)

Strzelczyk, Helen, "Oro Bay—New Guinea," Women's Army Corps Journal, 2(3), 22-26. (Courtesy of the U.S. Army Women's Museum Archives)

Sugarman, Tracy, "My War: A Love Story in Letters and Drawings" (New York: Random House, 2000)

Taaffe, Stephen R., "MacArthur's Jungle War: The 1944 New Guinea Campaign" (University Press of Kansas, 1998)

Theophane, Sister M., "New Guinea Adventures" (Rochester, NY: James Connolly Co., 1945)

Titus, Charles H., "The University and the New Veteran" (The Journal of Higher Education, Vol. 15, No. 2, February 1944)

Toliver, Oleta Stewart, editor, "An Artist at War: The Journal of John Gaitha Browning" (Denton, Texas: University of North Texas Press, 1994)

Treadwell, Mattie E., "The Women's Army Corps" (Washington, D.C.: Center of Military History, 1991) (first printed 1954)

Turkel, Studs, "The Good War: An Oral History of World War II" (New York: Pantheon Books, 1984)

Twain, Mark, "The Adventures of Tom Sawyer" (New York: Harper & Brothers Publishers, 1920)

Vader, John, "New Guinea: The Tide Is Stemmed" (New York: Ballantine Books, 1971)

Van der Vat, Dan, "The Pacific Campaign: World War II, The U.S.-Japanese Naval War, 1941-1945" (New York: Simon & Schuster, 1991)

Vincent, Francis, "Vincent's Semi-Annual United States Register" (Philadelphia, published by author, 1860)

Walker, Private Leatha, unpublished diary of a WAC in New Guinea, 1944-1945

Wallace, Paul Jefferson, "Guinea Gold History: Port Moresby, Dobodura, Lae and Rabaul" (published by author, 1971)

Watts, Sylvan, "New Guinea Aristocrats: It's an Ideal Life (for Natives) on Kwato Island" (Our Navy magazine, Mid-March 1945)

Ward, Geoffrey C., and Burns, Ken, "The War: An Intimate History, 1941-1945" (New York: Alfred A. Knopf, 2007)

Wetherell, David, editor, "The New Guinea Diaries of Philip Strong, 1936-1945" (South Melbourne: The Macmillan Company of Australia, 1981)

Wiles, Christina W., and McRae, Jean, "Prince George County Courthouse Historic District" (registration form for National Register of Historic Places, filed May 24, 2002; revised May 7, 2003)

Young, William H., and Young, Nancy K., "American History Through Music: Music of the World War II Era" (Westport, Conn., Greenwood Press, 2008)

Zufelt, Edwin J.H., "The Odyssey of the 411 Engineer Base Shop Battalion: 1943-1944" (1945)

NEWSPAPERS AND WEBSITES

MILITARY NEWSPAPERS

Arc Lite, published in North Africa by unknown unit, February 25, 1945

The Babbling Brooke, published aboard the U.S.S. General Brooke, troop transport, Vol. 1, No. 9 (4 September 1945)

Big G News, published aboard S.S. Christopher Greenup, a Liberty ship and troop transport, January 13, 1946

Bulldozer, published by the 757th Squadron, Engineers Parts Supply Depot, Milne Bay, New Guinea, June 26, 1944-Nov. 4, 1945

Club Chatter, published by American Red Cross Club, Newcastle, Australia, October 6, 1944

The Daily Observer of New Guinea, published at Base F, APO 322 (Finschhafen), Vol. III, No. 3 (January 3, 1945); Vol. III, No. 6 (January 6, 1945); Vol. III, No. 9 (January 10, 1945); Vol. III, No. 16 (January 18, 1945); Vol. III, No. 29 (February 2, 1945); Vol. III, No. 35 (February 9, 1945); Vol. III, No. 5 (March 9, 1945); Vol. III, No. 89 (April 13, 1945); Vol. III, No. 111 (May 9, 1945); Vol. 156 (June 28, 1945)

Damfino, published by 873rd Signal Co. Depot (AVN) at APO 322-1 (Finschhafen), September 1944 and March 1945

Guinea Gold: Vol. 1, No. 180 (May 16, 1943); Vol. 1, No. 239 (July 14, 1943); Vol. 1, No. 327 (October 11, 1943); Vol. 2, No. 18 (December 6, 1943); Vol. 2, No 29 (December 17, 1943); Vol. 2, No. 34 (December 22, 1943); Vol. 2, No. 62 (January 19, 1944); Vol. 2, No. 92 (February 18, 1944); Vol. 2, No. 99 (February 25, 1944); Vol. 2, No. 111 (March 8, 1944); Vol. 2, No. 115 (March 12, 1944); Vol. 2, No. 120 (March 17, 1944); Vol. 2, No. 126 (March 23, 1944); Vol. 2, No. 174 (May 10, 1944); Vol. 2, No. 186

(May 22, 1944); Vol. 2, No. 210 (June 16, 1944); Vol. 2, No. 220 (June 25, 1944); Vol. 2, No. 224 (June 29, 1944); Vol. 2, No. 227 (July 2, 1944); Vol. 2, No. 260 (August 4, 1944); Vol. 2, No. 296 (September 9, 1944); Vol. 2, No. 314 (September 27, 1944); Vol. 2, No. 317 (September 30, 1944); Vol. 2, No. 346 (October 29, 1944); Vol. 3, No. 235 (July 13, 1945); Vol. 3, No. 271 (August 15, 1945); Vol. 3, No. 313 (September 27, 1945)

Guinea Gossip, published by WACs at USASOS Headquarters (U.S. Army Services of Supply/Southwest Pacific in New Guinea, Vol. 1, No. 1, 17 December, 1944)

Gunto Graphic: Okinawa's Greatest, May 20, 1945

Jungle Journal, The (formerly Jungle Boi-Boi), published at Port Moresby, New Guinea, Vol. II, No. 1, March 26, 1944

Midpacifican: The Armed Forces' Newspaper in the Pacific Ocean Areas, February 3, 1945

Philippines Wing-Ding, published by 91st Photo Wing, Reconnaissance, Fifth Air Force, Vol. 1, No. 23, February 19, 1945

Pulse, The, published for 318th General Hospital unit, Vol. 1, No. 8, April 11, 1945

Rigel, The (Morning Star), Vol. 1, No. 29 (December 25, 1944); No. 254 (August 10, 1945); No. 255 (August 11, 1945); No. 260 (August 16, 1945); No. 269 (August 25, 1945); No. 278 (September 3, 1945); No. 288 (September 13, 1945); No. 293 (September 18, 1945)

"Sir"-Pent, published daily aboard the U.S.S. Marine Serpent, Vol. 14, No. 2 (October 27, 1946); Vol. 14, No.3 (October 28, 1946); Vol. 14, No. 4 (Oct. 29, 1946); Vo. 14, No. 15 (November 8, 1946—final issue of voyage from Japan to San Francisco)

Star of David, published at Finschhafen, New Guinea, Vol. I, No. 4, July 6, 1944

TopoGraphic News, published "somewhere in New Guinea" by 650th Engineer Topographic Battalion, Volume 1, Number 2, March 15, 1945

V-Mail Views: News, Views, and Gripes of 1605th Service Unit, April 1, April 15, May 1, May 15, June 1, June 15, July 1 and July 15, 1944

WAC Oversea-R, published by WAC unit in Manila, Philippines, Vol. 1, No. 14, 12 May 1945

Wing-Ding, The, published by 91st Photo Wing, Reconnaissance, Fifth Air Force, Vol. 1, No. 2, (April 15, 1944); Vol. 1, No. 4, (April 29, 1944); Vol. 1, No. 10, (June 24, 1944); Vol. 1, No. 11, (July 7, 1944); Vol. 1, No. 12, (July 24, 1944); Vol. 1, No. 13, (August 1, 1944); Vol. 1, No. 14, (August 14, 1944); Vol. 1, No. 15, (August 22, 1944)

★ ★ ★

DAILY AND WEEKLY NEWSPAPERS

The online archives of the following daily and weekly newspapers were consulted for this book:

• The newspapers available at www.accessible.com, including the Pennsylvania Gazette, the South Carolina Gazette, several African-American newspapers and the Richmond Enquirer.

• The newspapers and other material catalogued by Readex, a division of NewsBank Inc., including:

— African-American Newspapers, 1827-1998;
— American Broadsides and Ephemera, Series 1;
— American State Papers, 1789-1838;

— Civil War, The: Antebellum Period to Reconstruction;

— Early American Imprints, Series I, Evans, 1639-1800, and Series II, Shaw-Shoemaker, 1801-1819;

— Early American Newspapers, Series 1-7, 1690-1922;

— House and Senate Journals, 1789-1817;

— 20th Century American Newspapers, Series 1-3, 1923-2003;

— U.S. Congressional Serial Set.

• The U.S. newspapers found at www.newspaperarchive.com, especially those in Petersburg, Virginia.

• The dozens of newspapers archived by the Library of Congress at www. loc.gov/chroniclingamerica, including:

— these Virginia publications: The Alexandria Dispatch, the Richmond Dispatch, the Shenandoah Herald, the Richmond Times, the Richmond Times-Dispatch and the Virginia Citizen; and

— these District of Columbia newspapers: the Colored American, the Evening Times, the Hatchet, the National Forum, the Suburban Citizen, the Sunday Globe, the Sunday Morning Globe, the Sunday Washington Globe, the Washington Bee, the Washington Herald, the Washington Sentinel, the Washington Times, the Washington Weekly Post, and the Weekly News.

• The Camp Lee Traveller (later, The Lee Traveller), weekly newspaper of Camp Lee, from July 29, 1942 to February 12, 1947.
• The New York Times
• The Progress-Index of Petersburg
• The Richmond Daily Dispatch
• The Virginia Gazette
• The Washington Post

✮ ✮ ✮

MAGAZINE ARCHIVES

The online archives of the following magazines were consulted for this book:
Newsweek
The New Yorker
Time

✮ ✮ ✮

WEBSITES

Hundreds of online resources were consulted as part of the research for this
book. The following key websites may prove of special interest to readers:
http://aad.archives.gov/aad
www.ancestry.com
www.awm.gov.au
www.census.gov
http://chroniclingamerica.loc.gov
www.history.army.mil/
www.ibiblio.org/hyperwar/USA
www.loc.gov/vets
http://oralhistory.rutgers.edu/
www.pacificwrecks.com
www.qmmuseum.lee.army.mil/
www.quartermaster.army.mil/
www.vahistorical.org
www.ww2australia.gov.au/index.html

PARK CHASE PRESS A DIVISION OF:

CRMEDIA

CATHOLIC REVIEW MEDIA

Inform · *Teach* · *Inspire* · *Engage*

CRMEDIA.ORG · 443-524-3150

PARENT COMPANY OF:

The Catholic Review · Park Chase Press
Catholic Print Solutions · Cathedral Foundation Press
880 PARK AVENUE · BALTIMORE, MD 21201 · 1-888-768-9555

PUBLISHED IN AMERICA'S PREMIER SEE—THE ARCHDIOCESE OF BALTIMORE